Sensitive
Soul

"Cosmologists tell us the vast majority of the universe consists of dark matter and energy—'dark' because we cannot observe them, but they are vital to how the universe works. Jawer reminds us that the same is true of our personal universe—we, too, are permeated with forces we cannot directly observe but are vital to how *we* work. *Sensitive Soul* is a fascinating tour of the hidden influences that make us who we are and that hold the clues to some truly extraordinary abilities."

DEAN RADIN, PH.D., CHIEF SCIENTIST AT
THE INSTITUTE OF NOETIC SCIENCES

"Jawer's articulate writing, lucid descriptions, and remarkable case studies make this book not only a pleasure to read but a possible roadmap for people who always sensed that they lived in a different reality than their family and peers. *Sensitive Soul*'s compelling perspective will reassure emotionally sensitive people that they possess a gift, not a curse."

STANLEY KRIPPNER, PH.D., COAUTHOR OF
PERSONAL MYTHOLOGY

"Jawer is onto something vitally important: the astonishing individuality with which we think, feel, and process information. Backed by meticulous documentation and excellent science, Jawer weaves new threads in the tapestry of what it means to be human."

LARRY DOSSEY, M.D., EXECUTIVE EDITOR OF
EXPLORE: THE JOURNAL OF SCIENCE AND HEALING

"... invites us to put aside our preconceptions and approach the world of unanticipated influences with a sense of wonder. Jawer ties together research from seemingly disparate areas of study—from synesthesia to past-life memories to the feelings of pets—to demonstrate how emotion can align with sensitivity to unseen aspects of reality. The result is an important work filled with fresh insights."

JIM B. TUCKER, M.D., BONNER-LOWRY
PROFESSOR OF PSYCHIATRY AND NEUROBEHAVIORAL SCIENCES
AT THE UNIVERSITY OF VIRGINIA SCHOOL OF MEDICINE

"Jawer brings together many accounts of non-human animal sensitivities, suggesting that a connection with emotion may help explain some puzzling anomalies. His provocative ideas will no doubt spur readers to think more about these questions."

JEFFREY MOUSSAIEFF MASSON, PH.D.,
COAUTHOR OF *WHEN ELEPHANTS WEEP*

"This book takes up everything from ecology and child prodigies like Greta Thunberg to children who manifest birthmarks indicative of a previous death to the emotional, spiritual, and telepathic lives of cats, dogs, elephants, dolphins, and whales. What Jawer shows with such clarity is that the secret trigger to this hyper-connected cosmos is danger, distress, trauma, and, above all, embodied empathy, a kind of sixth sense that *feels* across space and time. Consciousness, it turns out, is not just conscious. It is *sentient*. In human terms, it is sympathetic, it cares, it loves. My response to this book was perfectly resonant with its extraordinary content and spirit. I wept. You will too."

JEFFREY J. KRIPAL, PH.D., ASSOCIATE DEAN OF
FACULTY AND GRADUATE STUDIES AND
J. NEWTON RAYZOR PROFESSOR OF PHILOSOPHY AND
RELIGIOUS THOUGHT AT RICE UNIVERSITY

"The insights of leading researchers and the accounts of highly sensitive individuals merge seamlessly, revealing human emotional biology as diverse, complex, and frequently uncanny. With his lively prose and intellectual curiosity, Michael Jawer has crafted a watershed volume on science, spirituality, and empathy."

C. C. HART, FOUNDING MEMBER AND SECRETARY OF THE INTERNATIONAL ASSOCIATION OF SYNAESTHETES, ARTISTS, AND SCIENTISTS

"*Sensitive Soul* brings to life the sense of wonder suggested by its opening sentence: 'Life is full of marvels.' By exploring the theme of emotional sensitivity through multiple lenses, Jawer paints a fuller picture of what it means to be human. He's not afraid to tackle such unusual phenomena as synesthesia (the blending of separate sensory modalities) or even reincarnation and relate them to such wide-ranging topics as autism and savantism. *Sensitive Soul* is an invaluable resource for explorers of these inner realms, and I recommend it highly."

ERIC LESKOWITZ, M.D., CODIRECTOR OF THE INTEGRATIVE MEDICINE TASK FORCE AT SPAULDING REHABILITATION HOSPITAL

"In this insightful and thought-provoking volume, Jawer bridges the gap between clinical research on the human emotional landscape and the unquantifiable mysteries that lie beyond. He includes the reader in his exploration of acute sensitivities and their underpinnings and offers plausible explanations for experiences that verge on the paranormal. Fittingly, he asks more questions than can be answered—as one can only surmise at the depths and complexities of the human soul."

NICK JANS, AUTHOR OF *A WOLF CALLED ROMEO*

"Jawer explores the relation between self, body, mind, and spirit, enunciating a view that they are not separate but are integrated. This book takes us to a deeper understanding of sentience in a nature and cosmos that evolved sentience."

MICHAEL FOX, BVETMED, PH.D., AUTHOR OF THE NATIONALLY SYNDICATED COLUMN THE ANIMAL DOCTOR AND THE BOOK *ANIMALS AND NATURE FIRST*

"Jawer has added a brilliant fresh layer and lens to sensory research. His work on thin boundaries should inform all researchers in the space, particularly those looking at synesthesia."

MAUREEN SEABERG, EXPERT ON THE SENSES FOR
PSYCHOLOGY TODAY AND COAUTHOR OF *STRUCK BY GENIUS*

"A wonder-filled exploration of the sensations that pulse within and compose our bodies, shaping our individual styles of empathy. Jawer induces a lucid attunement to the uncanny emotional makeup of our shared world."

DAVID ABRAM, PH.D., AUTHOR OF *THE SPELL OF THE SENSUOUS*

"*Sensitive Soul* makes a beautiful evidence-based case for living a life of wonder and curiosity. You will never see people and nature in the same way again."

SCOTT BARRY KAUFMAN, PH.D., HOST OF
THE PSYCHOLOGY PODCAST AND AUTHOR OF
TRANSCEND: THE NEW SCIENCE OF SELF-ACTUALIZATION

"This is a remarkable, informative book. Jawer has assembled a wealth of wisdom from science, anecdote, and personal experience into a rich tapestry and presented it with an engaging, empathic voice. If you struggle with any number of psychological or physical ailments, or are just curious to learn how the body and mind work in concert, I urge you to travel with this sensitive soul as your guide."

JONATHAN BALCOMBE, PH.D., AUTHOR OF *WHAT A FISH KNOWS*

Sensitive
Soul

The Unseen Role of Emotion
in Extraordinary States

MICHAEL A. JAWER

Park Street Press

Rochester, Vermont

Park Street Press
One Park Street
Rochester, Vermont 05767
www.ParkStPress.com

Text stock is SFI certified

Park Street Press is a division of Inner Traditions International

Cataloging-in-Publication Data for this title is available from the Library of Congress

ISBN 978-1-64411-082-9 (print)
ISBN 978-1-64411-083-6 (ebook)

Printed and bound in the United States by Lake Book Manufacturing, Inc.
The text stock is SFI certified. The Sustainable Forestry Initiative® program
promotes sustainable forest management.

10 9 8 7 6 5 4 3 2 1

Text design and layout by Priscilla Baker
This book was typeset in Garamond Premier Pro with Gotham and Museo used as
display typefaces

To send correspondence to the author of this book, mail a first-class letter to the
author c/o Inner Traditions • Bear & Company, One Park Street, Rochester, VT
05767, and we will forward the communication, or contact the author directly at
MichaelJawer.com.

This book is dedicated to four titans of subject matter so deserving of rigorous investigation and articulate exposition:

the late Ernest Hartmann;

the late William Roll;

and the very much alive and kicking
Stanley Krippner and Larry Dossey.

Each of these enterprising men allowed me full access to their outlooks and work products, and they encouraged me to develop and pursue my own. I would not have produced anything worthwhile in this field were it not for them. They have my gratitude, my esteem, and my fond affection.

Contents

Foreword

Christine Simmonds-Moore, Ph.D.

Michael Jawer is known for his fascinating findings regarding people who are environmentally sensitive. This is how I met him—following a presentation he gave that was related to his first book, *The Spiritual Anatomy of Emotion*. His research reveals that those who are environmentally sensitive may also be emotionally sensitive, for they frequently report seeing apparitions and experiencing other unusual perceptions such as synesthesia. (I experience a form of synesthesia myself.)

He and I continue to share an excitement for the concepts of sensitivity and thin and thick boundaries and believe that a deeper understanding of these traits can illuminate many aspects of human experience that challenge the dominant ways that "mind" is understood. In *Sensitive Soul,* Jawer captures something of the current shift in the zeitgeist that recognizes how easily the embodied mind can apprehend the minds of others (and share feeling states with them). He unpacks various individual differences in sensitivity and explores how emotion is at the heart of many exceptional experiences. This line of inquiry uncovers valuable clues to the nature of reality itself.

The full spectrum of human experience includes several truly exceptional phenomena that are explored here. It is noteworthy that these phenomena may, in their connection with emotion, enable us to understand sentience as a core component of consciousness. This is a valuable contribution.

The book rightfully emphasizes and articulates the centrality of the body (immune responses, interoception, and emotional processing) in our relationship with the world and the information that is held within it. The social/emotional aspect—*relationships* and *connectivity*—is, in Jawer's view, the most important ingredient. In this way, telepathy—the distant awareness of another's experience—is reconceptualized as a form of extended empathy. He recasts exceptional experiences as a property of intense emotion that is shared by humans and animals on our planet. The phenomena growing out of this wide "empathosphere" include prodigious skills, precocious awareness of information, apparent past-life memories, and mystical states of connection with nature (among others). The dots are thereby connected between neuroscience, embodied cognition, transpersonal psychology, trauma studies, parapsychology, and ecology (we are all part of nature).

The book also honors those who are not neurotypical, in particular those who are on the autism spectrum. Rather than strict categories of experiencers versus nonexperiencers, sensitivities and personality proclivities are examined along a continuum. Different forms of exceptional lived experiences are vividly portrayed by fascinating anecdotes, while academic research complements the anecdotes to provide context.

Sensitive Soul is a timely exposition of how some people simply have a different way of being in the world that renders them more sensitive to what are predominantly emotional influences that others may not have conscious access to. These so-called psychic experiences have been neglected by the mainstream but are part and parcel of the human experience. I am excited that Jawer has brought all of this together in a book that will appeal not only to a wide public audience but academics, students, clinicians, and all manner of "sensitives" as well.

CHRISTINE SIMMONDS-MOORE, PH.D.

CHRISTINE SIMMONDS-MOORE is an assistant professor of psychology at the University of West Georgia in Carrollton, Georgia. She has a Ph.D. in psychology from the University of Northampton in Northamptonshire, England. She is a coauthor of *Anomalistic Psychology* (Macmillan Insights in Psychology series) and editor of *Exceptional Experiences and Health: Essays on Mind, Body and Human Potential* (published by McFarland and Co.). Simmonds-Moore has received two awards related to parapsychology: the Gertrude Schmeidler Award (from the Parapsychology Association) and the D. Scott Rogo Award for Parapsychological Literature (from the Parapsychology Foundation). She is also the recipient of several grants from the Bial Foundation and has conducted research on many topics pertinent to exceptional experiences.

At the Confluence of Science and Wonder

The most beautiful experience we can have is the mysterious. It is the fundamental emotion that stands at the cradle of true art and true science.

ALBERT EINSTEIN

In any field, find the strangest thing and then explore it.
JOHN A. WHEELER (PHYSICIST AND COSMOLOGIST, 1911–2008)

Uncertainty is an uncomfortable position. But certainty is an absurd one.

VOLTAIRE

Life is full of marvels. When we are born, everything is new and we drink it all in. If our circumstances are fortunate, we are introduced to and grow into the world with the guidance of caregivers who gentle that world for us. Even if our circumstances are not fortunate the many novelties the world presents must still astound. As we grow and learn, however, the ratio of novelty and amazement to "been there, done that" eventually ebbs, to the point that we often take life for granted. The sheer repetition of the known comes to obscure what was once marvelous and eye-opening. But it needn't be so. As the sharp-eyed writer and humorist Douglas Adams once remarked, "The fact that we live at the bottom of a deep gravity well, on the surface of a gas-covered planet going around a nuclear fireball 90 million miles away and think this *normal* is obviously some indication of how skewed our perspective tends to be."[1]

In the same adventuresome spirit, this volume is intended to open our minds again to the curiosities that surround us but to which many of us have become immune. How, for example, do other sentient creatures experience themselves and the world at large? What might they feel? What senses do they have that are different or more highly developed than ours? How might they apprehend danger? Can some animals be damaged by trauma, much as we are? Do they have a sense of kinship to their fellows and a sense of connection to nature? If so, could this be characterized as a form of spirituality?

And what of our fellow human beings? There are certainly some exceptional ones around. When I use the word *exceptional* in this context I'm not referring to individuals who are high status, or high achieving, or who flout convention. I mean "exceptional" in the most rudimentary way: how differently they perceive the world—and perhaps themselves. I mean people who are born with or develop autism or synesthesia (overlapping senses); who display stunning capacities as child prodigies or as savants (savantism can also be suddenly and astoundingly acquired as an adult); who appear to remember, as children, another life; or who seemingly demonstrate uncanny psychic abilities. You might be surprised to learn that heightened physical and emotional sensitivities characterize all these different types of people. What can we learn about humanity in general—about the development of our brains, our minds, and ourselves—that might foster a widened appreciation of these exceptional individuals?

Additionally, I intend in this volume to explore the phenomenon of trauma. It is something that likely affects all mammals, but it affects different *people* in vastly different ways. Thus, there are distinct forms of post-traumatic stress disorder (PTSD) based upon one's brain wiring, physiology, and emotional type. Different minds and different selves respond to significant stressors differently. This phenomenon goes to the heart of how we are constituted.

It's been said that we live in two worlds. One is our inner world, which revolves around feelings, memories, dreams, reflections, longings, regrets, aspirations . . . and perhaps the most ineffable of all, our spirituality. The other is the outer world of time, space, and material things. Try as we might, we cannot fully convey the former to anyone else, even to our mate or our closest friend. The outer world, in contrast, is objectively describable and subject to scientific investigation.[2]

My further aim with *Sensitive Soul* is to bridge these two worlds: to explain the one to the other in terms each can understand. I'm convinced that one's interior, deeply felt, spiritual reality—while ultimately intangible—draws upon a physical, bodily experiential core that can be articulated scientifically. Likewise, I believe that science needs to understand that what can't be measured, made manifest, or even wholly defined is nonetheless deserving of attention. In fact, the more perplexing, astounding, or uncanny a perception is, the more it deserves scrutiny. If such experiences are happening to enough people, perhaps a fundamental form of human functioning is being overlooked.

I will have succeeded in my endeavors if this book impels you to *wonder* once more. None of us (as far as we know) wills herself or himself into the world—we find ourselves here trying to figure out what it's all about, and what our place in it is. The ideal is to not become inured to life's essential wonderment. Better to take a fresh look at the people, the animals, and the phenomena around us. What is called for is a sense of "skeptical enthusiasm," where novel ways of looking at things, unconventional ideas, and thoughtful provocation are all welcomed yet tempered by serious scrutiny. As one such enthusiast has written, "Revel in the mystery and drink in the unknown. It is where science and wonder meet."[3]

1
PTSD
A Window into the Intersection of Mind, Body, and Emotion

Hippocrates famously stated, "It is more important to know what sort of person has a disease than to know what sort of disease a person has." What he said was correct then and it remains correct today. If anything, the latest discoveries from the fields of medicine and psychology are demonstrating that it's the *intersection* of person and illness that will surely yield the most useful insights about the nature of chronic illness and, indeed, human nature itself.

Take the modern plague of post-traumatic stress disorder (PTSD), which is debilitating the lives of so many combat veterans (not to mention civilians traumatized by emotional abuse, natural disasters, or horrific events that are out of their control). Did you know that:

- Trauma experienced *before* a soldier goes to war—particularly in childhood—may play a greater role in the development of PTSD than the actual tour of duty. Some soldiers, in fact, report that they're in a better frame of mind after their wartime experiences than before, probably because of the camaraderie and feeling of support they receive from fellow soldiers.[1]

4

- PTSD isn't one syndrome—there are distinctive subtypes. Researchers have found, for example, that some PTSD sufferers (anywhere from 14 to 30 percent) show a unique pattern of dissociation.[2] (Dissociation is an extreme reaction to stress whereby a person feels strangely distanced from what is happening to him or her. Life may feel unreal or the person may feel distant from his or her own body.)
- Another variation of PTSD is one where sufferers develop obsessive-compulsive disorder (OCD) following the traumatic episode. Studies have found that anywhere from 4 to 22 percent of people with PTSD also have a diagnosis of OCD.[3]
- People differ greatly in their ability to recover from trauma. About two-thirds of people afflicted with PTSD eventually recover. Feeling supported by family members or caring friends seems to be a factor, as does the degree of communication between the emotional and reasoning circuitry in a person's brain. Animal studies suggest that having a "quieter" or less reactive stress handling system overall may also contribute mightily to resilience.[4]

When we think about PTSD, of course, we picture someone who reexperiences the trauma virtually as a replay—with the sights, sounds, smells, and, most importantly, fears registering in his/her psyche as if the remembered episode were taking place in the present moment. Since one-quarter to one-third of people exposed to the most violent or life-threatening situations *don't* develop these symptoms[5] (indeed, less than one-third of individuals who have spent time in war zones develop PTSD),[6] the question becomes: What distinguishes the people who *do* suffer from PTSD?

For a start, it may surprise you to learn that women are twice as likely as men to develop PTSD, or at least to come forward and be diagnosed with it.[7] So we might want to consider the myriad ways that women are more sensitive or more susceptible than men: to sensory stimuli; to autoimmune diseases; to pain; to conditions such as migraine, fibromyalgia, and irritable bowel syndrome that are characterized by pain; to anxiety disorders; and to emotional prompts in general. Emotion, in my opinion, holds the key to understanding PTSD, and chronic illness in general, because feelings have such a demonstrable influence on symptom severity and quite likely even the development of the types of conditions noted immediately above.[8]

But following the female trail a bit, we come across something odd. One would suppose that women, who tend to register and remember emotion more keenly than men, would be less likely to manifest the dissociative form of PTSD (since dissociation is a form of emotional distancing). However, that's not the case—women are also twice as likely as men to show a dissociative pattern, characterized by complaints of feeling emotionally numb.[9] A closer look, therefore, is needed at this particular subtype of PTSD. What are the differences in neural processing from the classic form of PTSD where the person reexperiences the traumatic event as if it's happening in the here and now?

Dynamics in the Brain and Body

The dissociative type of PTSD is one where, instead of having flashbulb memories of a traumatic event—along with a racing heart, shortness of breath, and all the other hallmarks of a brain and body on high alert—the person reports feeling nothing. He or she is seemingly unaffected by reminders of the disturbing episode, yet there is *some* influence since these individuals are bothered by a nagging sense of unreality at times. They feel not fully present, or strangely numb, or have the sense of not fully inhabiting their bodies. These symptoms add up, in the parlance of psychology, to conditions known as depersonalization and derealization.

Let's examine what's happening in the brain in each of these cases. In the more typical form of PTSD, the medial prefrontal structures that regulate the emotional, or limbic, part of the brain *undermodulate,* so that the limbic structures go hyper and the person becomes highly aroused. But in the dissociative form, the pattern is just the opposite. The medial prefrontal part of the brain *overmodulates,* causing the limbic structures to become inhibited and the person to profess that he or she feels nothing.[10]

In either case it's a matter of what neuroscientists and psychologists call dysregulation: an exaggeration or underplay of normal emotional activity. The type of dysregulation has actually been found to correlate with a particular part of the brain known as the insula, which is a prune-size structure, one in each hemisphere. The insula is where sensory information converges from throughout the body—from the skin, muscles, and internal organs—signaling sensations such as heat, cold, itch, tickle, ache, burn, pain, sensual touch, hunger, and thirst. The insula integrates such information to produce an impression about the body's overall "felt" state—how one feels at any given moment. Scientists call this information gathering process *interoception*—how the brain minds the body, one might say.[11]

The forward end of the insula in our right hemisphere (known as the anterior right insula) seems, in particular, to be where our felt sense is produced.[12] The right anterior insula also corresponds most closely to the severity of a person's PTSD symptoms. When someone is having a fearful flashback, that part of the insula is highly activated; when someone is feeling distant or nothing at all, that part of the insula shows very low activation.[13] A person's felt state, therefore—one's very sense of self—is tangibly diminished when he or she is in the throes of dissociation. The flip side is that people who are tuned in to their bodies (and who, consequently, are more *emotionally* attuned) actually have right anterior insulas that are more developed, as measured by the amount of gray matter residing there.[14]

It seems, then, that people who relive a traumatic episode in the here and now have more sensory information being collected via their insulas than people who dissociate when reminded of a trauma. The felt state of the former is literally more coherent and a whole lot more assertive. We could term these individuals "high reactors" versus the "low reactors" who effectively tune out. (All of these reactions are unconscious and instantaneous, of course; no one suffering from PTSD chooses their biology. The undermodulation or overmodulation of limbic structures occurs entirely outside of conscious awareness.)

Interestingly, it's been proposed that people become high reactors or low reactors based on the frequency and timing of the trauma they suffered. An individual who faced a single intensely threatening experience is, according to this theory, more likely to exhibit the highly reactive form of PTSD. Someone who suffered prolonged threats or injury is more likely to exhibit the low-reactive form. Likewise, someone who encounters a traumatic episode in adulthood, when he or she has better developed appraisal and coping skills, is more likely to manifest the high-reactive form of PTSD. A child, on the other hand—who is typically unable to evade a threat (especially the recurrent kind)—is more likely to manifest the low-reactive form.[15]

The Related Puzzle of Alexithymia

The dissociative form of PTSD points toward an even stranger condition, one known as *alexithymia*. This term describes people who seem not to understand that they even *have* feelings. Whereas for PTSD patients feeling distant or numb may be troubling and unpleasant, it's not characteristic of their lives. It comes and goes. People with alexithymia, however, seem permanently lacking in the ability to describe what they are feeling. Even their scariest or most trying experiences are apt to be recounted impassively, as if what happened made little or no difference.[16] It will come as no surprise that the facial expressions of people with alexithymia are typically wooden and their posture stiff. (These are reflections of their felt state.) And they will never indicate that what happened to them felt like anything.[17]

Neural evidence suggests that people with this condition are the lowest of the low reactives. Their medial prefrontal structures have no need to suppress emotional activity in the limbic region because there is a dearth of bodily and emotional input to begin with.[18] An alternate (and more charitable) view is that the person with alexithymia does indeed have sensory and feeling input to draw upon but cannot because his or her cognition is so fundamentally separated from what is being felt. The individual, in other words, is severely *dis-integrated*.[19]

How does alexithymia develop? As with the dissociative form of PTSD, it may take root in early childhood—except that no particular trauma and no recurring danger is needed in this scenario. If a young child's expression of emotions finds no validation on the part of his or her caregivers, so the explanation goes, he or she will be threatened by unbearable tension—and to become alexithymic is to foreclose on the possibility of such tensions arising. Never owning up to one's feelings, nor even to the fact that one *has* feelings, is a way for the developing child to protect himself or herself. Inexpressiveness will then become a way of being in the world. In adulthood, such people's tendency to intellectualize, to keep their body stiff, and to be highly organized will rigorously and routinely keep feelings at bay.[20] (The plight of people in this state is poignantly captured in the lyrics of the late singer-songwriter Warren Zevon, who declared "I'm gonna hurl myself at the wall/Cause I'd rather feel bad than not feel anything at all."[21])

If PTSD is a disorder of feeling—with the dissociative or alexithymic form on the one hand and the more common high-reactive form on the other—then here we clearly have distinct reactions to the scary, threatening occurrences that cause PTSD in the first place. We have people with different neural dynamics and, fundamentally, *different ways of feeling*. The differences in how people literally feel are, in my estimation, reflected in the distinctive brain patterns and not vice versa. The brain is part of an entire "bodymind" encompassing our rudimentary sensations, along with the material aspects of ourselves that allow us to process sensory input and ultimately feel things—namely, our skin, muscles, organs, and nerves. It is the *interconnections* between brain and body, head and heart, psyche and soma that, in their totality, make us who we are. Moreover, it is the *quality* of those interconnections that will distinguish how one person feels from the way any other person feels. (The pioneering discipline of psychoneuroimmunology is doing much to illuminate how these connections work.)[22]

It is ultimately fruitless, in my opinion, to seek the basis of individual differences in the brain alone. Although we can see differences encoded there, the brain is not the source of those differences. Likewise, it is erroneous to think that an approach to alleviating PTSD that works for one person will necessarily work for another. Hearkening back to Hippocrates, we need to know what *sort of person* has PTSD. More specifically, how do they feel? I mean literally: What are the bodymind dynamics involved? If there were a way to illustrate, fairly simply, the qualitative differences in bodymind functioning between one person and another, it would greatly illuminate conditions such as PTSD. It would also point the way toward treatments that would help the different kinds of people who are afflicted by the various forms of PTSD.

The Key: Feelings and Boundaries

There are two ways to get at the essence of how emotional experience differs from one person to another. The first is to look at feelings and the second is to look at people. Let's start by considering a metaphor that I believe is entirely appropriate: *feelings are like water.* As with water, feelings seem to have a movement or flow—they ripple up, settle down, seek a release, explode from within. The flow, by definition, is energetic; the very word *emotion* connotes movement.

Picture this movement as fast or slow, heavy or light, or any degree in between. Ascribe other qualities as well. For example, anger feels sharp. Sadness feels heavy. Joy feels expansive. Fear feels racing. Regret feels tugging . . . and so on. Now picture feeling, in general, as a stream within the body, in continuous motion. Imagine, further, that the flow *animates* us. (Of a lively person, for instance, we might easily say that he or she "seems very animated today.") We now have a way to picture feeling acting very much like water—bubbling up, pooling, meandering, cascading, receding.

The second way to get a handle on characteristic differences in emotional experience is to look at the individuals who are experiencing the emotions. We noted earlier that some people are high reactors and some low reactors (corresponding to two distinct types of PTSD). Another means of framing that essential difference is with a concept known as Boundaries. This is a measure of how much people are affected by various triggers—what "gets" to them, whether in the form of environmental stimuli (sights, sounds, smells, tastes, textures) or emotional stimuli. *Boundaries* conjures up the idea of a divide between inner and outer—but also a borderline *internally* between what's conscious and what's unconscious; what becomes evident to a person and what he or she is unaware of.

As propounded by the late psychiatrist Ernest Hartmann,[23] the concept suggests that everyone falls somewhere along a spectrum from thick boundary to thin boundary. Thick-boundary people seem thick-skinned: not much gets to them. By contrast, thin-boundary people seem thin-skinned: lots of things get to them. Thick-boundary people are stolid; thin-boundary people are sensitive. Internally, thick-boundary people are less aware of what they're feeling in general than thin-boundary people who are often supremely aware. Adjectives that tend to apply to thick-boundary people are *rigid, calm, deliberate, well organized* (they keep everything "in its place"), and *persevering.* Adjectives that tend to apply to thin-boundary people are *open, vulnerable, reactive, flexible* (they see "shades of grey"), and *agitated.* As with most dimensions of personality, most people are somewhere near the middle of the spectrum instead of at either extreme. (You can get a sense of where *you* are on the Boundary spectrum by taking an online quiz at http://youremotionaltype.com/boundaries/quiz.html. It takes no more than ten minutes and is scored automatically.)

Let's now combine the notion of feelings as water with the concept of thick and thin boundaries. I suggest that the flow of feeling is actually quicker and more direct in thin-boundary people and slower and less direct in thick-boundary people. Thus, individuals who are on the thin side of the spectrum will be quicker to realize what they're feeling—and to express or react to it—than individuals on the thick side of the spectrum for whom feelings are often "out of sight, out of mind." However (and this is important), *anyone* can ignore, repress, or dissociate from feelings that are especially intense or threatening.

An Improved Understanding of PTSD

If we can imagine feelings as being a *flow* through the bodymind, and given the understanding of boundary differences from person to person, we can now shed light on the remarkable finding that PTSD comes in at least two forms: a high-reactive and a low-reactive kind.

As we noted earlier, in the more typical (flashbulb) form of PTSD, the emotional or limbic part of the brain becomes hyperactive because the medial prefrontal structures that normally regulate this type of activity are damped down. A flashback occurs and the initial fear that the person experienced during the traumatic episode recurs in full force. The person's "felt state" (as registered in the insula) is substantial and is informed by all kinds of bodily input. *It is as if a wave of feeling is cresting, overwhelming the neural circuitry.*

By contrast, in the dissociative form of PTSD, the functioning of the limbic part of the brain is overregulated. As a result, the individual feels distant, numb, or nothing at all. His or her felt state is diminished, as a paucity of bodily information registers with the insula. *It is as if the flow of feeling has been minimized, diverted, or dammed up.* This state of things is episodic with PTSD but is clearly characteristic of alexithymia.

My conjecture is that the majority of people who suffer from PTSD are thin-boundary. These are people who feel things keenly and who respond strongly to physical and emotional pain in themselves as well as others. These are also people who register sensory stimuli (sights, sounds, smells, etc.) fairly vividly. Furthermore, the images and feelings contained in their memory are close at hand. The boundaries of people like this—the dividing line between them and the external world and the threshold between conscious and unconscious within—are fairly porous.

The 14–30 percent of PTSD patients that exhibit the dissociative form of the condition are another story. These are people who are not terribly conversant with their own feelings or, consequently, the feelings of other people. They're less apt to be affected by sensory stimuli. And their memories typically stay in the past; they're not readily brought to mind or ruminated upon. The boundaries of people like this—both between them and the external world and delineating between conscious and unconscious within—are relatively impermeable.

A good deal of evidence, both anecdotal and scientific, supports this assessment of PTSD. On the anecdotal side consider the following statement made by a combat veteran. The smell of gunpowder, he said, not only makes him feel hot, "It's as if my whole metabolism changes."[24] This is manifestly a thin-boundary person. What he experiences is intense as well as instantaneous. Additional biological evidence that most PTSD sufferers are high reactors is contained in a book that I coauthored with Dr. Marc Micozzi, *Your Emotional Type*.[25]

People with alexithymia, on the other hand, have been shown to be strongly thick-boundary,[26] suggesting the same is true for those who exhibit the dissociative form of PTSD.

A Major Change in Outlook

Once upon a time, conventional science and medicine just "knew" that the mind was different from the body . . . that the head's place was to rule the heart . . . that the nervous system, immune system, and hormonal system were entirely separate . . . that either nature or nurture was bound to be predominant in the development of human personality . . . and that certain conditions were all in a person's head. That someone could suffer "inexplicable" pain or fatigue (or that someone could get better from a placebo) was deemed to be "psychosomatic."

Today we know that just about all those assumptions are wrong. The mind, it turns out, is an amalgam of the brain *and* the body—two sides of the same coin.[27] The "rational" part of the brain, the neocortex, is literally bypassed in cases of emergency.[28] Meanwhile, our gut has its own nervous system that can take precedence over what the "upstairs" brain thinks.[29] The nervous, immune, and hormonal systems are in constant contact, influencing one another reciprocally.[30]

Nature and nurture have likewise been found to collude in the formation of personality; genetic predispositions either come to pass or not based on factors in the person's environment.[31] And a wide range of maladies—such as PTSD, ulcer, allergy, migraine, chronic fatigue, fibromyalgia, irritable bowel, and depression—demonstrates that *every one of us* is psychosomatic. That is, we're influenced by feelings, memories, and impressions that are no less real or valid for being outside of our conscious awareness.[32]

The flip side is that people who benefit the most from placebos are found to have certain personality traits, ones that we might expect from our understanding of boundaries. Would a thick-boundary person—one who views things as distinctly "me" or "not me," who is slower to recognize what he or she is feeling, and who's prone to being habitual or rigid—be more or less likely than a thin-boundary person to believe that a particular remedy will help, and *make that suggestion real?* If you said no, it's the thin-boundary person who benefits more from a placebo, you'd be right. People who are open to new experiences,[33] who show directness and resilience,[34] are the ones who gain the most symptom relief.

Thus it's time for two more sacred cows to be upended. One of these posits that all people are essentially the same, so that if person X has the same condition as person Y, then they both should derive benefit from treatment Z. The second presumption is equally simplistic and unimaginative. It maintains that someone either "has" an illness or does not . . . making him or her either "normal" or "abnormal."

What we're learning about PTSD tells us that both of these axioms are unsubstantiated. There are at least two flavors of this affliction: the kind where past fears are vividly reexperienced and the kind where the person goes numb. Additional subtypes of PTSD may yet be discovered. For now, though, we can see the condition as a confluence of several factors. These include gender (women are more likely to manifest PTSD), reactivity (high reactors disposed to one form, low reactors to another), the nature of the trauma itself (acute or chronic), the timing of the trauma (whether occurring in childhood or adulthood), and the kind and degree of support received by caring family members, friends, and/or therapists.

People aren't blissfully normal before they develop PTSD, nor are they irrevocably abnormal once caught in its throes. The type and severity of the PTSD varies along a spectrum, just as an individual's boundary type varies along a spectrum—from extremely thick to extremely thin. Where science and medicine can make the most headway is through an appreciation of the idea that *both* human nature and chronic illness lie along a continuum. By examining the necessarily complex intersection of the individual and his or her condition, we'll be able to learn the most about both and treat people most humanely and effectively.

Bit by bit, questioning—and questing—leaders in the fields of philosophy, psychiatry, and medicine are coming to this same view of things. They see that the old assumptions are painfully limited, increasingly ineffectual, and manifestly out of step with the accumulating evidence. They seek a "spectrum" approach to both person and illness, replacing the linear model that is today's convention.[35] Just as the body politic realizes that answers to our society's most pressing needs will not be found by pulling wholesale from party A or party B, so leaders of the new medicine are pushing for a framework that properly accounts for the complexity of human beings, the salient differences in bodymind functioning between people, and a full appreciation that we are not separate from our environment. All of us are embedded in nature . . . we are social creatures influenced by our fellows . . . and we are all sentient beings for whom feelings (even the unconscious or dissociated kind) are paramount.

Most of all we are unified beings, incorporating mental, emotional, physical, psychological, somatic, and spiritual functioning. When a given disorder stubbornly defies conventional treatment, it's wrongheaded to label and compartmentalize the problem as being either physical or psychological, and to prescribe more or different kinds of medication in the hope that the symptoms will just go away. The symptoms—of PTSD, alexithymia, chronic fatigue, chronic pain, depression, anxiety, and/or many other chronic conditions—are truly a call for attention. These conditions are inevitably *of* us, even if we would prefer them not to be.

Rather than treating them as alien and seeking to stamp them out, both patients and caregivers would do better to assess the "why" of the matter. "What is my boundary type?" "How did I become this way?" and "What is my condition telling me?" are all pointed and prospectively illuminating questions. Ideally and over time, the given disorder will be *integrated and transformed* rather than overcome. This will advance the person's long-term well-being rather than merely fix his or her current suffering.[36]

For PTSD and other excruciating dilemmas, it's an approach we should use—one that is not just pragmatic but recognizes the extraordinary diversity of human functioning.

2

Mirror Senses

Extraordinary Instances of Emotion Moving beyond the Self

Popular attention has come to embrace "mirror touch" and "mirror pain" synesthesia, which encompass a remarkable ability to feel what other people are feeling. The phenomena themselves have much to teach us about perception, what constitutes the self, and how empathy works.

They can teach us even more, however. Based on a thorough understanding of how feelings work within the human being, we shall see that mirror senses have much in common with phenomena we know a little bit better: migraine headache, phantom pain, and déjà vu. By considering the circumstances under which these occur, we can better fathom what is happening in cases that are characterized by the quality of extreme empathy.

But we'll go much farther than that. Having an appreciation of the dynamics of feeling in the human organism—and noting the different ways that feeling operates in different people—opens a new vantage point on the relationship between the brain and the rest of the body, the boundaries between self and other, and the nature of reality itself. Exploring this will be a fantastic journey!

Let's begin with synesthesia—the crossing over of the senses, such as hearing a color, seeing a sound, or tasting a shape. Synesthetes inevitably have much more interesting perceptions than the rest of us. Typically born with this condition, they presume that everyone experiences the world as they do—until it's brought home to them that not everyone sees the word *Wednesday* as indigo blue—even other synesthetes.

Possibly the most fascinating form of synesthesia is known as mirror touch synesthesia. This is where the person feels sensations that other people are presumably feeling regardless of whether those other people are physically there—standing right in front of oneself, for example—or whether they're on a movie or TV screen. The sensations follow from wherever the synesthete is directing her or his attention. These feelings may be anything from the play of a woman's hair across her face to the literal sting of a punch to the figurative sting of an insult. Research demonstrates that mirror touch synesthetes aren't making it up or speaking metaphorically. When they report pain—while viewing someone else in pain, for example—greater activity registers in the parts of their brain that relate to both physical and emotional hurt.[1]

Mirror touch synesthetes are, by definition, highly empathic individuals (experimental evidence backs this up),[2] gathering a plethora of impressions at every turn. It can be a most challenging condition to live with. Think of the necessity to distinguish—and disentangle—one's "own" feelings from those that others appear to be experiencing. By the same token, mirror touch synesthetes are poised to gather some remarkable information about their fellow creatures, not just human beings.

A Different Form of Knowing?

Consider a woman from Great Britain called Fiona (her pseudonym), who will be discussed in the account below. The narrator here is another mirror touch synesthete, an American by the name of Joel Salinas. (Joel, incidentally, made apt use of his synesthetic ability to diagnose other people by becoming a physician—and is now affiliated with the Harvard Medical School.) In his autobiography, he describes getting to know Fiona, who

> recalled an instance when she was temporarily living in a remote cottage in the farmlands of Essex. "I know this is going to sound really odd, but when I experience pain I also experience blue or orange. Orange is when it gets really severe. . . . My collie was still a puppy at the time, but almost overnight there was this thing where every time I looked at her I kept seeing these . . . snakes, oh I know it sounds odd, but I'd look at her and I'd have the synesthetic experience of these two snakes almost colliding, and I kept seeing this bluish-orange around her. Mind you, I didn't see them literally in front of me. . . . They were in my synesthetic mind's eye."

For two days she kept seeing the mental image of two colliding snakes and blue-orange around the collie. Though the dog appeared to be eating, drinking, and getting along just fine, Fiona maintained her suspicion that something was wrong. She described the experience of colors as "an almost instinctive feeling." After the second day, the collie became extremely ill. Fiona scooped her up and drove a long way to another farm where there was a vet. The collie had evidently been poisoned by a pesticide used on the farm where she lived. Once Fiona found out the specific kind of poison the vet was able to neutralize it. The collie was fine, but Fiona was stunned by her experience. She explained this calmly, matter-of-factly, though with a hint of hesitance, an internal skepticism. "It was the strangest thing. It was *almost* like I had this pre-sense. And I think my synesthesia had everything to do with that."[3]

Someone who didn't know anything about synesthesia might conclude one of four things: Fiona is lying; Fiona is a little "out there"; Fiona has strange, paranormal powers; Fiona is a little "out there" *and* what happened to her collie is an amazing coincidence.

But there's another way to look at this, which is to key in on Fiona's concluding statement: "I think my synesthesia had everything to do with that." Is it possible the neural cross wiring that's characteristic of synesthesia opens up a range of nonordinary possibilities, such that Fiona did discern something of an incipient illness in her dog? And could other forms of synesthesia, not just the mirror touch variety, open up the person, as it were, to forms of knowing, of apprehension, which bypass the rest of us?

Synesthesia and Anomalous Perceptions

Neurologist Richard Cytowic, who introduced synesthesia to a public audience in 1993 with his book *The Man Who Tasted Shapes* (and sparked a profusion of scientific interest),[4] noted at the time that synesthetes "seem more prone to [report] 'unusual experiences' than one might expect."[5] More recently, researchers in Spain have proposed that "healers" who claim to see auras around people are relying on a form of synesthesia.[6] A Swedish paper suggests a link between synesthesia and out-of-body experience (OBE).[7]

The most current research on such questions is being carried out by Christine Simmonds-Moore at the University of West Georgia in Carrollton, Georgia. A synesthete herself, her explorations have been prompted by the recognition that healers will sometimes claim that a part of the body they sense to be unwell appears as a certain color to them (red, for example). Other parts of the body that are healthy might appear to be a different color (such as green). As in the case of Fiona, instances of mirror touch synesthesia—as strange as they are—might seem for all intents and purposes like ESP or other "psychic powers." Flipped around, it's also possible that a genuinely psychic person could apprehend information gained anomalously in a manner reminiscent of synesthesia.[8]

One path Simmonds-Moore has illuminated is the key role that emotion plays in at least some forms of synesthesia. Take, for example, a synesthete named Harry (a pseudonym), who reports a wide range of both synesthetic and anomalous experiences. Harry associates colors with numbers, letters, and words (the most common type of synesthesia), as well as with days and months. He even experiences colors with different genres of music and mathematical concepts. Harry reports having an exceptional memory along with strong musical and mathematical abilities (memory having been shown to aid and abet these talents). He also says he perceives auras and has lucid dreams (this is where the dreamer knows he or she is in a dream and can even manipulate what happens in the dream). In his interviews with Simmonds-Moore, Harry equated the strength of his emotions with the strength of his synesthesia.[9]

Emotional Synesthesia

Numerous other examples provide ample evidence linking emotion to synesthesia—such as in the following cases, when colors, shapes, and textures are experienced:

- Penny is "visited" by colors based on the feeling tone of the situation she's in. On one occasion, a translucent red blob covered the back of her writing hand as she completed a difficult examination. Another time a warm blue light hovered above and to her left ("as if the sun were shining") while she wrote a letter on a subject that aroused strong emotion in her. A small blue light will often appear, she reports, when she puts her baby to bed.[10]
- Deni sees purple when she's upset with her kids and yelling at them. She relates that many years earlier she saw "orange sherbet foam" when kissing her boyfriend.[11]
- Dmitri's first intense sexual experience "was accompanied by huge, strong, geometrical shapes, spheres, cubes, and pylons that filled my mind."[12]
- Women synesthetes describe their orgasms as being accompanied by "brilliant flashes of colored lights," "two-dimensional, brightly

colored shapes moving against a black background," "neon pastels, intertwined like a rope or thick strands of licorice," or "a three-dimensional oil slick, myriad colors blended together exactly as it looks on the road after a rain."[13]

There is, in fact, a form of synesthesia known as "emotionally mediated synesthesia" or simply "emotional synesthesia." Examples can be found in the medical literature dating back to 1925. A synesthete in that era related the following: "Read of the death of a near neighbor; the newspaper suddenly turned green and took on a swirling motion; as I read the details the color faded somewhat but for several hours my imagery took on a greenish cast. Later in the day I picked up [a] magazine and discovered a reference to an old acquaintance. The green cast changed to colors characteristic of happier moods—rose, orchid, and cream yellow."[14]

A synesthete quoted by Cytowic in 1989 said: "It feels like an emotional bond. The feeling lasts a few seconds . . . sometimes I think I see the color and react emotionally; [with] others it may be reversed—I get an emotion and then see the color."[15] For another woman, people she had gotten to know were associated with a color. When presented with the given person's name or face, that color would spontaneously appear. Her feeling for the individual seemed to exert some influence over the color.[16] And a male synesthete saw halos around people that corresponded to his feelings about them; experiments confirmed that his perceptions were real, not imagined.[17] In each of these instances, the emotional biology of the synesthete herself or himself was clearly paramount, given that none of the people who evoked the emotionally shaded colors was physically present at the time.

Emotions, Colors, and Intuition

Let's step back for a moment and consider the known ways that we perceive emotion as color. First is a general observation: people tend to equate the concept of "lighter" with "higher" and "brighter" while equating the concept of "darker" with "lower" and "descending." This may simply be because the sky (from which light emanates) is above us whereas the ground beneath us is dark. In any case, these relationships are consistent for both synesthetes and nonsynesthetes.[18] Physiologically, human beings are adept at intuiting the feelings of others based on subtle shifts in blood flow—and minute changes in color—around the nose, eyebrows, cheeks, and chin. Indeed, nowhere else on the body are so many blood vessels so close to the surface of the skin. This suggests that human beings are not only programmed to express a multitude of fleeting feelings via the face but also that we have evolved to *detect* those changes in others.[19]

Our very language—our idiomatic expressions—point to the functioning of this system. A person can argue until he's "blue in the face." Someone can turn "green with envy" or go "green around the gills" with disgust. We can be "rosy cheeked" in health and contentment, yet also become "red-faced" with embarrassment. Our faces can turn ashen with dread or white with fury. Our moods, too, are known in cultural colors. If you're feeling down, you're "blue." But if all is fine, you're "golden." These expressions presumably didn't develop in a vacuum. Recent research suggests that they harbor some physiological truth, as touches of color characterize every expressed feeling via slightly different amounts in locations around the face.[20]

So are synesthetes simply better at facial recognition than everyone else? Are their memories better, too, so that merely hearing the name of someone they know conjures up an immediate emotional association that registers in color? This may be—but I suggest there's more to the equation.

For one thing, every synesthete's internal "palette" is different: One person's indigo Wednesday is another's chartreuse. Beyond that, how are we to interpret the mechanism manifesting in Fiona's "two colliding snakes"—a corollary to her perception of the bluish-orange disturbance in her collie? Likewise, how to interpret an account supplied by the "mind reading" entertainer Kreskin—a synesthete himself—who once felt compelled to stop a performance because he was convinced that an audience member he'd interacted with was planning to commit suicide? "I had sensed it," he relates, "almost the way one feels sick to one's stomach, an actual, physical sensation of queasiness that was immediately and consciously associated in my mind with death."[21]

It's probably no coincidence that in his twenties and thirties Kreskin served as a medical intuitive to an established physician.[22] His degree of intuition is mirrored, shall we say, in this account by the mirror touch synesthete Megan Pohlmann, a nurse at St. Louis Children's Hospital, who recalls one young patient thusly: "It was like we were so much on the same wavelength that I didn't even have to ask if his medication had headaches as a side effect. I just had an overwhelming urge to bang my head on something to make the pressure stop. A few hours later that's exactly what he started doing. It turns out that headaches were a common side effect of the drip he was on."[23]

Such perceptions are literally empathetic—a corollary to the hypersensitivity that's a trait of synesthesia in general.[24] Consider that synesthetes are wired in such a way as to literally gather more sensory information than most other people. Indeed, they're known to become overwhelmed by things such as a trip to the supermarket, with its barrage of stimuli: crowded aisles and plentiful sights, sounds, and smells (at least in the produce section).[25] Synesthetes aren't the only type of "highly sensitive person."[26] They're one distinct variety. I contend that a high degree of empathy—and its close cousin, intuition—inevitably accompany such sensitivity.

When Boundaries Are Thinned

If synesthesia as a condition evinces high sensitivity, we might ask if it works the other way around. Do other types of highly sensitive people ever experience synesthesia? I'm not sure this question has been investigated scientifically but it deserves to be. One potentially relevant finding is that synesthesia can be induced in highly suggestible individuals through hypnosis.[27] In fact, people who are highly suggestible tend to score higher in three personality measures: one known as openness to experience, another known as absorption,[28] and a third known as thin boundaries.[29]

Boundaries is a concept I have written about at length, and it seems logical to infer that people with thin boundaries would be more likely than the average Joe or Jane to experience synesthesia. Again, it's not apparent if this correlation has been systematically explored. But something else has been: the effect on the average Joe or Jane when *they have their boundaries thinned.* Two distinct types of such experiences have been examined. The first is the use of drugs, most notably LSD, mescaline, and psilocybin. These agents are known to produce synesthesia-like perceptions, though it remains unclear if the perceptions qualify as genuinely synesthetic.[30]

The second type of experience is completely involuntary and something no one would want to go through—a near-death experience (NDE). Interviews done with more than three thousand survivors of an NDE indicate that close to 80 percent of them experience a raft of major changes afterward, including synesthesia.[31] One study found that synesthesia arises in as many as two-thirds of cases.[32] Other reported aftereffects include unusual sensitivity to light and sound, increased allergies, electrical sensitivity, vivid dreams, heightened creativity and aesthetic appreciation, enhanced intuition, and an uptick in psychic experiences.[33] An increase in reported psychic experiences has also been found by American and Australian researchers.[34]

The fact that electrical sensitivity is prominent among these reports is significant.[35] In my own survey of highly sensitive people, I found that 37 percent of respondents claimed to be electrically sensitive, asserting that their presence affected computers, lights, or appliances in an unusual way. This contrasted with just 6 percent of a control group that did not assert native high sensitivity.[36] The numbers are considerably higher among people who have had an NDE. "A large majority" of such individuals report electrical sensitivity, according to longtime researcher P. M. H. Atwater.[37] Intriguingly, a 2008 study found that people who reported the most electrical effects tended to be those who related having had "deeper" NDEs—whereas people who reported the fewest electrical effects tended not to have had NDEs at all.[38]

Alterations of Consciousness and Emotion

A fascinating illustration is that of Tony Cicoria, an orthopedic surgeon who had an NDE upon being struck by lightning in 1994. He was famously the subject of a profile by the late neurologist Oliver Sacks, who focused on Cicoria's transformation, soon after the lightning strike, into someone obsessed with piano music.[39] Cicoria began hearing classical music in his head, which would intrude into whatever he was doing. The music would often come "in an absolute torrent" of notes with no breaks, overwhelming him. He became inspired—indeed, possessed—by what he came to call "the music from heaven."[40]

Cicoria also became much more spiritually inclined, reading every book he could find on NDEs, lightning strikes, and high-voltage electricity. He acquired "a whole library" on Nikola Tesla, the inventor of alternating current (who, by his own description, was extraordinarily sensitive).[41]

Concurrently—pun intended—Cicoria maintains that he became electrically sensitive himself. This included a penchant for sensing electrical buildups in the ground prior to a storm . . . having computers and watches frequently malfunction in his presence . . . feeling auras around people . . . apparently transmitting energy himself . . . and seeing apparitions and having other psychic impressions.[42] Cicoria is unassuming and down-to-earth about what happened to him.[43]

Reflecting on this case, Sacks considered that a sudden NDE must, of its very nature, induce neurobiological upheaval as well as profound alterations of consciousness and emotion. "One cannot suppose," he wrote, "that such events are pure fancy; similar features are emphasized in every account." He equated the surge of music in Cicoria's life to "a surge of emotionality, as if [feelings] of every sort were being stimulated or released."[44] Such major shifts in personality are widely noted by NDE researchers. The aftereffects amount to what I would term *a thinning of boundaries.* Thin-boundary people are sensitive and open, apprehending connections and commonalities much more than distinction and separations.[45] NDEs, I contend, are likely to thin an experiencer's boundaries in numerous ways. It is possible that during an NDE one's sense of self even expands into the surroundings—and that the experiencer "returns" with a greater appreciation for other people's feelings and perceptions and a more highly developed sense of empathy.

Synesthetes, perhaps, have such a capacity built in. Fiona's imagery of the two snakes when she was looking at her collie, for example—and her perception of a bluish-orange color (her internal code for pain)—may be a case of instantaneously apprehending what another is feeling. Kreskin's sensing of what he believed was an audience member's suicidal intent, paired with the physical sensation of queasiness, might be a similar case in point. Likewise, nurse Megan's overwhelming sense of pressure in her head—evidently mirrored in her young patient's headaches—could reflect this instant and instinctual empathy.

It remains to be seen if particular types of synesthesia (mirror touch first and foremost) are consistently associated with these types of experiences. But we would be wise to recognize that we don't know what we don't know. Accordingly, we should consider the distinct possibility that other forms of knowing—based on *dynamics of feeling*—may be available to some of us, at least at certain times and in certain circumstances.

The Processes of Synesthesia

My own conjecture (actually one voiced by an increasing number of researchers) is that synesthesia is simply a different manifestation of mental and emotional processes that are common to each and every one of us. As exotic as it may seem, synesthesia points toward the general way that feelings become associated with particular people. It's also representative of the way that metaphors become our typical mode of thinking about things and describing them.

Much of this has to do with childhood development. Consider a four-year-old boy who sees people in colors. The people closest to him have the boldest, most definitive colors, whereas people he doesn't know well do not yet have colors. Once a person does take on a color, that color doesn't change. This state of affairs reflects the universal and unconscious process of gathering impressions about people—"sizing them up"—and at a certain point, effectively deciding what our attitude toward them is. Accordingly, the colors that synesthetic children associate with given individuals tend to deepen and solidify as the children grow. By their early teens, these colors will stay the same. The "assignment" of synesthetic colors, then, reflects one's becoming emotionally intelligent—figuring out what other people are like and what can be expected from them. It's a process we all share.[46]

I will go farther by suggesting that synesthetic impressions may also reflect information *outside of ourselves* that, while available in principle to any one of us, registers in a more direct and unique way for someone sufficiently sensitive—such as a Fiona, a Kreskin, or a Megan. For example, a synesthete once stated that when she was around Alzheimer's patients, the colors she perceived were "washed out and runny." Another synesthete remarked that an acquaintance of hers no longer triggered any color experience—and that person passed away shortly thereafter.[47] What appears to be happening in such cases is that the synesthesia—or lack of it—amounts to an impression of the health and emotional availability of the other person. Whereas the rest of us would come away with a general sense of unease, the synesthesia amplifies such information and presents it in a unique way (or no way at all, if the person who is being observed is not long for this world).

Here are two more cases in point. Case 1: The synesthete tends to see a "color spike" or "small lightning bolts, metallic, silvery, bronzy" around people who turn out to be disagreeable. Case 2: The synesthete sees a given person as red, green, or black, connoting that they are (respectively) mad, sad, or sick.[48] In these instances, the individual is unknown to the synesthete so no characteristic colored aura has yet formed. For the rest of us nonsynesthetes, we might harbor a vague sense that the other person is "trouble" and perhaps someone to stay away from. The synesthete, however, gathers a strong impression that registers in a distinct shape and bold color. The process for everyone is unconscious and automatic. For the synesthete, it's so instantaneous as to seem like clairvoyance. It's not anything magical or spooky, but it *is* predicated on dimly perceived emotion—both the conveyance of essential information about "who" the other person is and the sizing up of that information.

Feelings Flow

I have emphasized that feelings are dynamic: they rise and fall, ebb and flow.[49] This dynamism manifests the fact that, in the innermost workings of our cells, human beings are fundamentally electrical creatures.[50] The etymology of the word *emotion* expresses this state of affairs; its Latin root means "to move or to excite."[51]

The essence of a feeling is to be in flux. You know that you feel something because it's qualitatively different from what you felt a moment ago, and it won't be precisely the same feeling as time goes on. And while feelings are mercurial, they act differently within different people at different times. Picture them as water: they can surge or get bottled up; meander or pool. I've proposed that the flow is characteristically faster and more direct in some people (those who are referred to as "thin-boundary") and slower and less direct in others (who are referred to as "thick-boundary").[52]

This is not meant as any kind of value judgment, since feelings will act differently within each of us at different times and in different circumstances. Nor is it necessarily "good" or "bad" to apprehend and react to a feeling more quickly or more slowly. However, as the late Ernest Hartmann explained, people can be grouped along a continuum—from extremely thick-boundary to highly thin-boundary—based on their preponderance to be more or less reactive, more or less sensitive.[53]

There's a clear connection with synesthesia given that the findings of Hartmann and others disclose that synesthetes are on the thin side of the boundary spectrum.[54] But just as synesthesia illustrates mental and emotional processes that occur in everyone, so too does the condition point up the *workings of emotion in general*. Three cases in point that deserve examination involve migraine headaches, déjà vu, and phantom pain. (I use these examples not because everyone has these experiences or because they're commonplace but to illustrate how feelings—their energy and flow—and the apprehension of them work.)

The Emotional Dynamics of Migraine

To begin, there are several interesting things about migraine. A phenomenon known as "aura" will sometimes presage a migraine (in about 25 percent of sufferers).[55] An aura is often visual, presenting as bright spots or flashes of light, zigzag lines, or shapes—not altogether different from what some synesthetes experience. But an aura is far worse, causing tingling or a feeling of numbness, dizziness, blurred vision, confusion, and difficulty speaking.

One thing migraine sufferers tend to have in common is that they're highly responsive emotionally, reacting quickly to stress.[56] Australian headache expert James Lance has observed that "the pain control system and the related neurotransmitters are different in [patients with migraine], being more sensitive to changes in the body itself or the outside world."[57] This is a critical point: Migraine sufferers are extraordinarily sensitive to their surroundings as well as their own internal "landscape" of feeling. Emotional prompts, both from without and within, can and do set the stage for a massive headache. Consider the following anecdote from Lance:

A patient of mine was having a heated argument with a girlfriend about the rebellious attitude he had towards his father when he had been a teenager, a subject that had distressed him in later years. At the height of the argument his vision started to blur, and soon he could see only the center of objects. This tunnel vision lasted for about 10 minutes, after which his characteristic migraine headache developed. Some weeks later he was attending a cinema and found that the film dealt with the same problem of the father-son relationship that had always troubled him. Within a few minutes his vision misted over, and tunnel vision was again followed by a headache.[58]

An especially compelling account comes from psychoanalyst Stephen Appel, who writes of his own longtime acquaintance with migraines and one experience in particular:

In a co-therapy session Rebecca, a vivacious young woman, paraplegic after an accident that occurred after she got married, was confronting her husband yet again: "Why don't we have sex anymore? I'm still interested." Yet again, her husband hung his head, saying little. Then a sudden change: he raised his head, looking directly at his wife and out poured a stream of cruel, cold truth-telling. "I'll tell you why. You think you're normal, but you're not. You won't hear this, but you're disabled. You just lie there; I have to do all the work. Do you know what it's like having sex with a handicapped person? It's not fun, I can tell you." . . . And so on for some considerable time. Then a tearful silence broken eventually by Rebecca in her characteristic upbeat, appealing voice. "Yes, but that's just an excuse, we can try can't we?" The session came to an end, and as the couple left the room I was struck by a powerful and debilitating migraine.

Here the pain, rage, humiliation, sweetness, desperation, frustration, fear, horror, and heartbreak in the room became too great for me to handle. Taken aback, I identified with everything, it seems: his feelings about living with a paraplegic spouse, her hurt at hearing herself described in this way, and his desperation at her denial. Stunned into silence by the suddenness and the sheer magnitude of this emotional load, I was unable to relieve it. . . . I got a migraine for my troubles.[59]

According to Sacks, who first became known for his study of the subject, migraine is "conspicuously a psychophysiological event . . . an oblique expression of feelings which are denied direct or adequate expression."[60] I agree but would frame the matter slightly differently. Put it this way: when a thin-boundary person is caught unawares by powerful feelings, a migraine may result. Indeed, Appel understands his own tendency toward migraine as being "blindsided, mugged if you like" by an upwelling of feeling. Once the person is able to acknowledge the arousal (and, if appropriate, express the feelings—literally *emote*), the migraine will, like a wave, crash over and recede. In fact, suggests Appel, attending to the waxing and waning of migrainous symptoms may help "measure the extent of [one's] repression and denial, or insight and relief." It seems to have worked in his case, as Appel says he has come to "recognize the early signs . . . transform these into [emotions]," and so he no longer suffers from migraine.[61]

The Gut's Own Nervous System

A migraine is typically thought of as a phenomenon taking place solely in the head. However, the premise that feelings flow throughout the body suggests that anything related to emotional expression (or emotional damming) ought to be examined from the standpoint of the human being as a whole: mind *and* body. It is high time, indeed, to dispense with the notion that mind is something entirely different from body.

Although the presumption that mind and body are different types of things has a four-hundred-year history—dating back to the French philosopher/mathematician René Descartes—plenty of old ideas (such as the Earth being flat or a given race being inherently superior to another) have rightfully been invalidated. We would do better to adopt the concept of *bodymind:* the whole of who a person is—immaterial (mental, emotional, psychological) as well as material (neural, molecular, biological).[62]

This overlap, this interconnectedness, is on display through the constant communication that goes on between our brain and our gut. The fact of the matter is that the gut possesses its own self-contained nervous system. Known as the enteric nervous system, it can operate in the complete absence of input from the brain or even the spinal cord. It is huge, encompassing more than one hundred million nerve cells in the small intestine alone. When you add the nerve cells of the esophagus, stomach, and large intestine the result is that the bowel contains more nerve cells than the spine. This makes the enteric nervous system effectively our "second brain."[63]

The enteric nervous system is a vast chemical factory where every type of neurotransmitter found in the "first brain" is represented. One impressive example: 95 percent of the body's serotonin—the neurotransmitter involved in regulating one's mood and reactions to stress—is manufactured in the bowel, from whence it travels to the head.[64] Indeed, the stream of messages between the one brain and the other is so continuous that scientists often refer to them as a single entity: the brain-gut axis. All of this dialogue suggests that the term *gut feeling* isn't merely a figure of speech.[65] The matters we "chew on," find "hard to digest" or "tough to stomach," or that make us "want to throw up" may have analogues in the gut. These types of misgivings, irritations, or upsets may even originate there.

How does all this relate to migraine? Consider that serotonin is an important factor in the development of migraine as it has a direct effect on cerebral blood vessels.[66] This would suggest that the gut plays a role. So does the fact that migraine can be triggered by a variety of foods and beverages—and that nausea, vomiting, diarrhea, and constipation can be symptoms. *Abdominal migraine* is the term given to a condition experienced by some children who often go on to develop migraine headaches as adults.[67] Strangely, while scientists admit they don't know what causes this malady, the neurologists who drive the science remain wedded to the notion that it must be a disorder of the brain.[68] But the fact that it's a *head* ache doesn't mean that it necessarily starts there. Given what we know of the enteric nervous system—and how people prone to migraine are sensitive to all manner of environmental and emotional triggers—theories that migraine may originate in the digestive system ought to gain (or regain) currency.[69]

Déjà Vu and Dissociation

Moving on to another prime example of feelings at work in the body-mind, we come to déjà vu—the bizarre sense that one has lived a particular moment before. It is, I suspect, an outgrowth of *dissociation,* the term used for the unconscious disregard of what one is feeling. Dissociation can be a coping mechanism for a stressful situation—including situations that don't appear stressful on their face but recall disturbing memories. Or it can be a more benign process through which one becomes absorbed in a given activity, whether it's reading a riveting book, having a pleasant daydream, or being immersed in work or a hobby. In these latter situations we not only lose track of time but, in a manner of speaking, we lose track of ourselves. We no longer are aware of our *felt sense.*

The felt sense is the awareness of our bodily state—of pressure and vibration, weight and balance, breathing, heartbeat, temperature, smell and taste, hunger and thirst, touch, smell, pain, pleasure, sexual arousal, and all other body-based perceptions. In the words of psychologist Peter Levine, the felt sense is "the medium through which we experience the totality of sensation. . . . [It] blends together most of the information that forms your experience. Even when you are not aware of it, the felt sense is telling you where you are and how you feel at any given moment."[70]

Scientists use the term *interoception* for the felt sense.[71] Paralleling the thick-to-thin boundary spectrum, people are known to differ in their interoceptive ability, ranging from all but oblivious to highly perceptive. While there are undoubtedly many ways to appraise or measure the felt sense, interoception researchers have adopted just one: counting heartbeats. A problem here is that focusing on this cardiovascular benchmark ignores other physiological signals that may, practically speaking, be more important than tuning in to your heartbeat.

Whether it's being conscious of a stiff neck or a stomachache, chills down the spine or goose bumps on the flesh, an aching back or a generalized anxiety, a heart "leaping" in joy or butterflies in one's stomach, the perception of body states is incredibly varied. Heartbeats have undoubtedly been chosen because they are the most regular and recurring bodily event compared to any other. And while studies do show a close correspondence between interoceptive ability and the perception of intense emotion,[72] there's conflicting evidence as to whether being good at counting your own heartbeats means you're more empathetic.[73]

It might be that interoceptive ability is a form of emotional intelligence,[74] except that whereas women are generally considered more emotionally intelligent than men, thirty years of research has shown that men tend to be better at this form of interoception.[75] Perhaps other forms of interoception will be shown to be more generally meaningful and to more closely relate to the overall "felt sense." For now, acuity in heartbeat perception seems mostly a barometer of *reactivity*—the thin-boundary tendency to realize that one is getting worked up over something.[76]

To return to the felt sense, dissociation is what results when one takes leave of it. Beyond daydreaming and the less consequential instances of dissociation, it can also function as a defense mechanism, avoiding or repressing something that is emotionally threatening. Déjà vu is, I believe, a form of dissociation.[77]

In a nutshell, here's how it might work. Say you are facing a situation reminiscent to some degree of something threatening or overwhelming that occurred earlier in your life. You might experience the faintest of recalls but immediately have that recollection severed by the part of you that wishes the memory to lie dormant. That vague and momentary recall would be experienced as déjà vu. (Freud proposed something similar: that déjà vu represents the momentary recall of a memory deeply repressed from childhood or infancy.)[78]

About two-thirds of people have experienced déjà vu.[79] As commonplace as it is, there is no accepted explanation for why it happens.[80] Nonetheless, one experiment provides support for my hypothesis. Researchers found that if subjects were shown a scene that was very similar to a scene that they'd been presented with earlier but could not recall, a feeling of déjà vu was sometimes sparked.[81]

Déjà vu, I suggest, can be considered the typical person's equivalent of synesthesia—a peculiar overlap of present and past, a spontaneous and compellingly different form of perception. This is not to imply that synesthesia is itself a symptom of dissociation but that both phenomena reflect the dynamics of feeling. Whereas synesthetes are thin-boundary individuals, it seems likely to me that the people who experience déjà vu most frequently are thick-boundary.

Boundaries in Phantom Pain

Our third example of "feeling flow" is the phenomenon of phantom pain. This is a challenging condition wherein people who have lost a limb will complain vigorously about strange sensations where their arm or leg, hand, or foot used to be. *Cramping, itching, burning,* and *shooting* are the adjectives most commonly used to describe this sensation. In every case the person is convinced that the limb (or whatever the body part may be) is still there. The sensations are so realistic that the afflicted individuals will often attempt to walk on their phantom leg or search for objects with their phantom hand. Sometimes a bunion on the foot, a watch worn on the wrist, or a ring that had been on one's finger can be felt just as it used to be. Phantom sensations can occur immediately after surgery or manifest after weeks, months, or even years. In some cases the symptoms abate only to return later. The phenomenon is quite common: estimates are that 50–80 percent of amputees have experienced it.[82]

What could distinguish this large group from the minority of amputees who don't experience phantom pain? My supposition is that the former are predominantly thick-boundary individuals and that the pain they feel is an artifact, a "relic" of the dissociative process. Initial evidence to this effect comes from Eric Leskowitz, a Boston-based psychiatrist and energy healer who directs the Spaulding Rehabilitation Network's Integrative Health Initiative.[83] Leskowitz treated two patients whose reaction to their respective situations differed quite a bit. These differences, I submit, shed light on their boundary functioning. The first patient, "Mr. A," was

> a 37-year-old cargo loader, who lost his left leg just below the knee after suffering a massive crush injury when a cargo dolly jackknifed into his leg. He developed stump and phantom pain which was not responsive to two years of rehabilitation treatments. . . . Formerly an avid athlete, he appeared to withdraw from life due to the loss of his old self-image as a hockey player and "tough guy." He was also quite invested in a Worker's Compensation suit against his former employer, which consumed much of his emotional energy.
>
> He described this process of releasing his pain as frightening to him. Somehow, he was holding on to the pain and preventing it from totally leaving his body. He realized that if he could no longer feel any pain in his phantom leg, he would have to experience the true absence of his leg for the first time since his injury . . . doing so would also involve accepting the fact that he would never play hockey again. He stated quite clearly that he was not ready to proceed with further energy healing, because he wasn't yet ready to accept his disability.

Contrast this patient's reaction and outlook with that of another patient, "Ms. B,"

> a 65-year-old widow whose severe diabetic peripheral vascular disease necessitated a below-the-knee amputation of her right leg. However,

she apparently misunderstood her surgeon's plans, because she went into surgery with the expectation that only two of her toes would be removed (the painful and gangrenous ones). Needless to say, she was shocked to wake up and find her lower leg missing. Within hours of her [surgery], she developed phantom pain of the two toes she had expected to lose. . . . She proved to be a feisty yet trusting woman who was primarily upset that her esteemed surgeon had so misled her. Part of her psychotherapeutic work with me involved venting her frustration, and also communicating her distress directly to her surgeon. These conversations allowed her to feel as though a load was lifted from her shoulders . . . [later] the phantom pain dissipated . . . she was pain free for the first time since surgery.

The differences between these two instances are striking. Mr. A desperately wished to retain his old self-image as the rough-and-ready hockey player whereas Ms. B. was able, after venting her anger and frustration, to accept her predicament. My inference is that to the extent a person can acknowledge and express the feelings that inevitably stem from such a traumatic surgical procedure, dissociation (and consequently, phantom pain) will be reduced. It's conceivable in such cases that thin-boundary individuals as well as thick-boundary individuals are affected. While the latter may have difficulty realizing that what they are feeling is significant, the former may be slow to appreciate the intensity of the feelings involved—a recognition, which, under less alarming circumstances, they would normally embrace.

Mirror Pain Synesthesia

An especially fascinating aspect of phantom pain is that some people with the condition are known to have become synesthetes themselves. They experience mirror pain synesthesia, a close cousin to the mirror touch synesthesia that we examined earlier. When observing someone

else in pain or when witnessing something known to be painful or inju-
rious being done to someone else (even if simulated and not really being
carried out), they feel pain in their own phantom limbs or stumps.
An academic paper on the subject offers several examples. One person reported painful "electric" impulses in his phantom foot when he
observed sutured wounds; another person reported phantom pain when
watching television images of amputation. A third person said his phantom foot "went crazy" when he heard a gruesome story. And a fourth
person felt pain, first in his stump and then in his phantom, when he
saw someone else who had been hurt.[84]

While not every mirror pain synesthete is an amputee, many are
known to have suffered other types of painful traumas before developing their predilection to experience another's pain. An expert on the
phenomenon, Bernadette Fitzgibbon of Monash University in Australia,
suggests that such trigger events can make some people hypervigilant
to pain and the threat of pain. They will automatically scan the environment for danger, fixating on potential sources and representing the
pain they come across as pain or discomfort within themselves. This
might be why one mirror pain synesthete also finds the sound of her
husband's power tools distressing: perhaps, unconsciously, they appear
as a threat. It might also explain her "general feeling of disquiet and
almost helplessness" when she sees another person suffering—the situation could effectively mirror her own helplessness as a patient in the
face of amputation.[85]

Undergoing surgery and being anesthetized (much less having a
limb, a hand, or a foot removed) are among the "tripwires" that Peter
Levine has catalogued as being the most stressful to human beings.[86]
All of these have one thing in common: being in a situation where the
ill effects are overwhelming, irreversible, or both. Put another way: It's
where one is on the receiving end of something extremely threatening,
harmful, or undesirable and has little to no control over it. Even if one
has the best surgeon in the world, has been fully briefed, and is entirely
confident that surgery is the right course of action, the surgeon is still

cutting through flesh, muscle, and bone and the surgery "still registers in the body as a life-threatening event. On the 'cellular level' the body perceives that it has sustained a wound serious enough to place it in mortal danger. Intellectually we may believe in an operation, but on a primal level our bodies do not."[87]

Everyone is different, of course, so there may be a few stout individuals for whom surgery is not nearly so daunting. By the same token, an operation itself might be a *catalyst* for mirror pain synesthesia but the stage could effectively have been set for the condition to assert itself years prior, if the given person were especially sensitive by dint of nature and/or nurture. Researchers who study highly sensitive people have repeatedly found that many such persons were highly sensitive as infants or young children.[88] However, any trauma severe enough at any age can conceivably result in hypervigilance.[89]

An Explanation of Mirror Pain

As I indicated earlier, "mirror" types of synesthesia—like other kinds of synesthesia—are increasingly being seen as different in degree from more typical neurobiological processes but not necessarily different in genre or class. So, as we all tend to recoil if we see someone being punched, and as we all tend to feel badly for someone who is grieving, we can view mirror synesthesias as extreme versions of the way that empathy generally works.

I want to reemphasize that the same principle ought to apply to the concept of emotion as flow—with the current characteristically speedier and more direct in some people and slower and less direct in others. If phantom pain is, as I've conjectured, a fundamentally dissociative phenomenon, affecting thick-boundary people more often and more profoundly than thin-boundary people, then the model might be extended to suggest that mirror pain experienced in a phantom body part is a thin-boundary "adaptation" on top of the dissociative "frame." Indeed, I interpret such mirror pain as a manifestation of the feeling flow asserting itself. It would be as if someone experiencing déjà vu (which I've presumed is another thick-boundary occurrence) were suddenly able to realize and express whatever apprehensions caused them to dissociate in the first place. It would be a literal breakthrough—an acknowledgment of the elemental nature of the feeling.

This is what I suspect is happening with mirror pain. The synesthetes who experience it are highly empathic but the current of their feelings has been short-circuited by trauma, hence the phantom pain. A reassertion of "that old feeling," however, makes clear the underlying dynamism of their bodymind. While mine is an unorthodox reading of what appears to be taking place, it is consistent with the evidence. One oft-cited paper addressing mirror touch synesthesia among amputees with phantom pain states that mirror touch sensations are reported by individuals who "show greater empathic emotional reactivity." In a parallel to my surmise that the feeling flow is revitalizing, the researchers speculate that these mirror touch synesthetes "could be predisposed to strengthening existing pathways between observed touch and felt touch."[90] In other words, constitutionally thin-boundary people have an energetic feeling flow that's aligned with greater empathy.

Mainstream neuroscience struggles to explain phantom pain—to say nothing of the mirror touch experienced by phantom pain patients. Most current theories of phantom pain suggest that it's a result of the central nervous system "rewiring" itself in a maladaptive way after amputation. Damaged nerve endings and displaced electrical discharges . . . hyper-excitability of spinal cord circuitry . . . reorganized neuronal networks . . . and alterations in sensory and motor feedback are all invoked as possible mechanisms, none of them mutually exclusive.[91] The fact that individuals with phantom pain commonly experienced intense, traumatic, or chronic pain *before* their operation[92] at least offers a consistent thread, suggesting that people so affected have been "primed" to notice and even expect their pain.

Blood Flow, Feeling Flow, Energy Flow

Importantly, it is recognized that phantom pain is often worse when the person is distressed. To the extent that emotion is brought into the equation, constricted blood flow and fluctuations in the sympathetic nervous system have been identified as likely agents. It's likewise understood that emotionally charged experiences—whether restricted to oneself or triggered by seeing someone else in pain—result in increased pain in the phantom body part but not elsewhere.[93] But beyond these observations and stabs at mechanisms, mainstream neuroscience still has an enormous mystery on its hands.

The identification of blood flow, in my estimation, sheds some light on emotion as the driver of this phenomenon. Blood flow has been implicated in the process of migraine, which, as we noted earlier, is another condition that's sensitive to feeling. Migrainous pain can be reduced through biofeedback and acupuncture, both of which (through different means) are believed to work by altering the blood flow.[94]

Such observations (and treatments), taken together, comprise a picture of what is going on. The flow of feeling in people with mirror pain synesthesia manifests in the phantom, which serves as a focal point for their natural empathy. Here, the thin-boundary personality reasserts itself after the trauma of amputation, which triggered dissociation in the face of the palpable, bodily threat of surgery and the resulting loss of a body part. Dissociation—the unconscious disregard of what one is prone to feel—transmuted the underlying energy of feelings into phantom pain. Whether those feelings were sadness, shock, disbelief, or anger, they were effectively displaced into a phenomenon—phantom pain—that successfully captures the patient's attention.

As articulated earlier, thick-boundary people like "Mr. A" (the hockey player) are apt to stay in this situation whereas thinner-boundary people like "Ms. B" (the feisty widow) may be able to shed their phantom pain by coming to terms with and literally expressing their intense, pent-up feelings. (While not an exact parallel, one particular study I came across points up the differing dynamics. Subjects who were more in touch with their feelings were quicker to object to their pain than were subjects who were more dissociated from their feelings. While the terms *thin boundary* and *thick boundary* were not known by the researchers, the concept I am getting at does seem to have applied.)[95]

Indirect evidence for the emotional core of phantom pain comes from the more-than-occasional success of treatments aimed at releasing the pent-up energy associated with the phenomenon. Eye Movement Desensitization and Reprocessing (EMDR), for example, a therapy looked upon with high regard by well-known trauma experts,[96] has been shown to be efficacious in resolving phantom pain[97]—as have treatments such as acupuncture and therapeutic touch.[98] In the latter case, the patient described a sensation "as though the pain were draining down his leg and foot. Within a matter of moments, he was pain free for the first time since his surgery."[99]

Vastly Heightened Empathy

It seems apropos to circle back to the subject this chapter began with—namely, mirror touch synesthesia. Only this time we'll ask, "Is it really synesthesia?" The question is triggered by the foregoing discussion of mirrored pain in stumps or phantom appendages. Would we say that people who experience this kind of pain have synesthesia (defined as crossed senses) or do they have an exceptional form of empathy?

Let's start by reconsidering what it's like to have mirror touch or mirror pain. First, I wish to note how many people may be affected by these conditions. Current estimates are that just 1.5 percent of the population has mirror touch while 17 percent—quite a bit higher—has mirror pain.[100] The distinction may effectively be meaningless, as can be gathered from the comments of people with one or both of these capacities.

Recall Megan Pohlmann, the nurse in St. Louis. She says that her empathy is so strong that she can read a room when she walks into it, feel the emotions of strangers before they speak, and suffer the pain of another person's injury. "If I see you, I *know* you," Megan says. "Just walking around every day I feel strangers hurting, and I feel it so thoroughly and completely." What is it like to have mirror touch? "[It] goes beyond putting ourselves in someone else's shoes. It's actually wearing the shoes for a while. It's feeling the water splash from puddles. It's feeling the wear and tear in the soles."[101]

This sounds, first and foremost, like a vastly heightened form of empathy. My interpretation is bolstered by the way Megan describes her approach as a nurse "tuning in" to her patients: "I visualize my personal space surrounding [theirs]. Then I can feel them more." Once she's done that, filtering out the sensed feelings of the other person can be challenging. One patient, for instance, suffered a panic attack and Megan felt herself starting to have one, too. At the end of her workday, she needs to meditate in the hospital's rooftop garden to regain her equilibrium.[102]

A British woman, Fiona Torrance, relates that while watching someone eat she will taste and feel their food in her mouth. If someone is happy, "it's like an orchestra and I feel extreme excitement and joy." Another person's anger, though, feels like "heat running between my chest and stomach." And the feelings aren't limited to people physically present around her. When Fiona went to see the movie *The Girl with the Dragon Tattoo,* she felt as if her body were being beaten when the main character, Salander, was being tortured.[103]

Mirror pain experiences can be even more bizarre. C. C. Hart, a San Francisco massage therapist, feels "shocking electricity—like bolts of fire" down the backs of her legs anytime she sees someone who's injured.[104] Interestingly enough, "electricity" is often mentioned by people with mirror senses.[105] I find this intriguing given what we noted earlier: electrical sensitivity as a common aftereffect of near-death experiences. If NDEs force a thinning of one's boundaries, the effects would be consistent with greater empathy—even, perhaps, with this type of "energy surge" experienced by some thin-boundary people equipped with mirror senses.

Mirror Senses:
More than Mirror Neurons

The standard explanation for mirror sensory synesthesia (though scientists are debating whether or not "synesthesia" is appropriate to invoke) is that the individual's mirror neuron system is hyperactive. Mirror neurons are brain cells that fire when one is undertaking an action as well as when observing the same action being taken by another (or when hearing a vocalization associated with the action).[106] It's hypothesized that they also fire when someone else is seen experiencing a distinct sensation or feeling—thus providing a perceptual pathway for the development of empathy. If you flinch when you see someone being hit, for example, that is thought to be the work of mirror neurons.

Since their discovery (in monkeys) was announced in 1996, scientists have speculated unabashedly about the role of mirror neurons. Some go so far as to say that these cells underlie the ability of humans to form a theory of mind about their fellows—to understand intentionality. Still other researchers speculate that mirror neurons explain why yawns and laughter are contagious, and how we can "catch" each other's moods. Interestingly, though, their existence in people has yet to be proved, since it's not normally possible to study single neurons in the human brain. Some scientists criticize as simplistic the attribution of an expansive role for mirror neurons since they're inevitably embedded in a complex network of brain activity. One writer dubbed them "the most hyped concept in neuroscience."[107]

It doesn't seem likely that mirror neurons are themselves the engine of empathy. I suggest instead that they're a sort of focusing device that trains our attention on others. When they fire, the signals they send must connect with our stored memories of how people tend to look or sound or act in the given situation. This connection is vital because some people are quite adept at deceiving through their facial expressions and gestures while still others are ambivalent, camouflaging the truth even from themselves. For all these reasons, it's unlikely that the functioning of mirror neurons can single-handedly explain mirror sensory synesthesia, let alone "regular" empathy.

Moreover, people with mirror senses go far beyond our typical notion of empathy. In a room of total strangers they can tell instantly who is depressed, who is angry, who has just received good news.[108] They themselves feel the warmth of others in love or find themselves saddled with another's pain. They feel embarrassed, elated, anguished. The experience is qualitatively different from merely identifying with someone or empathizing as a distinct individual. Their very boundaries get blurred.

Likewise, as medical professionals, they can instantaneously visualize—or infer, picture, or sense—what is likely wrong with the patient or client. This capacity goes well beyond a "gut instinct" or what we normally think of as intuition. Interestingly, the impressions aren't confined to the head. They are emphatically realized in the body as well. Think of Kreskin's sense of dread around an audience member; his initial feeling was "an actual, physical sensation of queasiness." Another mirror sensory synesthete, Maureen Seaberg, tells of a remarkable instance recently where she gathered highly accurate impressions of several students' aches and pains without needing to see the parts of their bodies that were hurting.[109] Some mirror synesthetes evidently have this ability—she and Kreskin are two of them.

A Case of Blurred Boundaries

This brings us to an alternate theory of mirror senses known as self/other representation. The idea is that individuals with mirror touch and/or mirror pain have innate difficulty separating the concept of "themselves" from that of other people. For example, another's face or arm or leg could be automatically and erroneously incorporated into the representation of one's own body. A prime example is the following, from a person with mirror touch reflecting on having watched the famous Romanian gymnast Nadia Comaneci during the 1976 Olympics: "As

Nadia moved through her routines, my body would twitch and my muscles would move as she moved, and my friends just considered me a freak, and I couldn't explain it, and I wasn't trying to do it, and I just found the more I watched her the muscles in my legs would fire, and my legs would move. I remember being not able to explain what I was doing or why I was doing it, or even really realizing that I was doing it, until my friends would point things out to me."[110]

The leading exponent of this view, psychologist Michael Banissy of Goldsmiths College, University of London, notes that blurred boundaries are effectively the result.[111] A useful example is the following: "If I were to attend to a lamp or a potted plant, I feel my body become many of their elements—the roundness of the lamp or the hollow round sensation of the lamp shade. . . . I sense my body shaped with the pointed characteristics of the branches of the plant and smooth portions corresponding to its leaves."[112]

Clearly this person's self-image is highly adaptable, one might even say porous. The individual fits Hartmann's description of a thin-boundary personality to a T. Thin-boundary people, in his view, have a less solid or definite sense of their skin as a body boundary; an enlarged sense of merging with another person when kissing or making love; a greater sensitivity to physical and emotional pain (in themselves as well as in others); a penchant for immersing themselves in something—be it a relationship, a hobby or task, a memory or a daydream; dream content that's highly vivid and emotional; and, overall, a mind that is "relatively fluid" compared to thick-boundary people.[113] Hartmann believed that his Boundaries concept would prove to reflect actual neurobiological differences.[114] As additional data are gathered from synesthetes and others who fit the profile, I am increasingly convinced that he was right.

Psychosomatic Plasticity

Perhaps the most remarkable characteristic of highly thin-boundary people is their capacity to generate bona fide physical reactions to a thought, idea, or suggestion. Hartmann documented this ability through an experiment. He told a group of subjects to imagine that they were sitting by a fire with one hand near the fire, and then that they were holding an ice cube in that hand. The thin-boundary individuals produced a significantly greater change in the skin temperature of their hands than those with thick boundaries.[115] (His finding—not in thin-boundary people *per se* but in individuals experiencing self/other confusion—has been affirmed elsewhere.)[116]

Other researchers studied what they termed the *fantasy-prone person*, remarking that "a striking characteristic . . . is that their vivid fantasies and memories are at times associated with physical concomitants."[117] The examples that they pointed to parallel what Hartmann noted, such as spontaneously becoming ill on seeing violence on television or in the movies, being affected by imagined heat and cold in the same way as actual heat and cold, and experiencing an orgasm purely as a result of one's sexual fantasy. The lead researcher, Theodore Barber, called this phenomenon *psychosomatic plasticity,* defining it as "an extreme capacity to turn suggestions . . . into bodily realities."[118] *Psychosomatic plasticity* resembles a term that neuroscientists have offered as a variation on Banissy's theme of confusion in self/other representation; people with mirror senses, in their view, have "an abnormally plastic self-representation" that allows them to merge, in their own minds, into the observed other.[119]

Neuroscientists, of course, share a conviction that the brain is where all of our experiences originate and where all of our perceptions necessarily reside. I submit that this view constitutes a prejudice, thereby limiting our ability to understand the phenomena in question. A different view is held by others, such as philosopher George Lakoff, who astutely notes that "Our brains take their input from the rest of our bodies. What our bodies are like and how they function in the world thus structures the very concepts we can use to think . . . the mind is inherently embodied."[120] In a similar but more poetic vein, naturalist Diane Ackerman gives homage to the "gorgeous fever" that is sensation itself. Human beings, she writes, "Ache fiercely with love, lust, loyalty, and passion. And we . . . perceive the world, in all its gushing beauty and terror, right on our pulses." In contrast, the brain itself "is silent, the brain is dark, the brain tastes nothing, the brain hears nothing."[121]

Feelings as Messengers

Let us consider that feelings are not merely manifestations of various brain states. Instead entertain the idea that feelings exist in their own right, as fluid messengers between raw sensation and mental activity—between what we take in through our senses and what we recall, value, believe, and otherwise know about ourselves and the world around us. Feelings are thus essential in "making sense" of the situations we're in and in literally "minding" who we are and what we do.

Here's an analogy. If you wanted to understand the United States, would you concentrate solely on Washington, D.C.? True, that jurisdiction is its capital, the seat of its government, and its political nerve center. But is the "real" America located there? No more so than in Wichita, Kansas; Tampa, Florida; Philadelphia, Pennsylvania; or Bismarck, North Dakota—and perhaps less so. The citizens of those places and many others send their elected representatives to Washington. The representatives bring something of the history and values of the given place to the nation's capital and, in turn, help make decisions for the good of the nation (theoretically, anyway). They are akin to messengers, shuttling back and forth. Envision those messengers as your body's feelings. They traffic with the brain but aren't located exclusively there. Just as the U.S. could not be a nation without input from all of its cities, counties, boroughs, and towns, so the individual is manifestly more than her or his brain. Each of us requires the sensory input and feelings generated in the rest of our body. Ultimately we are the amalgam of our neural circuitry and our physiology (psyche and soma), with feelings partaking of both.

This continual interaction—and the way it manifests in psychosomatic plasticity—is on display in instances of hypnotic suggestion, in at least some cases of allergy, in blushing, migraine, psoriasis, and the placebo effect.[122] Some hypnotized subjects, for example, can develop an allergic reaction when they come into contact with a substance that they aren't truly allergic to but which they have been told will trigger allergies. Conversely, they can avoid an allergic reaction when told that they aren't allergic to a certain substance when they actually are.[123] A related finding—and a stunning one at that—is that a group of mediums (who by definition demonstrate self/other confusion) had a rate of autoimmune disorders seven times greater than average and an incidence of migraine nearly two-and-a-half times the average.[124] In each case, it's likely that the individual is highly thin-boundary. (Experimental confirmation has been found, not in expressly thin-boundary people but, intriguingly, in people with induced self/other confusion.)[125]

The Bodymind Speaks

A marvelous example of psychosomatic plasticity is provided by neuroscientist Antonio Damasio in his celebrated book *The Feeling of What Happens*. He relates an encounter between himself, his wife Hanna (a fellow researcher), and the pianist Maria João Pires. She told them that

> When she plays, under the perfect control of her will, she can either reduce or allow the flow of emotion to her body. My wife . . . and I thought this was a wonderfully romantic idea, but Maria João insisted that she could do it and we resisted believing it. Eventually, the stage for the empirical moment of truth was set in our laboratory. Maria João was wired to the complicated psychophysiological equipment while she listened to short musical pieces of our selection in two conditions: emotion allowed, or emotion voluntarily inhibited. Her Chopin *Nocturnes* had just been released, and we used some of hers and some of Daniel Barenboim's as stimuli. In the condition of "emotion allowed," her skin conductance record was full of peaks and valleys, linked intriguingly to varied pas-

sages in the pieces. Then, in the condition of "emotion reduced," the unbelievable did, in fact, happen. She could virtually flatten her skin-conductance graph at will and change her heart rate, to boot. Behaviorally, she changed as well.[126]

The above is a case where the person involved is conscious of what she is doing. Other instances are distinctly different—the bodies of the people involved are effectively "speaking" their feelings, circumventing the conscious mind:

- A woman with multiple personality disorder had been abused by her father. Only one personality "knew" about the abuse. Whenever this personality emerged, burn marks would appear on the woman's arms. Once she shifted from that personality the burn marks would go away.[127]
- Another woman's skin would break out in large hives whenever she was around someone domineering. Most of her problem involved her mother-in-law, with whom she had a difficult relationship. She would even break out in hives if she went to the mailbox and found a letter from her mother-in-law. When she talked about her mother-in-law in the psychiatrist's office, boils on her skin would form right in front of him.[128]
- A still more unfortunate woman was regularly beaten by her husband. As their sons grew up, they kept the father from physically beating their mother. He then began to attack her with words. Whenever he unleashed a barrage of verbal abuse, bruises and black-and-blue marks would appear on her skin in the very places where she had previously received bruises from her husband's beatings. A psychiatrist watched the bruises appear on the woman's arms when she talked about the verbal abuse.[129]
- When hypnotized, a woman raised blisters on the back of her left hand, always in the same place. When questioned later, she indicated that the area where the blisters had formed coincided

exactly with an area of her hand that she had burned six years earlier with hot grease.[130]

These examples are very strange, but no stranger than the fact of people feeling phantom limbs, phantom rings on fingers, or phantom bunions on feet. All are explicable, I propose, through a different model than we are used to—one much closer to the model of bodymind functioning developed by the pioneering discipline of psychoneuroimmunology. This field recognizes that the nervous system, the immune system, and the endocrine system are in constant communication. The dialogue between them is rapid-fire and reciprocal; the language spoken is electrochemical. Electric impulses convey across neural circuitry while scores of hormones, neuropeptides, and other molecules relay chemical messages throughout the body and brain. (The even newer field of neurogastroenterology is training a lens on the brain-gut connection.)[131]

Imagine, if you will, a stream of water rippling over rocks, in continuous motion. Imagine, too, that the stream has various sources and tributaries, fed by springs and emptying into various channels and pools. That stream is the ever-present flow of feeling. It is sourced by all the cells in our body that create and sustain energy. Its course is nerve fibers and the bloodstream itself; its tributaries are the muscles, organs, and skin. If thin-boundary people do have a feeling flow that is more rapid and direct, they are the most likely candidates to manifest psychosomatic plasticity.

Moreover, Hartmann's work suggests that they are most likely to retain visceral, emotional *memories* of pain. This would seem to be reflected in the four reports of psychosomatic plasticity above—as well as by evidence that individuals with self/other confusion may anticipate pain more readily because it's familiar and accessible to them.[132]

From Mirror Sensing to Sense of Self

The fact that approximately one in five people reports the experience of mirror pain (and the figure may be higher still)[133] suggests that mirror sensing is relatively common. The 20 percent figure happens to parallel the proportion of highly sensitive people estimated by psychologist Elaine Aron.[134] She believes that such sensitivity has arisen for sound evolutionary reasons. Other species, she says, are made up of "roving" and "sitting" individuals. The rovers boldly seek out such necessities as food, warmth, and shelter while the more sensitive sitters hang back. "They notice potential danger sooner," writes Aron. "Clearly the two [dispositions] work best in combination."[135]

An independent study suggests that people do naturally fall into these two groupings. In their book *The Long Shadow of Temperament*, psychologists Jerome Kagan and Nancy Snidman found that approximately one-fifth of young children are "high reactors" who demonstrate obvious distress when novel stimuli or situations are presented.[136]

By the same token, a variety of experiments disclose that most anyone can be induced to feel that they have lost ownership of their body or parts of it. Through what is known as the "rubber hand illusion" and other tricks, people can be made to feel that another's hand is theirs, or see their body from behind, or other such oddities.[137] Even full out-of-body experiences have been experimentally prompted.[138] As we've seen, real-life "jolts" such as a lightning strike or a near-death experience can equally force such perspectives upon us. In a more benign way, people are sometimes moved to feel at one with their surroundings, whether it's a child prompted by an encounter with the natural world[139] or an astronaut prompted by the awe-inspiring view from his spacecraft. Ecstatic music and dance represent a time-honored pathway for inducing extraordinary perceptions; drugs such as ketamine and LSD can do the same artificially.

The closer we look at the self, the more precarious or malleable it seems to be. There is really no alternative to asking, in the words of one science observer, "What the hell is going on?"[140] Neuroscience tries its best to shed light on the "how" of becoming disembodied— via self/other confusion, a failure to integrate sensory information within the brain,[141] or problems with the vestibular system.[142] By the same token, the essential mystery—"What" is being experienced outside ourselves?—remains.

Going beyond the Body

I wish to return to a frame of reference discussed much earlier: namely that at different times and in different circumstances one's boundaries can thin and one's sense of self effectively expands beyond the body.

This is not exclusively my idea. Essentially the same thing was proposed by the adventuresome parapsychologist Michael Grosso. His touchstone was the extent to which a person is identified with his/her body. Similar to the boundary spectrum, Grosso sets out a range wherein a person can feel fully and completely embodied (on one end of the spectrum) or disembodied and depersonalized (at the other end of the spectrum). He hypothesizes that people are "placed" differently along this continuum at various points in their lives depending on their characteristic neurobiology (i.e., the way they're wired) as well as what is happening to them at any given moment.

For example, a woman meditating quietly may at first be attuned to her felt sense and reasonably anchored in her body (e.g., by being mindful of her posture, her breathing, the feel of clothing on her skin, and nearby sounds). But as her meditation progresses, she may become more contemplative, paying less attention to the external world—even to her own feelings—and focused more and more on thoughts and mental images. At this stage, says Grosso, she is less embodied and more dissociated. As her felt sense diminishes, the possibility of having an out-of-body experience increases.[143]

Neuroscience, in its way, is aligning somewhat with this view. The suggestion has been put forward that in the absence of a strong felt sense, the perception of what is *external* to oneself becomes predominant.[144] In other words, when the felt sense is impeded, we apprehend much more readily—and identify with—that which is external to us. In extreme cases, when we are forcibly jolted out of our normal felt sense, we may even take the perspective of being outside of our own bodies. Some people are prone to such perceptions by virtue of being thin-boundary; those who experience mirror senses are in this category. Distortions of the felt sense can also occur through dissociation. A prime example is phantom pain, with the most compelling cases being those where the amputee experiences another person's pain (either real or simulated) in his or her own phantom limbs or stumps.

All of this begs the question of what constitutes the self. The self is evidently a composite and a process as much as a thing.[145] It inevitably starts with and is keyed to the body. It encompasses the brain, of course, but far more, given that the brain relies on a myriad of biological inputs from everywhere in the sensing, feeling organism. The felt sense is essential to identity and awareness, as is the energy of feelings themselves as they flow throughout the individual.

What Pain Has to Teach Us

Through the course of this chapter, we've seen that not just synesthetes but several other types of people experience exceptional kinds of empathy and, on occasion, some very nonordinary perceptions (such as NDEs and out-of-body perspectives). My opinion remains that while these people are clearly exceptional, they are most definitely not unique. In fact, the mental and emotional processes involved in their experiences are common to all human beings. While we may differ depending on where we are on the thick-to-thin boundary spectrum, the biology of emotion and the energy inherent in feelings is entirely consistent from person to person. Thus, through the exceptional types of people we've surveyed, there is much we can learn about "life, the universe, and everything" (in the immortal words of the late Douglas Adams).

Recall Fiona's "almost instinctive feeling"—accompanied by a blue-orange color around her collie—that the dog was seriously ill. Recall the palpable sense of pressure in Megan Pohlmann's head, mirroring her young patient's headaches. Recall Kreskin's sense of queasiness accompanied by his impression of an audience member's suicidal intent. And recall Maureen Seaberg's highly accurate visualizations (as she tells the tale) of several students' aches and pains, literally sight unseen. In any other context, these experiences would be labeled ESP or clairvoyance. But take away the labels and simply consider the phenomenon. I am reminded of a quote by Leonardo da Vinci: "The deeper the feeling, the greater the pain." The current of feeling in these individuals runs deep. As such, their tendency to resonate with another's injury, illness, or distress is far beyond the norm.

Pain is not just about the feeling of being hurt. In evolutionary terms, it's explained as a way for an animal to escape, heal, and ultimately survive. The remembrance of the pain or discomfort serves as a potent reminder to avoid situations that could bring about similar pain in the future. Furthermore, the expression of pain is a social signal. Other animals, seeing the pain, infer potential danger and learn to avoid the given hazard themselves.[146]

I would add that pain—especially the psychic kind (versus merely physical)—is essential to personal development and self-actualization. Much as a fever signifies that the body is fighting off an infection, painful or "negative" emotions inform us that we are in the midst of a difficult situation and that learning needs to occur if we are to grow.[147] For all these reasons, the apprehension of pain at a distance betokens, at one and the same time, an advanced capacity *and* a core element of humanity.

A Wider Spectrum of Reality

A final lesson to be gleaned from the exceptional perceptions that some people have (or that they suddenly acquire) concerns the very nature of reality. The following statement, by two synesthesia researchers, puts it well: "All of us, synesthetes and non-synesthetes alike, sense just a small fraction of outside reality. For example, we do not perceive the electromagnetic spectrum in its entirety, but merely a tiny slice of it.

The rest of the spectrum—carrying TV shows, radio signals, and cell phone conversations—flows through our bodies with no awareness on our part. We are utterly blind to it."[148]

It is equally stunning to realize that as solid and unchanging as we imagine our very "self" to be, that sense of self can shift in an instant. We've seen the evidence that when our felt sense is disturbed we are much more likely to perceive what is outside of ourselves, even beyond our body. Just as with the electromagnetic spectrum, this is not typically part of our awareness. Yet our consciousness can sometimes be displaced into this wider spectrum. Again, Grosso anticipated the idea when he proposed that by removing our accustomed bodily awareness, the universe may effectively open to our inspection.[149]

Like Tony Cicoria, we are agape when it happens. Where is the music coming from? From whence the heightened sensitivities, the newly found creativity, the enhanced empathy, the intuition and psychic propensity? These things necessarily seem incredible, inexplicable, otherworldly—yet they typically become as much a part of the transformed person as she or he was before.

The implications of this wider realm speak of true wonderment.

3

The Resonance of Perception

Instinctive Sensing as a Crucible for the Anomalous

The late Donna Williams was a remarkable person. Raised in Australia, she was autistic but didn't know it until diagnosed at age twenty-six. Up to that point she had been regarded as exceedingly strange. *Retarded, robotic, mental, stupid, disturbed,* and *crazy* were some of the words used to describe her, starting with her own family.[1]

In many respects, Donna was encased in her own world. She had a fascination for shiny objects and the feel of different fabrics.[2] She would see patterns and spaces, losing herself in what she gazed upon or felt herself a part of.[3] She loved making collections of things and endlessly ordering them.[4] She largely saw parts of people—hands, arms, faces— and didn't easily connect the whole person together, let alone her or his motivation.[5] Similarly, the meaning carried by gesture and intonation was often lost, with the sounds of words alone having an impact.

Donna constantly dealt with a barrage of sensation, finding high-pitched sounds, bright lights, and even the most basic touch intolerable.[6] It didn't help matters that her parents could be violent and abusive. Emotion scared her,[7] and she coped by further withdrawing on the one hand and developing a pair of trusty personas on the other. She also, it turned out later, was allergic to various foods; her behavior and demeanor improved to some extent when this was addressed.[8] Donna ultimately became able to feel her feelings rather than being scared by them and retreating into her private, inaccessible world.

A Web of Sensory Impressions

In her memoirs, Williams strikes several themes that are highly useful in understanding what it's like to be autistic—and that bear on much that I have written and speculated about (including the anomalous). Her first key point is that people on the autism spectrum view themselves and the world primarily through a web of sensory impressions, not mental constructs.

People with autism spectrum disorder (ASD) are apt to experience things first and foremost as sensory phenomena, being drawn by the literal impressions themselves rather than by the person or thing in its totality. Most people know a comb, for example, as an object that has utility with hair. It happens to be flat and has teeth and is often black. For an autistic person, however, that same comb might be fascinating for the scraping sound it makes when run across a surface. Whereas most people regard patent leather shoes as stylish conveyances for walking, a person with ASD might value them for their shiny, smooth surface, which can be licked and, when bitten, leaves indentations. Whereas a normal child values a bike for its overall look and, even more, for the places it can take its rider, someone on the autism spectrum might be fascinated by its silver spokes, its black tires that have a certain "feel" when pressed, or its smooth forest-green seat. And whereas most people identify a chandelier by its ability to cast a lot of light as well as its crystalline quality, someone who's autistic might be swept up in its multifaceted reflectiveness, its tinkling sound, and the way it breaks light into many prismatic colors. In the same way, individuals with autism tend to perceive other people, animals, even insects, based on characteristic colors, smells, vocalizations, and movements rather than taking them in as "wholistic" organisms.[9]

A second, fundamentally related point is that people with autism will often merge into the web of sensation they are witnessing. They "resonate" with whatever is being experienced, losing their sense of body boundaries so that they seem to become one with the object.[10] "Suddenly," observes Williams, "there is no you and what had been you just becomes a tool, like a sponge through which this sensing or resonance is taken in. What is sensed is not taken in by the conscious mind and there is no thought and no reflection, no wonder and no curiosity. There is just a journey into whatever is being sensed."[11] She recalled losing herself at a young age in her bedroom wall, for example, based on its surface texture and density—its unique pattern of "wall-ness."[12]

In this regard, people with autism are similar to people who are fantasy-prone; the latter, too, find immense appeal in sensory stimuli and can feel as if they have become one with whatever they are regarding.[13] There is also a marked similarity to individuals who rate high in absorption, a personality trait reflecting the tendency to become lost in contemplation or absorbed in a task.[14]

"Resonance" in Autism

A theory that has particular relevance here is known as the "intense world" hypothesis. It posits that people with autism are bombarded at an early age with sensory stimuli and that they subsequently withdraw from the world in order to cope. The theory is the brainchild of Henry Markram, director of the Center for Neuroscience and Technology and codirector of the Brain Mind Institute at École Polytechnique Fédérale de Lausanne (EPFL). Markram developed this theory with his wife, researcher Kamila Markram, and their former associate, Tania Rinaldi Barkat. It emerged out of years of frustration with the Markrams' son,

Kai (who is now in his twenties). The concept they hit upon is described most eloquently by Maia Szalavitz in her article "The Boy Whose Brain Could Unlock Autism." She writes:

> Consider what it might feel like to be a baby in a world of relentless and unpredictable sensation. An overwhelmed infant might, not surprisingly, attempt to escape. Kamila [Markram] compares it to being sleepless, jetlagged, and hung over, all at once. "If you don't sleep for a night or two, everything hurts. The lights hurt. The noises hurt. You withdraw," she says. Unlike adults, however, babies can't flee. All they can do is cry and rock, and, later, try to avoid touch, eye contact, and other powerful experiences. Autistic children might revel in patterns and predictability just to make sense of the chaos.[15]

The intense world theory presumes that the world autistic people perceive is one of constant sensory overload. This is because their brains are hyperconnected. Rather than one cell having connections to ten other cells, it might be linked to twenty. So the world is experienced as "a barrage of chaotic, indecipherable input, a cacophony of raw, unfilterable data."

It's worth noting that emotional stimuli are as prominent as physical stimuli in that barrage. Donna Williams called it "an intense, uncontrollable empathy." Around someone with a broken leg, for instance, she "felt their pain in my leg." Similarly, "I could feel when people had . . . emotional pain whether they displayed it or not. . . . I felt it within me and [my] connection to my own feelings . . . simply switched off as though some frequency had interfered with my aerial."[16] The mechanism, as she describes it, is one where too much information is coming through and the person can either attend to the external stimuli or the internal stimuli but not both at the same time. It's an "involuntary adaptation," in Williams's words.[17] In the exchange, it would inevitably seem as though "either 'I' did not exist and other things existed or they existed and 'I' did not."[18]

Williams did not just resonate with people and things—she resonated with places, too. "Sometimes," she writes, "it is . . . possible to sense a lingering 'feel' to a place just as we might smell a lingering smell on the carpet from a beer-swilling party . . . or experience the lingering 'touch print' of a handshake that has already left a few seconds ago."[19] In this respect, people with ASD may be highly sensitive persons, the appellation developed by psychologist Elaine Aron. As Aron puts it, "Most people walk into a room and perhaps notice the furniture, the people—that's about it. Highly sensitive persons can be instantly aware, whether they wish it to be or not, of the mood, the friendships and enmities, the freshness or staleness of the air, the personality of the one who arranged the flowers."[20]

Just as Temple Grandin proposed in her book *Animals in Translation,* Williams thinks it likely that many animals have this same type of highly attuned sensing ability. If so, we can imagine animals experiencing the world as people with autism tend to—as a "swirling mass of tiny details" (in Grandin's evocative phrase).[21]

We Could All Be Born Autistic

My proposition is this highly attuned sensing is the "default" setting of human beings, beginning in utero. Gradually, through infancy and childhood, this fluid and multimodal way of perceiving is superseded (in most people) as neuronal connections mature and sense perception becomes more discrete. The process may be akin to synesthesia, which, as science now surmises, results from extraordinarily dense and far-flung neuronal connections. Just as it's possible that we're all born synesthetes, it is equally possible that we're all born autistic.

Some people, because of a combination of nature and nurture, retain this mode of perceiving to a far greater extent than others. The types of individuals I mean are those who are fantasy-prone, or who find themselves easily absorbed into various situations or pursuits, or who are suggestible or who have thin boundaries. For them, it takes little or no effort to slip into a reverie, to empathize intensively, to "merge" into something or someone else. It's easy for them to conjure up a memory with such clarity and vividness that the recollected situation seems to be taking place all over again. Williams considers this form of perception to be "a very pure state," preconscious and independent of directed thought or judgment.[22]

Lest you think that such traits are childish and have no application in the real world, I would suggest otherwise. The ability to perceive broadly and empathize deeply is well suited to any creative endeavor, whether writing or any form of art or science. It is a decided advantage in counseling and psychological studies, not to mention in criminal investigations where the character and tendencies of those involved are of critical importance. Political and social activists may likewise benefit. Indeed, many people on the public stage undoubtedly possess these talents. One is Meryl Streep, the acclaimed actress. In an interview, she acknowledged being highly sensitive and having thin boundaries. "I have my antenna out, what can I say?" she explained. "That's my job as an actor. I'm hyper-alert to all signals. My boundaries are not so clear. I sort of bleed out into whoever I'm talking to."[23]

Other types of entertainers, too, leverage these personality traits to their advantage. The late impressionist David Frye, who was popular in the 1960s and 1970s sending up presidents Johnson and Nixon, explained the secret to his success: "I would begin to believe I was [the person he was mimicking]. I would make his facial expressions, imitate his voice. I would get vibrations from just a brief meeting with [that] person . . . and hours later I would still be feeling them."[24]

Gathering Others by Their Edges

Williams, who became an adept author and communicator, said that she got to know people, places, and things by what she called their "edges." By this she meant the degree of congruence between her essence and the essence of any "other" based on feeling. To what degree does she register an attraction or acceptance or, alternatively, an opposition or repulsion? "This is instinct," she explains:

> Animals have it and they sense it about people. . . . It is that sensed something that makes the hairs stand up on your arms or makes you shiver or pull away or makes you grimace and tense up in spite of no obvious, physically perceivable sign of threat. Some animals seem to "know" before they even smell another creature. I believe that what they sense is the congruence of a capacity for resonance with what is sensed, the lack of it or the . . . dissonance. I believe they sense what I came to call . . . edges.[25]

To my mind, edges correlate with thin and thick boundaries. As propounded by the late Ernest Hartmann, boundaries reflect the characteristic way individuals process stimuli. As discussed in the first chapter, people with thick boundaries come across as stolid or rigid; people with thin boundaries come across as reactive or vulnerable. Boundaries are essential to life because, without them, organisms would literally merge into one another or into their surroundings. One has to be able to differentiate self from other. Our immune systems operate on just this principle.

On a nonbiologic (but scarcely less important) basis, one needs to distinguish what is likely to be healthful, supportive, or convivial from what could be dangerous, harmful, or painful. Feelings are an ideal way to do this. While we base our judgments on facts wherever possible, we also gather information from "squishier" sources. What does your gut tell you? What does your intuition suggest? When we talk of being "sympatico" with someone or a certain situation "not feeling right," we are using the language of sense impressions and emotion. We continuously take the measure of another person's mood, his or her energy in any given circumstance, how they (or the place or thing in question) comes across to us.

Inevitably these impressions are affected by subjective criteria that we are consciously unaware of: memories, ideals, desires, motivations, disappointments. But this is not to say that the impressions so gathered or the decisions made upon them are of questionable validity. Just the opposite—as living, feeling, mindful creatures, we are continually drawing on our cumulative life experience to try to make the right call in any given situation. And through our demeanor, attitude, mood, and characteristic energy in the given circumstance, we inevitably send out signals of our own. These "edges" or boundary indicators will be there for others to decipher and assess.

Williams suggests[26]—and I agree, based on abundant available evidence—that people with thin boundaries are more likely than others to have anomalous experiences.[27] This is not because they have some sort of arcane psychic powers but because they literally take in more information at a preconscious level.

Blindsight and Everything We Miss

Here is a remarkable example of how much there is to perceive—and how many of us typically filter it out. The experiment (you may have heard of it) involves a video of two teams passing around a basketball. One team is dressed in white shirts and the other in black shirts. Viewers are asked to count how many times the white team passes the ball. Most people count correctly but, in so doing, miss a strange development: in the middle of the video someone dressed in a gorilla suit walks into the game, pauses to look right at the camera, beats its chest, and then walks away. The tendency to miss the gorilla is known as *inattentional blindness*.

A few people, when this video is played, do see the gorilla immediately. They are the ones, I would wager, who are thin-boundary—who are primed, neurobiologically, to notice environmental details that pass others by. My proposition is supported by evidence that people who score low on a personality trait known as "openness to experience" (and which, in turn, is related to having thick boundaries)[28] are more likely to experience inattentional blindness.[29] It stands to reason that the opposite is also true: that individuals who are more open to experience (and thinner boundary) will perceive some things that other people miss. As one researcher puts it, "The 'gate' that lets through the information that reaches consciousness may have a different level of flexibility. Open people appear to have a more flexible gate."[30]

Another even more startling experiment was conducted in 2004 at Rice University.[31] The subjects agreed to be temporarily blinded through magnetic pulses that affected their visual cortex. During this momentary blindness they stood before a computer screen, on which flashed either a vertical or horizontal line. In an accompanying test, a red or green ball appeared on the screen. When the subjects were asked what they had seen, all reported they'd seen nothing—and, of course, they should not have been able to. When asked to guess which way the line was oriented, however, they were correct 75 percent of the time. And they were right 81 percent of the time on the color of the ball. By chance, both those figures should have been roughly 50 percent. While some volunteers said they'd been guessing randomly, others reported "having a feeling" about what was on the screen. Their higher confidence tended to correspond with a more accurate guess.

Visually, this phenomenon (both with the Rice University experiment and the gorilla experiment) is known as *blindsight*. It's well studied by now, with the eye/brain connection receiving serious scrutiny. But what of our other senses? And what of emotion itself? Is it possible that some of us are more thoroughly "wired" to gather sensory and felt impressions based on information, as in the computer screen experiment, that shouldn't, by all rights, be accessible?

Temple Grandin believes that most people are too busy deciphering incoming stimuli to necessarily apprehend it accurately. Their brains "use the detailed raw data of the world to form a generalized concept or schema, and that's what reaches consciousness. Fifty shades of brown turn into just one unified color: brown."[32] It's an entirely autonomic process. So most of us end up seeing what we expect to see in any particular situation. But certain people—the high sensitives of the world—

will access that raw data and attend to it by other means. Williams called it "peripheral perception"[33] and her "shadow sense."[34] It is indirect, fragmentary, attuned to tone rather than words, pattern and movement rather than substance. It is more like daydreaming than paying attention. "It is this shadow sense," related Williams, "with which I can sometimes sense the boundaries of a room even without reliance purely on sonics. . . . What is mapped out is the 'feel' of the experience."[35]

Grandin herself cites a curious example. She notes that a student of hers, Holly, "has such acute auditory perception that she can actually hear radios that aren't turned on . . . [she] can hear the tiny little transmissions a turned-off radio is [still] receiving. She'll say, 'NPR is doing a show on lions,' and we'll turn the radio on and sure enough: NPR is doing a show on lions. Holly can hear it. She can hear the hum of electric wires in the wall. And she's incredible with animals. She can tell what they're feeling from the tiniest variations in their breathing."[36] If this is not anomalous, I don't know what is. Yet it's not crazy. It's fascinating, and it can and should be investigated by science. The individuals prone to these perceptions hold the key.

The Personal Agency of the "Will"

We would do well to ponder what combinations of factors produce exceptionally sensitive people—whether it's people with autism, people with synesthesia, savants, gifted children and child prodigies (about whom many intriguing tales are told), children who vividly recall what appear to be memories of another life, or people who seem to engender anomalies themselves. As I shall discuss in the next chapter, a strong case can be made that such personalities are the outcome of something gone amiss during development: an infection, accident, or other stressor that occurs during gestation, a trauma suffered in childhood . . . in effect, an intrusion or shock to the system. However, there's another way of looking at how people with extraordinary sensitivities develop. It's counterintuitive but is explored by Williams in her conception of will.

By *will,* she doesn't mean a last will and testament. She means personal agency, a sense of self somehow independent of the body. Her will was the vehicle for her "shadow sense" to engage—the means by which she claims to have been able, at a very early age, to sense "the surface, texture and density of material without looking at it with physical eyes or touching it with physical hands or tasting it with a physical tongue or tapping it to hear its sound. It was as though some part of me, of my 'be-ing' could see without my eyes, hear without my ears, touch without my hands, and feel . . . without my body making direct physical contact."[37] Her will was the agency through which young Donna would lose herself in her surroundings.

In close connection with these perceptions, Williams offers several examples of ostensible out-of-body experiences, though she recollects these as wholly ordinary and not in the least bit mystical or spooky. For example, "As a young child, people would enter my room and sometimes, without even looking, I'd merge with them and my sense of 'entity' . . . left the room with them when they left again. When my body called me back, it was as though I'd had a sharp perceptual shift. It was as if I was surprised to find myself back in my own body."[38] Later, as a teenager, she would gravitate in this way toward various people and places where she was likely to feel comforted beyond her tumultuous and sometimes scary home life:

I didn't do this with imagination. I didn't fantasize what I'd like to say or do. I simply found myself feeling physically in these places or with these people. I could not see myself there and I did not interact with the people I'd been drawn to. Yet I did feel myself moving up the stairs to my friend's flat, through the front door and into the kitchen. I could sense the smell of the room and the noises in the room. I could "hear" and "see" as my friends moved about and went on with things.

What I'd seen and heard was generally quite trivial: someone doing the dishes, getting something to eat, going to bed. What . . . surprised me was that, upon checking with these friends without prompting them about what I'd experienced, the events had apparently happened in the same order in which I'd seen them at the time I'd "been there."

Two of the strangest experiences among these were one when I "visited" my friend but found myself in a different house. I moved from room to room and found what felt like her room. When I saw her again she told me she'd moved house and I told her I knew. She was surprised at this and asked how. I described the house and the layout of the rooms and my description had been precisely in accordance with where her family had moved.

The other experience was after leaving a house I'd lived in for two years. In the two months before I'd left I'd moved bedrooms and had stayed in one with a sliding door. After having left, I continued to dream that I was living in that house. About a year later I saw the person who remained living there who proclaimed I'd "never left." I asked what this meant and was told that for some time afterwards, every morning, around the time I'd usually get up, the door would slide itself open. It occurred to me then that what others call "ghosts" were possibly sometimes merely unintentional out-of-body experiences.[39]

The Roots of Dissociation

As intriguing as Williams's out-of-body experiences may sound, the simplest explanation is that she was engaged in what's called magical thinking—the apparent evocation of what one *wants or needs* to have happen. It's well established that magical thinking, belief in the paranormal, and anomalous perceptions can all be conditioned by trauma, particularly chronic childhood abuse, which Williams endured.[40] Fantasy and imagination—as much as she denied it—clearly serve as an attempted "escape route" from recurring abusive treatment. The illusion that the child holds some special, invisible capacity to influence people or events is reassuring, and from the comfort of this fancy flows a willingness to believe in strange powers generally. Over time, the child may grow into an adult who is not only interested in things psychic but believes that he/she actually experiences them.[41]

A case in point is provided by psychiatrist Lenore Terr, who has extensively investigated early trauma and its consequences. Some children, as she's documented, learn to dissociate, to "go somewhere else." Consider a boy Terr refers to as Frederick, age seven, whose "stepfather had been throwing him against walls while [his mother] worked the evening shift." Here is how he reacted:

> Frederick glanced down at the playground pavement one day and saw blood. After several seconds of searching for a wounded companion, Frederick realized that it was *he* who was bleeding. The boy realized he could feel no pain.
>
> In a psychotherapy session I asked Frederick how he could make this sort of thing happen. "It jus' happens now," he said. "I used to pretend I was at a picnic with my head on Mommy's lap. The first time my stepdaddy hit me, it hurt a lot. But then I found out that I could make myself go on Mommy's lap [in imagination], and [his stepfather] couldn't hurt me that way. I kept goin' on Mommy's lap—I didn't have to scream or cry or anything. I could *be* someplace else and not get hurt."[42]

Now, though, consider a different twist. Just as the tendency to dissociate is undoubtedly provoked by trauma, it could just as easily—and even earlier in one's life—be occasioned by an innate sensitivity to one's environment. Just as a child can have no control over the unpredictable or abusive treatment inflicted on her or him, an infant can have no control over an inborn sensitivity to bright lights, loud noises, intrusive smells, or harsh, tactile sensations. Dissociation could eventually become a personality trait through the simple urge to take refuge from such environmental influences.

A seminal study from 1949 provides evidence for this. Children from three months to seven years of age were observed rhythmically rocking themselves or covering their eyes and ears from unwelcome stimuli: odors, sounds, colors, textures, temperatures. Their feelings also appeared to be easily hurt, so that (as the investigators commented), "They were 'sensitive' in both meanings of the word: easily hurt, and easily stimulated. . . . Variations in sensory impression that made no difference to the average child made a great deal of difference to these children."[43]

It's conceivable, then, that dissociation is a natural outcome of high sensitivity, whether or not trauma is inflicted later on. Absorption and fantasy proneness (the tendencies, respectively, to become swallowed up in an experience and for mental and emotional journeys to be experienced as real as reality) could be similar, expected outgrowths.

A Wellspring for Anomalous Perceptions

I want to propose something rather provocative now. Namely, that the environmental and emotional sensitivities that are a hallmark of so many extraordinary people—as well as the dissociation and absorption that inevitably occur—are the crucible from which anomalous perception can genuinely result. I am certainly not the first to propose this. Kenneth Ring, who has researched near-death experiences, suggested that "sensitives with low stress thresholds" . . . through "their difficult and in some cases even tormented childhoods . . . have come to develop an extended range of human perception."[44]

This is not to preclude much more prosaic and undoubtedly more common factors such as suggestibility, magical thinking, preexisting paranormal belief, anxiety, discomfort with ambiguity, mental illness (such as schizoid personality disorder), and simply mistaken environmental cues. But it suggests that beyond such factors, highly sensitive and thin-boundary people can legitimately apprehend stimuli in the external environment unnoticed by the rest of us who are more, shall we say, neurotypical. The "gorilla" experiment and the Rice University experiment referenced earlier are among a plethora of findings that suggest our standard means of apprehension fall short of providing a comprehensive view of the world—let alone a comprehensive view of our own sensory capabilities.

With regard to the sort of out-of-body experiences (OBEs) described by Donna Williams, let's consider a means of evaluation based on *the extent to which a person is identified with his/her body.* On one end of our evaluative spectrum would be people who typically feel fully embodied; at the other end of the spectrum would be people who at least sometimes feel disembodied or depersonalized (i.e., lose touch with the sense of feeling itself). Just as with the Boundary spectrum, we can hypothesize that different people are "placed" differently along this continuum at various points in their lives, depending on the way they're wired along with what is happening to them in the given situation. Using the example provided in chapter 2, someone meditating may be attuned to their felt sense in the initial stages of meditation but as the meditation progresses, become more contemplative and much less aware of bodily signals and the world around them. The result: greater dissociation and the increased possibility of having an out-of-body experience.[45]

Parapsychologist Michael Grosso, who has proposed this "continuum" approach, suggests that a person having an OBE might be "a spatially extended entity, occupying and then slipping out of the body, like a handkerchief plucked from a vest pocket."[46] Even more radically, he suggests that we should think of the body as being one point in an extended field of consciousness. Remove our accustomed bodily awareness and—just possibly—the universe opens up to a completely different form of inspection.[47]

Dissociation and Body Awareness

Sometimes dissociation is thrust upon us, irrespective of one's boundary type, sensitivities, or any other measure. The following is a case in point. It was reported by a young race-car driver whose vehicle had been thrown thirty feet in the air during an accident: "Everything was in slow motion and it seemed to me like I was a player on a stage and could see myself tumbling over and over in the car. It was as though I sat in the stands and saw it all happening . . . but I was not frightened. . . . Everything was so strange. . . . I remember being upside down and looking backward. And I saw the man who won the race pass under me. The guy looked up, and I remember that he had an amazed look on his face."[48]

What is happening here? In the face of surprise, shock and, perhaps, terror, the race-car driver is dissociating. For a few seconds, he is farther to one side of the scale of embodiment than he has probably ever been in his life. The result bears all the hallmarks of an out-of-body experience.

Dreaming, too, is a dissociative process—if for no other reason than the brain is disconnected from bodily sensation during rapid eye movement (REM) sleep. We actually depersonalize nightly! Occasionally, people may be stunned by a strangely telepathic or precognitive dream. This seems to indicate that our private dream world can extend out in time and space, much like an OBE.

Williams offered support for these conjectures when she suggested that a person's "will"—her or his individual essence—may be variably tethered to body awareness. One person will be fully engaged with her or his senses while, for another person, the reliance on conscious awareness is more tentative. Some people—here she refers to individuals with autism as well as those with other developmental challenges—may simply require more time and patience to become fully functional human beings. As children, they "haven't got fully into their bodies," resembling "someone who has fallen down a few rungs of the ladder but is still holding on a few rungs down."[49] But "those who appear not to seek to make sense of their environment may not necessarily be 'retarded,' disturbed [or] crazy . . . but may, in spite of not using the same [sensory] system everyone else uses, still have one of their own. They may . . . actually continue to use a system that others have left behind very much earlier."[50]

The Centrality of Emotion

In reflecting on all we have covered, I return to the overarching theme of my longtime research into personality and personality differences: namely, the centrality of emotion in the formation and expression of self. I am reminded of Williams's frequent mentions that she was afraid of feelings and repelled by touch for much of her life but that, just the same, she would "resonate" with people and places without conscious effort. ("Some people could capture me emotionally without trying. Merely to be touched by them or looked at could overwhelm me with feelings.")[51] In speaking of people's edges, she often references the energy of their moods or dispositions. ("Edges are about the 'feel' carried by people . . . about variations in the flow and nature of energy.")[52]

The word *emotion,* of course, comes from the Latin *emovere,* meaning "to move from" or "to move out of." Indeed, feelings originate from minute but essential movements within our bodies: the transmission of nerve impulses, the release of neurotransmitters, and the circulation of hormones. Such movement requires energy within cells, and the movements themselves connote energy. As our emotions are expressed, therefore, energy is conveyed and energy is released. (Or, if our feelings fail to be expressed, energy is held within and effectively repressed.)

Connected with these reflections are various quotes I've collected over the course of my work that brim with relevance:

- "She really brightens up a room as soon as she walks in. My grandma is ninety-two years old but, whenever I'm around her, I feel younger, happier, and more energetic. There's just something about her."[53]
- "Our boss is just a downer. We know he's down even before he walks in the door. Even the dog can feel him coming and hides. We say that he's PMS: pretty mean-spirited."[54]
- "I have three children, and my autistic child is my most

empathetic." (This from a mother who, when she first read about the intense world hypothesis, said, "This explains Benjamin.")[55]

- "I found that the physical body actually keeps emotions from getting in." (This from a woman who had a near-death experience as a result of a car accident.)[56]
- "Abnormal is defined only in relation to normal, and the definition of normal, like beauty, often lies in the eyes of the beholder."[57]
- "What might be called 'spirit' . . . eventually evolves into what people know as emotion."[58]
- "One sees clearly only with the heart; what is essential is invisible to the eye."[59]

Emotion is elemental to our existence. It allows us to recognize other people's states of mind and, just as often, signals to us the degree of satisfaction with our own situations and lives. The expression of feeling cements bonds between people—far more than does the transmission of thoughts and ideas. Emotion plays a pivotal role in our preconscious, as it flows and manifests in associations, imagery, and dreams. Ultimately, feelings are essential to judgments of self-worth and the meaning of our lives.

The people most sensitive to emotional energy are those whom the rest of us find the most difficult to understand. But, I submit, they have access to a gateway to greater understanding of our embodied existence and the universe we are born into.

Perhaps we can agree with the well-known skeptic Michael Shermer when he comments that "there is no paranormal or supernatural; there are only the normal and the natural—and mysteries yet to be explained."[60]

4
Unspooling the Thread
Connecting Four Remarkable Personality Traits

Having a heightened reaction to sensory stimuli is a feature of several conditions that don't seem to have much in common but which have become the focus of a great deal of scientific curiosity. These conditions—one might even call them personality traits—include

- synesthesia (overlapping senses, such as tasting a sound or hearing a color)
- autism (a seeming lack of ability to empathize, which occurs on a spectrum ranging from less pronounced to severe)
- savantism (having an extraordinary mental ability that coexists with significant mental and social deficits)
- prodigiousness (displaying a talent in an otherwise unfettered personality that is so advanced it's almost uncanny).

High sensitivity is not just an intriguing characteristic in its own right but a vital clue to what may be happening in different conditions that continue to perplex the more they are studied. I first noticed the overlap of environmental sensitivity with various health conditions (e.g., allergies, migraines, chronic pain) around 2005, when I was conducting a study into people's reports of anomalous perceptions—such as seeing apparitions and sensing energy around people. I was not familiar, at that time, with synesthesia, nor had I thought that autism might be connected with sensitivity at all. But the results of my inquiry—gathered from the reports of the original sixty-two survey participants—indicated that environmental and emotional sensitivity might be a salient feature of a number of intriguing health conditions and personality traits.[1]

The more evidence arrives from independent scientific research, the stronger becomes my suspicion that these disparate conditions have a common heritage in the brain and in the body. It is entirely possible that what happens to a developing fetus—based on what the influence is and when it happens—plants the seeds for these different personality predilections. The fact that environmental sensitivity is a noteworthy feature of all these conditions, however, leads me to believe that the genesis is the same. In other words, being highly sensitive is an illuminator of the path we all take to becoming individuals.

Consider that our genes and our environment intertwine, beginning in the womb, to shape who we'll become. If the convergence is smooth, a person will not ultimately demonstrate high sensitivity. But if there are major bumps in the road—if the mother is affected by illness, by accident, by deprivation, by trauma—then a penchant for overreacting to sensory stimuli (or the related tendency to "lose oneself" in sensory-induced reverie) will ultimately result. Being highly sensitive is an echo, so to speak, of that process.

The more we look into pronounced sensitivity, the more we can learn about the forces that sculpt us into unique human beings. That uniqueness is especially evident in synesthesia, autism, savantism, and prodigiousness, all of which (and more) will be explored next. Interestingly enough, the trail leads into spiritual terrain and to the ultimate question of how we got here. The road is long and a bit winding; we begin with a foray into synesthesia.

The Curious Case of Synesthesia

Synesthesia is a remarkable blending of senses that in most people are separate and distinct. While those of us born without the trait may say metaphorically "This wine tastes wonderfully dry" or "I sure feel blue today," the synesthete actually experiences such perceptions. For her or him (more likely the former, as synesthesia is much more common among women), a taste can be round or pointy, a word can taste like potatoes, the sound of a violin can be felt on the face, a letter or number or even a smell can have its own vivid and recurring color.

Hypersensitivity is an oft-noted aspect of synesthesia. One woman puts it this way: "Like many synesthetes, I have a heightened appreciation for all kinds of sensory phenomena. . . . I tend to get overloaded quickly: like there's just too much sensory perception coming in at one time, and I have a hard time sorting it out and coping with it. . . . Shopping can do it. Being in a store where there's a lot of noise, colors, smells—it's just too much."[2]

What causes synesthesia? Neuroscientists believe it results from extraordinarily dense connections in the brain—and, furthermore, that everyone has the capacity to be synesthetic. This latter view has evolved rather recently. The prevailing view used to be that each sense is processed separately in the cortex (the outer layer of the brain), with sensory information only coming together later. But this "uni-modal" model is now being questioned. It could be that cortical regions respond to and integrate information from several senses at once. Alternatively, it could be that our cortices are primed to process just one sense but information from other senses modulates or adjusts the signal from the primary sense.[3]

Consider, for instance, what happens when someone suffers a stroke and while one sense becomes impaired, another type of sensory information comes to the fore. The case of Sherrilyn Roush is particularly interesting. After a stroke, her skin became sensitive to sound. "My entire body rebels at certain pitches," she relates, adding that even in her quiet apartment she'll sometimes have to wear ear plugs in order to concentrate. Since robust connections between brain regions have been found in people who are *not* synesthetic as well as those who are, our senses appear fundamentally more interconnected that scientists ever knew. Someone like Roush doesn't have to be born synesthetic (as most synesthetes are)—she can acquire it.[4]

If this is the "how" of synesthesia, the "why" remains a mystery. An intriguing theory has been advanced by two Canadian researchers, Daphne Maurer and Catherine Mondloch. They suggest that all of us are born perceiving across sense modalities and that we learn to differentiate senses in reaction to the cognitive logjam we experience as babies.[5] Looking at it the other way around, Simon Baron-Cohen of Cambridge University pictures synesthesia as a breakdown in the normal maturation of the brain.[6] The two views aren't necessarily incompatible. If all of us are born synesthetes, cognitive maturation would imply that connections between brain regions are "pruned" during infancy. If this process is interrupted or impaired, the person would remain synesthetic.

Here we encounter the first of many intriguing correspondences between synesthesia, autism, savantism, and prodigiousness. Synesthesia has been found to occur in more than twice as many people with autism (18.9 percent) as in the general population (7.2 percent). And sensory hypersensitivity is common to both.[7]

Sensory Processing Disorder

A paper presented at the International Meeting for Autism Research (IMFAR) in 2014 verified what many parents of kids with an autism spectrum disorder (ASD) had already come to know—that children with some form of autism often overreact to sensory stimuli.[8] As with other studies that have shown that synesthesia is demonstrably "real" in the brain,[9] being overwhelmed by sensory input is also evident in brain scans of kids with ASD. The researchers found that while separate sensations were processed normally, sensations occurring at the same time were not. The implication: people with ASD (especially children, who are not as accustomed to bustling stimuli as adults are) have legitimate challenges regulating their reaction to things happening in quick succession.[10]

In this respect, autism is similar to a condition known as sensory processing disorder (SPD). A psychologist and occupational therapist, A. Jean Ayres, first described the condition in 1972 as revolving around difficulty handling information coming through the senses: not just the five obvious senses but the equally critical proprioceptive and vestibular senses. These tell us, respectively, where our limbs are in relation to the rest of our body and how our body is oriented in space. Kids with SPD may be extremely sensitive to touch but not able to tell *where* the touch is coming from, for example. Their balance may be shaky and they may tend to bump into other people and things. They may not use the left and right sides of their body in a coordinated manner, and have trouble carrying out new or unfamiliar movements. Learning to write, color in the lines, put puzzles together, hit a baseball, ride a bike . . . all of these may prove problematic for a child with SPD.[11]

As the research proved forty-two years after Ayres intuited it, some children's brains have difficulty interpreting a sensation, especially if it comes on the heels of another, different sensation. While most of us take this for granted, kids with SPD feel overwhelmed, frustrated, confused, and/or tormented by stimuli on an ongoing basis. These feelings translate into problematic behavior: irritability, jumpiness, full-blown tantrums.

To their parents, teachers, and peers, this behavior occurs for no apparent reason. The children come across as some combination of withdrawn, inattentive, annoying, disrespectful, stubborn, unruly, or unpredictable. They may be considered learning disabled or written off as discipline problems. They may also be labeled autistic—though it's believed that most children with SPD are not autistic because they don't experience breakdowns in the three areas that typify autism: language development, social affiliation, and empathy. Three-quarters of kids with ASD, however (at least according to one oft-cited study) show significant signs of SPD.[12]

In such children, for whom the moment-to-moment overlap of sensations may be something like a "traffic jam in the brain,"[13] environmental sensitivity abounds. Things are perceived as too loud, too bright, too fast, or too tight.[14] They may report what sounds like synesthesia, saying things such as "I don't like that shirt. It's too spicy on the inside." And such children often have highly reactive immune systems and a greater incidence of allergies than typical kids do.[15]

This package can be pretty intense for parents to deal with. But what of the traditional picture we have of the autistic child—the boy (it's mostly boys) who has become withdrawn and uncommunicative? It turns out there's probably much more going on *there* that's intense, too.

Sensory Overload: A Crucible for Autism?

Adam, a boy with ASD, is at the playground with his mother and a friend of his mother's. It's a typical scene: Some adults are playing basketball and racquetball, moms are pushing strollers, and younger children are running around, giggling and yelling. A Little League practice is going on, a breeze is blowing, and, just outside the playground, there's plenty of traffic.

In the midst of all this, Adam is in his own world. Suddenly he excitedly shrieks and points in the direction of the traffic. His mom's friend manages to catch the words "white police truck" being said again and again. The friend stops, listens carefully, and hears a faraway siren. In the midst of the playground commotion, Adam has evidently tuned out all of it in order to isolate a sound that must initially have been many blocks away. His mother couldn't hear it, and her friend just barely could.[16]

This anecdote illustrates what may be happening in cases of ASD—particularly instances where the child or adult in question has a more severe form of the condition. People who seem to be tuned out of social interaction may, counterintuitively, have become that way not because they have a deficit of empathy or mental/social apparatus, but because they have fled from *too much* sensory and emotional input.

Such is the inference of the "intense world" theory presented in the last chapter. It surmises that the person with autism, in order to rise above the torrent of "frightful and oppressive noise," must become expert at detecting any patterns that present themselves. "To stay sane," that individual would "have to control as much as possible, developing a rigid focus on detail, routine and repetition. Systems in which specific inputs produce predictable outputs would be far more attractive than human beings, with their mystifying and inconsistent demands and their haphazard behavior."[17]

Recall the finding that the brains of kids with ASD register individual sensations normally but overreact to sensations *occurring at the same time.* This seems consistent with the intense world presumption: the more stimuli, the more information is shared by neural connections, and the more reaction is ratcheted up.

Now think back to Adam in the playground. He blocked out everything else so he could concentrate on one sound—a far-off police siren. No doubt this strategy succeeds in protecting the autistic child from an overload of stimuli. But it comes at a significant cost—and not just in lost "face time" with other children and adults around him. There are critical stages in neural development when certain kinds of external input are essential for the growing brain. If the opportunities for interaction with the outside world are minimized during these periods, social and language impairments may arise. Thus, in seeking a measure of comfort and predictability in his environment, the infant who was initially prone to autism may well cement it by unwittingly sabotaging his social, linguistic, and emotional skills.[18]

Yes, emotion is a big part of the equation. The IMFAR study

found that the amygdala—the brain's emotional "sentinel"—is one of the regions that reacts strongly to concurrent stimuli.[19] If the amygdala reacts this way to a sound or a texture, imagine how it would react to a yelp of pain, a gasp of surprise, or a pointed accusation. The intense world view posits that people with ASD dial themselves down in the face of a barrage of feelings—their own as well as the feelings of others. Again, this is counterintuitive. But I am struck by the comment of one particular mother that her autistic child is actually the most empathetic of her three kids. And Kai Markram (son of the researchers who developed the intense world hypothesis), when asked if he sees things differently than others do, responds emphatically: "I *feel* them different."[20]

Roots of Sensitivity in the Womb

If we accept the validity of the intense world theory of autism—and many people with ASD do[21]—it's fair game to ask whether the hyperconnectivity and hyperreactivity of the autistic brain is preordained by genetics or whether environmental influences may have some bearing here.

In answering this question, let's start by dismissing the outmoded assumption that it's either/or. To assert that nature is more important than nurture or vice versa is like saying that the length of a rectangle is more important than its width.[22] Each makes an essential contribution to the rectangle's area, and you can't have the whole without both of them.

That rectangle should really be a triangle, based on an increasing amount of evidence suggesting that a third leg—immune function—plays an essential role in at least some cases of ASD. Over the past decade, teams at three major research centers have demonstrated that immune system disorders are more common in the parents of children with ASD.[23] Their work has also demonstrated that the mothers of some autistic children, when pregnant, make antibodies that cross the placenta and affect proteins in the fetal brain. (Antibodies are proteins the body makes in response to viruses and bacteria. They're also associated with autoimmune conditions such as lupus and rheumatoid arthritis—and they may also result from maternal stress, infections, and environmental exposures during pregnancy.)[24] These antibodies bind to particular proteins in the fetal brain, interfering with cell signaling and neuronal growth and otherwise disturbing brain development and organization.[25] While this process is believed to apply to just a quarter of all cases of ASD, the documentation behind it is convincing.[26] The implication? The "intense world" of the infant who develops ASD is, at least in some cases, less a matter of genetics and more of immune system influence and other factors (such as maternal stress) during pregnancy.

On a parallel track, neurobiologist Lisa Boulanger of Princeton University has been investigating another possible immune influence on the developing brain. Scientists now know that certain immune system molecules, instead of scouting for germs, influence the connections between neurons. One of them, known as C1q, appears to prune synapses in the normal course of development. (Humans are born with more synapses than needed; weak and unnecessary connections are gradually eliminated during childhood.) But if C1q and other such proteins are diverted from their usual job—say, because of a virus in a mother's body when pregnant—their impact in the child's brain won't be sufficient. Indeed, in animals it's been found that a deficit of such proteins is linked with extraneous neural connections.[27] And a surfeit of neural connections is implicated in both autism and synesthesia.

The prospect raised here is that a maternal infection during pregnancy—or, for that matter, the occurrence of stress, trauma, injury, deprivation, or exposure to environmental toxins—could cause the child's brain to be hyperconnected, setting the stage for extraordinary sensitivity.[28] The nature, severity, and timing of the occurrence would presumably have much to do with the condition or personality trait ultimately manifested. Population studies indicate, for example, that ASD may result if a pregnant mom develops an infection during the second trimester.[29]

There's yet another way that the immune system exerts an influence on the developing brain. It's through a set of cellular players that until recently scientists had written off as being inconsequential—despite the fact that they outnumber neurons by a ratio of 9 to 1. These players are called glial cells. *Glial* is Greek for "glue," and historically scientists believed they served as figurative spackle and caulk for the neurons they surround. But now glial cells are garnering lots of attention, for it seems they carry out an intricate and ongoing communication with neurons. They begin life as immune cells, migrate to the brain, and there do any number of critically important things. These include surveying the entire brain for signs of injury, gobbling up invading pathogens, and clearing away cellular debris to speed repair. Glial cells also seem to trim away immature, weak, or unnecessary neural connections.[30] They are extremely dynamic, constantly on the move—and they're increasingly implicated in autism.

Glial cells have been found in the cerebral spinal fluid of people with autism, and at greater concentrations than control subjects.[31] If they're busy pruning synaptic connections, this would be the opposite effect of the immune activity we surveyed earlier. While those processes would lead to *more* neural connections and the likelihood of hypersensitivity, the action of glial cells in the fetal brain would *cut back* on synaptic connections. So the picture is not at all uniform, matching the phenomenon of ASD, which is hardly uniform either. ASD, after all, stands for autism spectrum disorder, and people on one end of the spectrum (the Asperger's side) are affected much less notably than people on the other end.

Scientists speculate not only that the combination of these various factors—genetic, environmental, immune—influence where on the autism spectrum a person will be[32] but also that their interaction has a bearing on gender differences in autism and other conditions.[33] It's puzzling that synesthetes are predominantly female and persons with ASD are overwhelmingly male, and yet large numbers of both are plagued by sensory overload.

Perhaps one view at least can be agreed upon, as articulated by pediatric neurologist Martha Herbert of Harvard Medical School. ASD, she says, is not a disorder *of* the brain but a disorder that *affects* the brain. The entire body is presumably involved.[34] Indeed, one's entire sense of self may be involved.

Autism and Sense of Self

One of the most flat-out fascinating books on autism is Temple Grandin's *Animals in Translation*.[35] Grandin, a professor at Colorado State University, is undoubtedly the best-known person with ASD in the world because of her ability to communicate what it's like to be autistic (at least her form of autistic) through her books, interviews, and talks.

She states that many animals are effectively autistic because they process their perceptions concretely, without interpretation—as do people with ASD. While the rest of us proceed through our days reliant on generalized concepts assembled through experience, people with ASD (as well as the farm animals she works with closely) perceive the world as a "swirling mass of tiny details."[36] This makes sense given the finding that children with ASD have difficulty interpreting a sensation, especially if it's paired with another, different sensation. This is why they get overwhelmed and find it easier (and comforting) to concentrate on one thing at a time. To the rest of us they may seem zoned out or disengaged. They retreat inward, away from the sensory "noise" and the bustle of unpredictable human interactions.

I propose that the way we process environmental and emotional stimuli has a direct bearing on our sense of self. Not just how we come across to other people (our personality) but how we sense—and thereby conceptualize—ourselves.

Evidence for the validity of this statement can be seen in a remarkable report from a few years ago. The research found that people with a high-functioning form of autism have a weaker sense of self than people who do not have ASD. Furthermore, the weaker the sense of self is, the more pronounced are the ASD symptoms.[37]

Recall Ernest Hartmann's framework of Boundaries, and the salient differences between thick- and thin-boundary people. I will venture to say that people with Asperger's have thinner boundaries than those who have a more severe form of ASD. This is because the latter are more armored, more protected, and have firmer delineations of thought and feeling. Interestingly, it seems that the children of fathers who are in technical occupations are more likely to have ASD—and children whose parents were *both* in technical occupations have a higher risk of having a more severe form.[38] This finding would not have surprised Hartmann at all, as his studies yielded consistent correlations between boundary type and occupation. (Examples of thin-boundary occupations are artist, musician, fashion model; thick-boundary occupations include military officer, salesperson, lawyer.)[39]

Sense of self, it turns out, has a lot to do with two more conditions that scientists—along with regular folks—find astounding: savantism and prodigiousness. If you remember the movie *Rain Man* with Dustin Hoffman, you'll know what the first is all about. And if you recall the film *A Beautiful Mind* with Russell Crowe, you'll recognize the second.

Synesthesia and Autism Experienced Together

Daniel Tammet is a mathematical and linguistic genius. He has memorized pi to more than 22,500 digits, and he speaks eleven languages—one of which he learned in a week for a TV special that he subsequently appeared in. He can multiply enormous sums in his head in a matter of seconds. A standard job, however, is not for him, in part due to his obsessive adherence to ritual, down to the precise times he drinks his tea and the exactly forty-five grams of porridge he allocates for breakfast each morning.[40]

Daniel is a high-functioning autistic (Asperger's) savant. And for good measure, he's a synesthete. He doesn't calculate numbers as much as experience them. For him, each one has a color, a shape, and a texture. The number 1 is like a shining light; 2 has a flowing, violet color; 3 is green; 5 like a clap of thunder; and 37 is lumpy. This capacity enables him to perform astonishing feats without conscious calculation, the answer materializing in his mind's eye. As he explains, "When I multiply numbers together, I see two shapes. The image starts to change and evolve, and a third shape emerges. That's the answer. It's mental imagery."[41]

Unlike most other prodigious savants (of whom there are fewer than one hundred in the world),[42] Daniel can and does describe articulately what life is like for him. He's written three books, appeared on *The Late Show with David Letterman*, and keeps up a busy schedule of lectures. He also collaborates with neuroscientists who are fascinated by his capacities and what can be learned from them.

Life has become easier for Daniel as he's gotten older and has learned to live with—and surmount, to a great degree—his communicative disabilities. Growing up was difficult. As a child, he shunned eye contact, banged his head against walls, flapped his hands when excited, and often didn't speak to other children at all. "One of the downsides to having an autistic spectrum disorder," he remarks, "is that you find it very difficult to relate to other people. To do things that most people take for granted, like knowing how to read body language, how to make eye contact, when to laugh at a joke."

When teased or bullied, "I would put my fingers in my ears . . . and I would count to myself, very, very quickly in powers of two . . . on and on into the millions and the numbers would form patterns in my mind . . . colors, patterns, shapes and textures. It would just be a beautiful experience . . . and the [other] children . . . were kind of perplexed and just walked away. How could they bully someone who didn't know how to be bullied?"[43]

To this day, Daniel is compelled to notice details. He'll count the stitches on someone's shirt but not necessarily remember the gestalt of their face when next they meet. He finds it difficult to go to the beach because there are too many grains of sand to be counted, and a trip to the supermarket is problematic because his attention is drawn to the shape, texture, and arrangement of the items on display. But in his mind, "words, colors and numbers blare with color, emotion, and personality."[44]

Until he taught himself the art of getting on with people—which he's now quite accomplished at—Daniel "had no sense of other people. They were really just like wallpaper," he remembers. In contrast, "silence was a beautiful thing for me; it was a kind of silvery texture around my head like condensation running down a window pane. And when someone made a noise, a knock on the door, a car horn blaring on the street below, it would be a shattering of that experience . . . [it was] physically painful."[45]

As noted earlier, sensory hypersensitivity is common to autism as well as synesthesia. Scientists point to a proliferation of white matter tracts connecting different parts of the brain in both conditions. In autism, there is an increased volume of such connections between local regions, while in synesthesia the connections are more long-distance.[46] In either case, one can presume that some combination of genetics and environment—the latter quite possibly exerting an influence during fetal development—is at work.

Making of a Savant

Savant syndrome is the name of a rare but extraordinary condition in which someone with serious mental impairment (often some form of autism) displays a spectacular "island of genius" amid the overall disability.[47]

Take, for example, a child who is mute and noncommunicative but has the bizarre ability to do any jigsaw puzzle placed in front of him, picture-side down, with machine-like rapidity. Just by looking at the shapes of, say, two hundred pieces, he can quickly put the puzzle together. Or consider another savant, blind from birth, who, at fourteen years old, played Tchaikovsky's Piano Concerto no. 1 from beginning to end flawlessly, having heard it just once. Or the late Kim Peek (who inspired Dustin Hoffman's role in the film *Rain Man*), who would read books extremely rapidly—one page with the right eye and the other with the left. He also memorized literally thousands of books after having read each of them just once.[48]

What all savants have in common is prodigious, almost uncanny memory. This type of memory, while deep, is also narrow, linked solely to their particular ability. These abilities cluster into five major categories: music, art, lightning calculation, calendar calculation, and visual-spatial ability (such as the jigsaw-puzzle kid, or a man who can hit golf balls with enormous accuracy, so much so that they all land within a few feet of one another).[49] Brain damage, generally in the left hemisphere, is endemic to nearly all congenital savants. (Some people acquire savant-like skills later in life; these nearly always appear in the aftermath of a head injury. We'll take up the "acquired" savant momentarily.) About half of the individuals with savant syndrome have an autism spectrum disorder (ASD), while the other 50 percent have some other form of central nervous system damage or disease. Peek, for instance, lacked a corpus callosum, the bundle of fibers that connect the brain hemispheres. He also had substantial other central nervous system damage.[50] Not everyone with ASD, of course, will have savant abilities. Just one out of ten people with ASD does.[51]

The best explanation of what happens in the brain of a savant (whether congenital or acquired) is this: Damage occurs to the left side of the brain, with higher-level memory circuits also sustaining damage. Parts of the brain that are undamaged are recruited to compensate, as are lower-level memory capacities. Rewiring occurs, and dormant capacity from the newly wired area is released. Darold Treffert, formerly of the University of Wisconsin—and the world's leading authority on savants—terms this process *the 3 Rs:* recruitment, rewiring, release. The capacities that savants draw upon come from fast, preconscious mental activity; this isn't the executive-level reasoning that most of us engage in. In general, creativity and cognitive flexibility are severely limited. In their place: automatic, rigid, rule-based processing.[52]

Why are almost all savants male? One theory suggests that any number of disorders involving the disruption of the brain's left hemisphere (such as savantism, autism, dyslexia, delayed speech, stuttering, and hyperactivity) will inevitably occur much more often in boys. This is because the left hemisphere typically completes its development later than the right hemisphere—making it susceptible to prenatal influences for a longer period. In the developing male fetus, for example, circulating testosterone can slow the growth of the left hemisphere. This can trigger "recruitment," with the right hemisphere becoming bigger and more dominant.[53]

Perhaps the most incredible manifestation of savant syndrome is that of the "acquired" savant. Here, prodigious skill—especially in art or music—emerges as a complete surprise in people who have suffered a head injury, stroke, dementia, or other form of brain damage. Take the fifty-six-year-old builder who, after surviving a stroke, "began filling several notebooks with poems and verse; he had never written poetry prior to that time. Following that, [he] began to paint expansively and expressively, spending almost all of his time painting and sculpting."[54]

Or consider the forty-two-year-old orthopedic surgeon who, in the aftermath of being struck by lightning, developed an insatiable desire to listen to classical piano music—a complete departure from his longtime taste for rock. Tony Cicoria (whom we met in chapter 2) sought out Chopin recordings and had such a strong desire to play them that he taught himself how. Close on the heels of this impulse, he started hearing music in his own head—"an absolute torrent" that would intrude into whatever he was doing. It became "enjoyable, addicting, and overwhelming." Over several years, he wrote down transcriptions of what he was hearing, ultimately recording and performing his own Lightning Sonata.[55]

The evidence suggests that acquired savant syndrome occurs the same way as the congenital kind—from damage to the left side of the brain. The 3 Rs spring into action: recruitment, rewiring, and release. Exceptional abilities that were previously dormant rise to the surface. More accurately, they take over someone's personality, impelling him or her to express these new capacities.[56] Treffert believes that acquired savant syndrome indicates latent ability in everyone—that all of us have some "Rain Man" capacity within.[57]

The implications may be even greater than that. To get at them, we need to take a closer look at how savants and prodigies (who have savant-like abilities but without physical or mental impairment) know things they never actually learned.[58]

Knowing What You've Never Learned

All savants, whether congenital or acquired, demonstrate spectacular—and quite sudden—ability. Some of these capacities are the counting and calendar curiosities we've come to associate with savants, such as indicating unerringly what day of the week a given day falls on or counting pi to the 22,500th digit. In these cases, the savants know the rules of math without knowing that they know them, and without having been taught. Other savants—and child prodigies, for that matter—do even more astounding things. Alonzo Clemons, notwithstanding no training in art, sculpts intricate, true-to-life figures of animals in motion with merely a glance at an image on television or in a book.[59]

And consider the story of Jason Padgett, who in his early thirties was brutally attacked by muggers. They kicked him repeatedly in the head, causing a concussion and sending him to the hospital. But the next morning, after having been sent home, something very strange happened. While running the water in the bathroom, Jason noticed "lines emanating out perpendicularly from the flow . . . it was so beautiful that I just stood in my slippers and stared." When he extended his hand out in front of him, it was like "watching a slow-motion film," as if each successive movement were in stop-motion animation.

He soon became obsessed with every shape he saw, from rectangular windows to the curvature of a spoon. He also developed synesthesia, with numbers generating colorful shapes. Jason also began envisioning complex images which, when he drew them, were recognized as fractals—beautiful shapes in which every element is the same as the whole. Before the mugging, Jason had no interest in drawing, no math training, and no college degree. He was a self-described "goof." Now he sells his drawings for top dollar and is committed to teaching others about the beauty of math.[60]

Just as stunning is musical prodigy Jay, now in his teens:

Jay [began] to draw little cellos on paper at age 2. Neither parent is musically inclined, and there never were any musical instruments, including a cello, in the home. At age 3, Jay asked if he could have a cello of his own. The parents took him to a music store and, to their astonishment, Jay picked up a miniature cello and began to play it! He had never seen a real cello before that day. After that experience he began to draw his miniature cellos placed on musical lines. By age 5 he had composed five symphonies. By age 15 he had written nine symphonies. His fifth symphony, which was 190 pages and 1328 bars in length, was professionally recorded by the London Symphony Orchestra for Sony Records.

Jay says that the music just streams into his head at lightning speed; sometimes several symphonies running simultaneously at the same time. "My unconscious directs my conscious mind at a mile a minute," he told [a reporter].

Where does Jay's musical genius come from? How did he know about cellos, and how to play them at age 3 when never exposed to one before? How did he instinctively . . . "know" the rules of music when he had never studied or learned them?[61]

Scott Barry Kaufman, a psychologist who studies creativity, suggests that savants and prodigies have a greatly enhanced ability to do what each of us does every single day without being aware of it—absorb the implicit rules of different subject matter. Music, for instance, consists of highly structured sequential regularities. Kaufman believes that savants and prodigies have "an innate predisposition" to identify and internalize these redundancies.[62]

This makes sense from several perspectives. On the one hand, all savants and prodigies draw upon truly massive memory. Whereas the source for savants is low-level and precognitive, prodigies excel in working memory, a higher-level ability to hold multiple pieces of information in mind while completing a task.[63] By the same token, both savants and prodigies display a surpassing attention to detail. Savants arguably pay attention in a less conscious way than prodigies do—but if this predilection for "homing in" on information is reminiscent of autism, that's no coincidence. About 50 percent of savants have an autism spectrum disorder; in one intriguing study, half of the prodigies either had ASD or had a close family member who did.[64] Where prodigies are concerned, Kaufman theorizes they're born with a genetic disposition to embrace structure and beauty. Some find it in music, others in art, still others in math. Their families encourage these tendencies, so nature and nurture reinforce one another, producing prodigious talent that advances itself through practice.[65]

I wonder about this explanation, though, in light of the *suddenness* with which prodigious interests assert themselves—or for that matter, the suddenness with which acquired savants find their lives overtaken by obsessions that were it not for injury or illness would be completely foreign to them. Kaufman's theory suggests (to me at least) that savants and child prodigies are in the natural order of things. Autism, extraordinary attention to detail, stupendous memory . . . his explanation frames these as "to be expected." Yet I'm bothered by the frequency with which the affected individuals (or the moms who were pregnant with them) were beset by injury, accident, or trauma. And I return to a recurrent theme of my work—sensory sensitivity and literally feeling too much.

Earlier we examined the intense world hypothesis and various ways that hypersensitivity could be engendered in the womb. While being highly sensitive undoubtedly confers some advantages, it's an ongoing challenge for many people. It can be distracting, frustrating, exhausting, overwhelming. My sense is that extraordinary sensitivities—and uncanny abilities—often result when something goes awry with the developmental process. It's not a bad outcome, just an unlikely one.

I want to advance a different way of understanding how autistic traits, savant skills, and prodigious talents might appear. While not intending to invalidate any of the mechanisms that have been proposed, I suggest bringing something fundamental yet profoundly overlooked into the equation: *emotion*.

A Genetic Imprint of Fear?

Fear is the most elemental emotion. A threat to self-preservation triggers a panoply of sympathetic nervous system activities: our senses go on "red alert," our pupils dilate, our muscles tense, and respiration is increased. The body prepares to fight, flee, or freeze. (The latter is not as well-known a response but is amply illustrated in the animal kingdom, e.g., "playing possum.")

The part of the brain instigating all this activity is the hypothalamus. In moments of anxiety or threat, it prompts the adrenal glands to release the hormones adrenaline and noradrenaline. The hypothalamus also stimulates the pituitary gland to release a hormone called ACTH; carried to the adrenal glands, it causes the release of other hormones. One of these is cortisol, which serves to marshal bodily energy (and also has an effect on the immune system over time). This entire stress response system is known, in shorthand, as the hypothalamic-pituitary-adrenal (HPA) axis.

You'll soon see why the HPA axis is germane to sensitivity. For now, let's consider how extreme fear registers not just in a given animal but how it can actually be transmitted to its offspring—and even to its offspring's offspring.

The research was conducted by a team at Emory University, and it set off shock waves throughout the behavioral science community.[66] In the first phase, mice were trained to be afraid of acetophenone, a fruity smell that's used in cherry, jasmine, honeysuckle, and almond flavorings. The researchers paired this fragrance with an electric shock to the mice's feet, so that the scent soon became a warning signal. Their noses adapted accordingly, generating more of a particular kind of neuron keyed to the smell. Their brains adapted as well, growing an expanded recognition area for it. So far, all of this is basic Pavlovian conditioning and neural adaptation.

The offspring of these mice, however—who had never before been exposed to the smell—*also* showed increased fear and startle responses to it. Somehow the learned association was transmitted from one generation to the next. The brains of these offspring also had more of those same neurons, so their noses were more sensitive to the fruity smell. Amazingly, even the third generation of mice was similarly affected.

The researchers took care to verify that the results were not attributable to the mouse pups learning anxiety from the behavior of an anxious parent. The mice showed no fear reaction to other scents or other types of warnings. To confirm this, the scientists took sperm from the first set of mice, implanted it in females from another lab, raised them in isolation, and *still* found an increased sensitivity to the original scent.

Identical results have been affirmed by other researchers in Switzerland.[67] That such changes happen over just a single generation indicates that random DNA mutations are not involved, since such Darwinian adaptation takes place slowly over many generations. Epigenetics, a relatively new concept in which environmental influences alter gene expression, seems to be at work.[68]

If the same findings hold for human beings, we're left with the amazing implication that fearful experiences can make a man's children—and even his children's children—more sensitive to the same stimuli that evoked fear in *him*. His progeny may also be more highly reactive in general, given studies linking trauma with an intensified startle reflex.[69] If this is the case for fathers, imagine what effect a pregnant *mother's* fearful experiences might have on the child she is carrying. After all, she and her child are "locked in the closest of biological embraces" via the placenta.[70]

To return to the HPA stress response, it's entirely possible that a pregnant mother's fearful reactions—especially if chronic—could effectively "program" her child to be anxious, high reacting, and environmentally sensitive. Alternatively, as I've indicated, it's conceivable that any number of things affecting a mom during pregnancy—infection, injury, an autoimmune illness, general deprivation, exposure to environmental toxins—could cause her child's brain to become hyperconnected, setting the stage for pronounced sensitivities. The conjunction of neural connectivity, fear, and sensitivity has been clearly demonstrated in rats with overly connected neural networks. Although they learn faster than normal rats, they're also more anxious, showing aberrant social behavior and increased repetitive behaviors (much like humans with an autism spectrum disorder). Furthermore, while ordinary rats become scared of an electrified grid when a shock is paired with a particular sound, hyperconnected rats come to fear not just the sound, but the whole grid and everything connected with it—including colors and smells.[71]

It's worth noting here that Kai Markram displayed a veritable terror of trying new foods when he was young. He can recall, to this day, exactly where he was sitting at a certain restaurant when he once tried to force himself to eat a salad.[72] Similarly, a researcher who worked with highly gifted children observed that several of them "were terrified of germs and would visualize them flowing through their bodies, destroying their health."[73]

Just as most adults can vividly remember where they were and what they were doing when the World Trade Center was attacked on September 11, 2001, I propose that fear—that most primal emotion— can "imprint" certain people with a virtual snapshot of what was taking place around them when something traumatic occurred. Their brains and their bodies may be especially sensitive to begin with[74] or, as suggested by the Emory study, their parents or grandparents may have had a particularly fearful experience. Child prodigies manifest this process to a great degree.

The Sensitivities of Prodigies and Gifted Children

In *Nature's Gambit,* his illuminating extended study of six child prodigies, Tufts University child development expert David Henry Feldman recounts several very strange anecdotes told to him by parents of these children. One of them, Adam (pseudonyms were used to maintain confidentiality), related what seemed to be memories of his own birth, including reaction to the bright lights of the delivery room and the placement of a suctioning bulb into his nose. He also related apparently prenatal memories, such as the sound of his mother's singing and "the walls closing in on me—they hurt." What makes this latter point so remarkable is that his mother's pregnancy was beset by numerous complications, including uterine contractions that threatened to terminate the pregnancy from the fourth month onward.[75]

Among prodigies and extremely high IQ children, there is an overrepresentation of complicated pregnancies, long labors, and premature births.[76] One example: the mom of Jake Barnett (a renowned math and physics prodigy) was hospitalized multiple times before giving birth. In another notable case, a mother of an eventual prodigy had an accident while pregnant. However, hers was not just any accident. She fell as she was helping her husband fight off an intruder who was trying to break into their house.[77] Talk about a fearful experience!

There is also an increased occurrence, among mothers of prodigies-to-be, of preeclampsia,[78] a condition marked by a sudden rise in blood pressure and swelling of the face, hands, and feet. Preeclampsia generally occurs during the late second or third trimester and may be caused by an underdeveloped placenta. That, in turn, may be due to a genetic defect whereby the mother's immune system treats the placenta like an invader.[79] Another study has found that exposure to environmental toxins increases the risk for both preeclampsia and premature birth.[80] Clearly the role of the immune system in conditions marked by environmental sensitivity cannot be overlooked.

Just as preeclampsia is associated with more than its share of child prodigies, so is it also significantly linked to the development of autism.[81] The placenta may actually be a biomarker for autism. Researchers have found that the more abnormal folds a mother's placenta has, the more likely the child will have autism and the more severe the condition. Such creases seem to be the placenta's way of responding to a variety of stressors—placental folds are akin to a check-engine light, a marker of something, somewhere, being wrong.[82]

Although the seeming retention of *in utero* memories is not something all prodigies share, virtually all of them have a finely tuned sensitivity to feelings—their own feelings as well as those of others. On the one hand, their own feelings are intense. As with many children with autism or sensory processing disorder, their outbursts can be too much to handle. One mother of a prodigy reflects that her son "just felt more from the time he was born. He . . . had so much emotion and feeling inside of him."[83] Claudio, at age two, wept uncontrollably when he heard his father playing Rossini's Stabat Mater Dolorosa. Years later, Claudio related that from an early age he felt connected to each note of music he heard and "just knew" that music was an expression of his soul.[84]

By the same token, prodigies' sense of connectedness with other people and with life in general disposes them to be "the most morally sensitive and generous individuals I've ever met," says psychologist Joanne Ruthsatz, who's been studying child prodigies for the past fifteen years.[85] This global sense of responsibility and altruism begins early. Take Rachel, who at age eight asserted that she could communicate with animals. "I can!" she said defiantly. "I can see it in their eyes and they sense my caring."[86] Prodigies—and other highly gifted children, for that matter—are likewise protective of others and have a deeply felt sense of justice. They can become terribly upset if a classmate is wronged, and they take personally issues such as war, poverty, homelessness, global warming, and environmental degradation. They may even cry at the violence in cartoons.[87] "Very sensitive beings" is the succinct way Susan Daniels, a noted educator of gifted children, puts it.[88]

A renowned case in point is climate change activist Greta Thunberg. At age eleven, she wept while watching a school video depicting the Great Pacific Garbage Patch. This area (as of 2018) was three times the size of France, encompassing 79 thousand tons of plastic among its appalling conglomeration of human-generated debris—an amount that continues to increase exponentially.[89] While other students were evidently able to accept what they had seen, Greta was not. She went into a prolonged funk, refusing to eat more than token amounts and crying every day. The video, along with other information that Greta had absorbed about climate threats, caused her to "disappear into some kind of darkness."[90] It took several years for her to emerge from this depression, finally embarking on the path that has made her the world's best-known climate activist. In the interim, she was diagnosed with Asperger's syndrome.

Such special children will often pose probing, existential questions, indicative of an understanding that they've come into a world much greater than themselves. They may even report transcendent or spiritual experiences. Elizabeth, for example, while sitting on a cliff overlooking the Pacific, felt her mind transported beyond the ocean, beyond the Earth, and beheld what she described as "the total interconnectedness of the universe." And Ian spoke of feeling holes in the fabric of the universe with the extinction of every species. These are truly striking expressions of empathy.[91]

Lisa Simpson, of the television show *The Simpsons,* is, funnily, the public face of all these qualities. But twenty years before *The Simpsons,* a pioneering Polish psychiatrist by the name of Kazimierz Dabrowski catalogued such personality traits in a cluster that translates from the

Polish as "superstimulatability" or "overexcitability." The five characteristics he identified are: an abundance of physical energy, sensory hyperreactivity, vivid imagination, intellectual curiosity and drive, and a deep capacity to care.[92] The combination of all five manifests as an emotional complexity and intensity. It's been described as a wholly different way of experiencing life: "vivid, absorbing, penetrating, encompassing, complex, commanding—a way of being quiveringly alive."[93]

Clearly these highly gifted children are blessed in numerous ways. Their penetrating intellect, their acute and prodigious memory, their reservoir of energy, their passion and drive, their empathetic embrace of others—all set them apart. Savants, too, are set apart, but through their particular and often bizarre abilities. Synesthetes are likewise a curiosity, pointing toward the marvels of heightened connectivity between brain regions. If all these conditions develop in the womb, they are in some sense "throwbacks" to capacities we all could have if our own prenatal development had been disadvantaged or interfered with in a major way.

Before continuing, I wish to present a caveat. Given that each person is unique, I don't mean to imply that *everyone* who's autistic, gifted, a synesthete, and so on is going to be off the charts empathetic, morally sensitive, and generous in outlook. Nature and nurture combine to produce an exceedingly wide range of individuals, each with his or her own quirks, limitations, and shortcomings. No parent of a child with any of the exceptional traits considered here should expect that child's personality to reflect the rather generalized picture we've been developing. As with any assessment of personality, the individual's mileage will surely vary.

The Most Astounding Aspect of Prodigies

Are there still other capacities that only a few of us humans have access to? I believe there are. Take Randy, a child prodigy, who was seven when he abruptly announced the following: "Truth is the word of being.

People who are questioned by the being word must be answered. People who do not answer by the being word are afraid of their death. People who do say the being word open a new life. Truth is the word of being."

When asked by his mom whether he'd remembered this passage from a book he might have been reading, Randy said no, that he'd not read it anywhere. Puzzled and astonished, his mother wrote down the passage word for word.[94]

Another out of the blue discourse was delivered to the late psychologist Joseph Chilton Pearce by his five-year-old son. Pearce was teaching humanities at college, engrossed in theology and the psychology of Carl Jung. One morning, as he was preparing at home for an early class, his son came into his room, sat down on the edge of the bed, and launched into a twenty-minute lecture of his own about the nature of God and man. His son, Pearce recollects,

spoke in perfect, publishable sentences, without pause or haste, and in a flat monotone. He used complex theological terminology and told me, it seemed, everything there was to know. As I listened, astonished, the hair rose on my neck; I felt goose bumps, and, finally, tears streamed down my face. I was in the midst of the uncanny, the inexplicable. My son's ride to kindergarten arrived, horn blowing, and he got up and left. I was unnerved and arrived late to my class. What I had heard was awesome, but too vast and far beyond any concept I had had to that point. The gap was so great I could remember almost no details and little of the broad panorama he had presented. . . . He wasn't picking up his materials from me. I hadn't acquired anything like what he described and would, in fact, be in my mid-50s . . . before I did. [95]

Later that day, when his son returned from school, he had no recollection of the event.

Moriah, age two and a half, was in school when she suddenly came to her teachers sobbing for her children and begging desperately for us to find them. This went on over the course of a couple of weeks. . . . During each episode she would try to tell us more of what she thought we needed to know in order to find them. She named the French village where she lived and described the round barn where she raised "fire horses." We could tell that she truly believed if she could make us understand where they were that we could find them . . . she identified five children by name—three girls and two boys. . . . Had Moriah not been so distraught and obviously grieving, we most likely wouldn't have thought much of her saying she had children. But, because of the sorrow and real emotion, we knew there was something to it. Moriah during that time also described her passing. I don't think she knew that as anything more than the last thing she remembered and it was vague; she said she was traveling on the road in her wagon, and she hit a boulder and remembered that she flipped off the road.[96]

Adam, a precocious eighteen-month-old, was getting a bath after dinner. Suddenly he sat bolt upright in the tub, screaming "The men! They're coming!" His eyes appeared fixed on some distant object and he seemed unaware of who and where he was. When asked by his mother who "they" were, he replied with mounting hysteria that men in uniforms and guns were coming to get him. His mom tried her best to assure Adam that he was safe in his own house, in a warm, soapy bathtub. Then, as suddenly as the episode began, it ended, with Adam seemingly unaware that anything out of the ordinary had taken place.[97]

In these cases, young children blurt out statements about things that obviously move them but seem very much beyond the pale of what they've read or encountered. As with savants, whether congenital or acquired, these children know things they've not actually learned.

Treffert's explanation is that savants—and prodigies, and all the rest of us as well—come with genetic memory, or what he calls "factory installed software." Unconscious knowledge and the latent ability to do all sorts of things, he proposes, is in us based on what our family members knew and did themselves. According to his theory, we don't all have the same memory bank; discrete knowledge and talent is distributed along a bell curve similar to just about every other capacity that people have. But when a savant skill suddenly appears, or a complex religious or philosophical statement is made, or when a child recalls what seems to be a past life, the person is channeling an out-of-awareness ancestral memory.[98] It's roughly the same capacity as the instinct that enables geese to fly in a V formation. They don't think about it, they just know to do it.[99]

Treffert's idea is controversial. It can be disparaged as unscientific, since genes code for proteins that may ultimately express a biological trait (eye color, for instance)—a far cry from coding for particular types of knowledge.[100] The point of his theory can also be questioned. Even if specific types of knowledge enhanced survival and were, therefore, passed along to succeeding generations, where is the survival value in knowing the things that savants do? What is the survival value of learning to play a complex piece of music sight unseen . . . of drawing animals in extremely realistic detail . . . of reciting pi to the thousandth place?[101]

I propose an alternate explanation, based on the fact that the special individuals being explored here—synesthetes, people with an autism spectrum disorder, acquired savants, and child prodigies—often have something else in common besides environmental sensitivity. That something else is psychic sensitivity. And while the possibility of anomalous perception may rub a lot of people the wrong way, science is an ongoing quest where we must realize, in all humility, that we don't know what we don't know. Anomalies, in the words of neuroscientist V. S. Ramachandran of the University of California, San Diego, "show the depth of our ignorance."[102]

Following these "outlier" experiences may, counterintuitively, lead us toward a fuller understanding of how certain people can know things, do things, or perceive things that are so surpassingly extraordinary.

A Psychic Element to Autism?

In *The Soul of Autism,*[103] author Bill Stillman provides dozens of examples of people with an autism spectrum disorder who have had a spiritual, psychical, or anomalous experience—call it what you will. Stillman, who himself has Asperger's syndrome, writes about these perceptions with a firsthand knowledge. The late Donna Williams (whom we met in the last chapter) recounted her own autistic and psychic experiences, connecting them with sensory sensitivity and thin boundaries.[104] Even among savants, anomalous perceptions are not unknown. A large-scale study of child savants in the 1970s turned up a few whose parents reported that their son or daughter had extrasensory perception.[105] A more recent cataloguing by Treffert indicates a similar smattering of cases.[106] Experiments conducted by neurospsychiatrist Diane Hennacy Powell provide evidence of telepathy among several young autistic savants, suggesting—in her estimation—an alternate, very direct mode of apprehension in children who are hampered in their verbal communication skills.[107]

I suspect that such accounts reflect a genuine difference in sensory processing—and, consequently, a different sense of self. As we've seen, accumulating evidence suggests that people with ASD (or, for that matter, with SPD) are, from an early age, bombarded by sensory input that they have trouble discriminating. Their boundaries, we might say, are thinner than those of other people for whom the distinction between "outer" and "inner" is more constant, more firm. But even among individuals living with such a condition, there is a continuum between high-functioning and low-functioning forms. People with high-functioning forms of ASD or SPD will have somewhat thicker boundaries and a more fully delineated conception of self. People with low-functioning forms will be more likely to withdraw into their own world, dissociate from feelings and sensations that become overwhelming, and become less engaged and communicative.

As I proposed in my first book,[108] thin-boundary people are most likely to *report* anomalous perceptions whereas thick-boundary people are more likely to *engender* anomalies. Perhaps the most outstanding illustration of the latter is Matthew Manning, a sixty-year-old Brit who, at the age of eleven, began to find himself at the center of a series of increasingly powerful poltergeist displays. They began with the "mere" unaccounted for movement of a silver tankard and flowerpot and then, when he was fifteen and living in a seventeenth-century home in Cambridgeshire, escalating to furniture lifting off the ground and household objects variously levitating or hurtling through the air. Even more bizarre,

> The signatures of dead people—several hundred of them, all in different hands—began to appear, roughly scrawled, on Manning's bedroom wall. The first was signed by one Robert Webbe, a 17th-century figure who left a message that indicated, as Manning puts it, that he "seemed to have no idea that he was dead." On one occasion . . . Derek Manning [Matthew's father] ushered the whole family into the garden, with his son's bedroom roped off, leaving a pencil on the bed. When they returned after ten minutes, another inscription had been added. Some of the names, which were systematically photographed, appear in historic parish registers; others were of unknown provenance.[109]

The story becomes stranger still. The family moved to another house, whereupon, in his brother Andrew's words, the poltergeist "just erupted, like a volcano under the house. When it got very bad I went to sleep in my sister's bedroom. The house had no carpet because we had just moved, and that made it all the noisier—bangings, crashings, thumpings. We had no explanation. We just hoped it would stop." When Manning was sent away to school, his parents and siblings experienced "a tidal wave of relief that he had left."[110] But the boarding school then suffered through a similar predicament. One of Manning's former classmates recalls: "There were 24 of us in bunk beds. Things just started to happen. Water appeared from nowhere. I remember my bed moving when there was nobody near it. On one occasion, this pile of dinner plates came crashing down, out of thin air, and shattered on the floor. Where they came from, who knows? Matthew was frightened. I was bloody terrified. It was the sort of experience that, unless you've been through it, you can't begin to comprehend."[111]

The tale takes one further turn. While working on an essay, Manning found that his hand began to produce writing that was not his. This took him quite aback at first. But then, after producing a long composition, he noticed that the poltergeist activity ceased for about twenty-four hours. So he deliberately tried the strange exercise again. "A lot of what came through," he recalls, "was nonsense; other things purported to be messages from people who had died. . . . I had always imagined that the automatic writing, whatever it was, was probably flotsam that was coming out of my unconscious. . . . But when I began writing in [fluent] Chinese and Arabic . . . well, that did freak me out a bit. Because those languages were not, so far as I was aware, present in my subconscious."[112]

Nor was Manning any kind of artist. Upon being prompted by his mother to "channel" artwork, though, he produced a number of pictures reminiscent of artists ranging from Albrecht Dürer (a renowned sixteenth-century painter and printmaker) and Aubrey Beardsley (a nineteenth-century author/illustrator) to Pablo Picasso. The drawings "seemed to be a striking mimicry . . . even though flawed in some technical detail, their style and execution faithfully mirrored the original model."[113] This remarkable capacity is exactly what distinguishes savants—but Manning, like Daniel Tammet, is not obviously impaired and is, in fact, quite at home as a conversationalist.[114] So does he have any touch of autism?

It's hard to say but, like Tammet, he might have had a more pronounced form of autism as a child. Manning is recalled as "an introvert who . . . absolutely refused to talk to strangers. When scolded for mischievousness, he would withdraw into a corner and remain there, sometimes for hours, curled up in total isolation." Some years later, the headmaster of his boarding school described him as "a loner and rather lethargic."[115] Manning might well have grown out of this inwardness given the many interviews and public appearances he undertook in his late teens and twenties.

When we consider what could possibly produce someone like Matthew Manning, it's significant that, three weeks before he was born, his mother suffered such a severe electrical shock that she feared she might lose him.[116] This reinforces my contention that challenges to normal development in the womb may be the most certain precursor of the conditions we've looked at—whether synesthesia, autism, savantism, prodigiousness, environmental sensitivity, or the attunement to / generation of anomalous experiences.

If this is so, there are broader implications that I would like to speculate upon. Given that personality can be influenced to such a large extent during gestation; might we "rewind" the process and imagine the possible origin of individual human lives?

Children Who Remember Other Lives

The ultimate "truth is stranger than fiction" accounts are to be found in *Return to Life: Extraordinary Cases of Children Who Remember Past Lives,* a book by Jim Tucker, a psychiatry professor at the University of Virginia.[117]

Tucker follows in the footsteps of the late psychiatrist Ian Stevenson, who for decades scrupulously investigated cases of young children who, around the world, spontaneously volunteered—in great detail—recollections that seemed to be about someone else's life. Much of the time the person being spoken of had died violently or unnaturally. (Earlier I referenced one such instance, where a two-and-a-half-year-old girl became distraught over her inability to find "her" children and described "having lost "her" life in a road accident.) Between them, Stevenson and Tucker compiled more than 2,500 cases; 70 percent of them fit this pattern.[118]

In many of these accounts, the person being spoken of could be identified through the specificity of information volunteered. Here's a look at two very impressive (and recent) instances. For the first, I'll quote extensively from a story done for the *University of Virginia Magazine* by Sean Lyons.[119] It conveys, among other things, a sense of how befuddled parents are in such a situation—in this case, the parents of young Ryan Hammond:

> When Ryan was 4, he began directing imaginary movies. Shouts of "Action!" often echoed from his room. But the play became a concern for Ryan's parents when he began waking up in the middle of the night screaming and clutching his chest, saying he dreamed his heart exploded when he was in Hollywood. His mother asked his doctor about the episodes. Night terrors, the doctor said. He'll outgrow them. Then one night, as his mother tucked Ryan into bed, Ryan suddenly took hold of her hand. "Mama," he said. "I think I used to be someone else."
>
> He said he remembered a big white house and a swimming pool. It was in Hollywood, many miles from his Oklahoma home. He said he had three sons, but that he couldn't remember their names. He began to cry, asking his mother over and over why he couldn't remember their names.
>
> "I really didn't know what to do," she said. "I was more in shock than anything. He was so insistent about it. After that night, he kept talking about it, kept getting upset about not being able to remember those names. I started researching the Internet about reincarnation. I even got some books from the library on Hollywood, thinking their pictures might help him. I didn't tell anyone for months."
>
> One day, as Ryan and his mom paged through one of the Hollywood books, Ryan stopped at a black-and-white still taken from a 1930s movie, *Night After Night*. Two men in the center of the picture were confronting one another. Four other men surrounded them. His mother didn't recognize any of the faces but

Ryan pointed to one of the men in the middle. "Hey Mama," he said. "That's George. We did a picture together." His finger then shot over to a man on the right, wearing an overcoat and a scowl. "That guy's me. I found me!"

The book didn't provide any names of the actors pictured, but she quickly confirmed that the man Ryan said was "George" in the photo was indeed a George—George Raft, an all but forgotten film star from the 1930s and 1940s. Still, his mother couldn't identify the man Ryan said had been him. She wrote Tucker, whom she found through her online research, and included the photo. Eventually it ended up in the hands of a film archivist who, after weeks of research, confirmed the scowling man's name: Martin Martyn, an uncredited extra in the film.

Not long afterward, Tucker and the family traveled to California to meet Martyn's daughter, who'd been tracked down by researchers working with Tucker on a documentary. Tucker sat down with the woman before her meeting with Ryan. She'd been reluctant to help but during her talk with Tucker, she confirmed dozens of facts Ryan had given about her father.

Ryan said he danced in New York. Martyn was a Broadway dancer. Ryan said he was also an "agent," and that people where he worked had changed their names. Martyn worked for years at a well-known talent agency in Hollywood—where stage names are often created—after his dancing career ended. Ryan said his old address had "Rock" in its name. Martyn lived at 825 North Roxbury Drive in Beverly Hills. Ryan said he knew a man named Senator Five. Martyn's daughter said she had a picture of her father with a Senator Ives, Irving Ives of New York, who served in the U.S. Senate from 1947 to 1959. And yes, Martin Martyn had three sons. The daughter of course knew their names.

The second case is equally remarkable.[120] It involved two-year-old James Leininger, a Louisiana boy who loved toy planes. But he started to have repeated nightmares of a horrible plane crash. He would kick his legs up in the air, screaming "Airplane crash on fire, little man can't get out." Then during the day, he would slam his toy planes into the family's coffee table while yelling "airplane crash on fire," to the extent that there were dozens of scratches and dents in the table. James talked about the crash, relating that "he" had been a pilot and that "he" had flown off a boat. His father asked him the name of the boat and he said "Natoma." When his father remarked, "That sounds Japanese to me," James replied "No, it's American." James went on to say that "he" had piloted a type of plane called a Corsair, that "his" nickname was Little Man, and that "he" had a friend on the boat named Jack Larson.

After years of painstaking research, James's father learned that an American aircraft carrier, the *USS Natoma Bay,* had supported operations at Iwo Jima during that World War II battle—and that it had lost one pilot there, a young man from Pennsylvania named James Huston. His plane crashed almost exactly as James had described: It had been hit in the engine, exploded, crashed into the water, and quickly sank. And the pilot in the plane next to his when this happened was named Jack Larson.

It's nearly impossible to conceive how children so young should have such vivid "memories" or how they (or anyone connected with them) could have known anything about such obscure figures from the past, whether it be Martin Martyn or "Little Man" James Huston. Nor do such children appear to be abused or suffering from any trauma connected with their current life. Moreover, the families in these cases are faithful Christians for whom the concept of reincarnation is foreign.[121] The parents, besides being vexed in the extreme, are inevitably reluctant to have their children's cases publicized for fear of being mocked.[122]

These types of memories typically fade, by the way, around six years of age, according to Tucker. The kids involved usually express a desire as well to fully embrace the life they're in now.[123]

However, the degree to which these children show heightened emotion in recounting these apparent memories is a tip-off that something truly significant is going on. A boy like James Leininger shows all the hallmarks of PTSD at age two; why should he? We can get a sense of the answer by realizing how fear—that most elemental of feelings—puts our entire being on red alert. To begin with, the pupils dilate, muscles are tensed, and respiration is increased as the body prepares to fight, flee, or freeze. Meanwhile, the HPA axis springs into action by releasing a cascade of hormones that serve to marshal bodily energy. If we are indeed in mortal peril, our entire bodymind tenses like a spring ready to snap. Our senses are honed to a fine edge; we notice every detail that could affect our existence.

But consider what would ensue if all that energy had no outlet—if, because of a sudden accident or foul play, someone could neither fight nor flee but was trapped in freeze mode? We know that rats that are given even a mild shock somehow transfer the fear associated with the particular stimulus on to their pups, and even to their pups' pups.

Could there be a mechanism, somewhere between life and death, where memories associated with the struggling person's circumstances are preserved? It would be akin to the echoes, preserved down the eons, of the Big Bang observable through faint but distinct background radiation. Except in the cases we are considering, the intensity of the person's feelings—his or her life energy, self-awareness, and *being*—might somehow be captured in a fusion of space and time. This "imprint" might become available for another, nascent life-form—not "his" or "her" memories (as in reincarnation), but a transmutation just the same.

Tracing Back to Our Germination

As mentioned earlier, highly sensitive or gifted children were scrutinized by Dabrowski, who dubbed their personality traits as amounting to "superstimulatability" or "overexcitability." The sheer *drive* that these types of kids have in common has been remarked upon by Feldman and others who have since studied them.[124] In a similar way, savants—whether congenital or acquired—are impelled to do what they do, whether it's painting, sculpting, playing or composing music, or memorizing zip codes, historical dates, or entire phone books. And children with apparent past-life memories likewise seem transfixed by the recollections that, for a time anyway, dominate their existence.

I've noted the highly intuitive and empathetic—even empathic—nature of many of these kids. Not only are they attuned to the feelings (indeed, sufferings) of other people and animals, but they grasp the fundamental interconnectedness of life on this planet. Some of them deliver spontaneous soliloquies on the nature of truth and reality. And some of them know other things they couldn't possibly know.

Ryan Hammons was aware that his grandmother had lost a premature baby shortly after giving birth—a matter never discussed with him.[125] Little Augie Taylor remembered "himself" as his grandfather Gus (who had died before he was born), astounding his parents with the statement "I had a sister but she died. She turned into a fish . . . some bad guys." In fact, his grandfather's sister was murdered years before and her body dumped into San Francisco Bay. It was a matter never mentioned to him (understandably so); it was barely discussed in his own father's immediate family.[126] In an altogether different way, Matthew Manning didn't know Greek, Chinese, or Arabic, but nonetheless expressed these languages through his automatic writing.

It seems likely that the special people we have been considering retain some access to information independent of personhood, locale, culture, or time period. The traits that Dabrowski identified, either singly or in combination, serve as markers for those who remain "tapped in" to this reservoir in some way. An accident or act of God (e.g., car crash, stroke, lightning strike, etc.) that occurs to a normal adult can also rewire the brain so that a similar effect is achieved. All this suggests that our typical waking consciousness is highly circumscribed. Perhaps William Blake was right when he stated, "If the doors of perception were cleansed, everything would appear to man as it is—infinite."[127]

Gestation does not mean just the development of an embryo between conception and birth. It is also defined as the development of an idea or plan in the mind.[128] Suppose this idea or plan comes to fruition in the form of individual human beings and is "seeded" by a greater mind, or via the mystery and majesty of life itself? The Greeks called this seed your *daimon;* the Romans termed it your *genius;* the late Jungian psychologist James Hillman refreshed the concept as the *acorn.*[129] Through whatever forces of nature, nurture, epigenetics, and soulfulness it springs, it is invariably *you*—your form, your pattern, your blueprint. Neurons and glial cells, nerves and organs, muscles and bones, head and heart, psyche and soma—these will coalesce around the unique design. The daimon, furthermore (according to classical sources), will have its way. It will impel the person toward her or his destiny.

That there is a seed, and through it a connection with the source of life itself, is evident in the types of people we've been surveying. Often their gestation was affected by some quirk: an illness, an accident, a deprivation, or a trauma visited upon the pregnant mother. In these circumstances it's as if the curtain is peeled back to reveal the blueprint forming. The process, having been short-circuited in some way, produces a child who is more closely connected with the universe, with the web of sensation and emotion, than he or she would otherwise be. (This is even true in the apparent abyss of severe autism. Just because such people live behind what's been called an opaque "glass wall" doesn't mean they aren't highly attuned.)[130]

Most of us—the common folk—believe our consensus reality is the sole and absolute reality. But I suspect we are (in the words of Yale University physician David Katz) merely "sequestered within the limited terrain of a reality that is itself lost in a far greater reality beyond our perception."[131]

As for myself, I harbor some sensitivity, such as a habitual startle at loud noises and a preoccupation with whether I have unintentionally made others feel bad. Growing up, I recall crying as I read a copy of a newspaper from 1945, realizing how stunned and grief-stricken people were at the sudden death of Franklin Delano Roosevelt, their leader through the Great Depression and World War II. Likewise, I became immensely sad one evening as I perused a promotion from Time Life

Books detailing (in evocative pictures and prose) how the Civil War cost tens of thousands of young men their lives in fierce battles that neither side could often claim, convincingly, to have won.

But perhaps the oddest thing that I remember happening—even into adulthood—is the sense that would dawn on me every now and again that I was part of a great immensity. Not an immensity reflective of the world we know but one that seemed to reveal itself around and beyond this one. When this sense enveloped me, it was both surprising and strangely reassuring. I would also get the feeling, once in a while, that there was something that had preceded my everyday world—that a curtain obscuring a vast but perceptible "then"-ness had been parted slightly. The sensation was akin to déjà vu, but not quite. (Interestingly, the last time it happened I had just finished watching a movie about a man who regained his full memory after "scraping by" on bits and pieces of it. The effect was extraordinary.)

Perhaps I was flashing back, as it were, to a long-lost reverie of the womb. But who's to say I did not somehow manage a glimpse into the "seed ground" from which we all come? If so, it was a unique privilege that may not come to me again. But other people—synesthetes, savants, those with an autism spectrum disorder, the highly sensitive, the gifted, the prodigious, the psychic—do have a degree of access, I believe. So we should pay proper attention to what they have to tell us. What we stand to learn could go well beyond the biological and the neurological, into the metaphysical and the meaningful.

5

Living Closer to the Bone
Felt Connections, Nature, and Soul in Non-Human Animals

If you're a pet owner—especially if your companion is a dog or cat—then you know without question that these animals have feelings. They can exhibit surprise, jealousy, happiness (consider a dog who hasn't seen you for a while), affection, contentment (think of a cat purring on one's lap), fear, agitation, annoyance (cats particularly), perhaps even guilt or shame (dogs at least).

While animals don't have language akin to humans, with words and symbols infused with particular meanings, they can certainly gather what's going on at a *feeling* level. Here's an illustration, courtesy of *Washington Post* columnist Gene Weingarten, concerning his late dog Harry:

> My wife . . . acts in community theater. One day, she was in the house rehearsing a monologue for an upcoming audition. The lines were from Marsha Norman's two-person play "Night, Mother," about a housewife who is attempting to talk her adult daughter out of suicide. Thelma is a weak and bewildered woman trying to

change her daughter's mind while coming to terms with her own failings as a mother and with her paralyzing fear of being left alone. Her lines are excruciating.

My wife had to stop in mid-monologue. Harry was too distraught. He could understand not one word she was saying, but he figured out that Mom was as sad as he'd ever seen her. He was whimpering, pawing at her knee, licking her hand, trying as best he could to make things better.

"You don't need a brain to have a heart," Weingarten concludes.[1]

Neurologically speaking, Weingarten was selling Harry short. The parts of the human brain that process feeling—collectively known as the limbic system—have their counterparts in other animals' craniums and nervous systems.[2] The late and esteemed neuroscientist Jaak Panksepp, best known for his research into emotion, declared that "the evidence is now inescapable: at the basic emotional level, all mammals are remarkably similar."[3]

One might even argue that other mammals are *more* aware of feelings than are human beings, because they possess a "primary" form of consciousness. They are aware of themselves and their environment but less burdened by complexities such as reflection and rumination that typify human consciousness. They live closer to the bone, one might say, than we do.

One animal behavioralist, Jeffrey Masson, has remarked that animals possess feelings of "undiluted purity and clarity"—at least at times—compared to the "seeming opacity and inaccessibility of human feelings."[4] A former psychoanalyst, he wonders if the human ego doesn't get in the way of our experiencing feelings as directly and undistilled as other creatures do. Masson draws attention, for instance, to the capacity of some animals to express pure, unbridled joy.

Take birdsong. Anyone who has awoken to hear birds twittering on a spring day catches a sense of what feeling might be present in them beyond any fundamental communications function or territorial pronouncement.[5] Naturalist Joseph Wood Krutch conjectured that "Perhaps certain of the animals can be both more joyful and more utterly desolate than any man ever was."[6] He also opined that "Whoever listens to a bird song and says, 'I do not believe there is any joy in it,' has not proved anything about birds. But he has revealed a good deal about himself."[7]

With regard to the "desolation" to which Krutch referred, I clearly recall a lion my daughter and I once saw confined within a rather small chain-link fence: it was pacing back and forth monotonously and with an evident degree of frustration. An animal denied the use of its natural abilities—to hunt, to soar, to climb, to dash—is almost surely forced into a pathos made worse by its inability, through language, to explain its predicament to itself.

The flip side, as Masson provocatively suggests, is that "language sets [feeling] at a distance . . . the very act of saying 'I am sad' with all the connotations that the words have, pushes the feeling away a little, perhaps making it less searing and less personal."[8] For all these reasons, he concludes that animals may well feel things more intensely than we do.

The Fact of Feelings in Mammals

Panksepp's opinion was that all mammals are "brothers and sisters under the skin" since we share the same fundamental neurology and physiology.[9]

His conclusion is based on several factors. First, biochemicals such as oxytocin, epinephrine, serotonin, and dopamine—which manifestly influence human feelings—are found in other animals, too.[10] Second, the more primitive parts of the human brain, including the limbic portion that mediates feeling, have their counterparts in other animals' craniums and nervous systems.[11] Third is the existence of mirror neurons—cells in the brain that fire in response to the same actions that one has performed being performed by *someone else*. Mirror neurons play a key role in empathy, and they function not just in humans but in other species, ranging from monkeys to mice.[12] Fourth, most mammals are social creatures—and if an individual is going to live with others, it's very useful to have feelings. Getting along, after all, involves communicating key messages as well as the ability to decode the essential messages others are sending *you*.[13]

There's one additional reason to infer that animals feel. The brain, over millions of years of evolution—both in humans and in vertebrates—grew from the bottom up, with its higher, thinking centers developing out of lower, more ancient parts.[14] As Daniel Goleman, author of *Emotional Intelligence*, points out, "There was an emotional brain long before there was a rational one."[15] The parallel to non-human animals should be clear.

Incidentally, Voltaire, the eighteenth-century French writer and philosopher—who didn't have the advantage of access to modern brain science—was typically outspoken on the subject of animal feelings. He addressed himself to "you who believe that animals are only machines. Has nature arranged for [an] animal to have all the machinery of feelings only in order for it not to have any at all?"[16]

Less than one hundred years later, Charles Darwin, in his book *The Expression of the Emotions in Man and Animals,* boldly speculated on the range of feelings animals may possess. Today, evolutionary and behavioral scientists are giving credence to what he observed and intuited. Evidence has accumulated of many species (dolphins, dogs, wolves, horses, chimpanzees, sea lions, baboons, elephants) feeling sorrow, grief, or dejection; parrots being cranky;[17] rhinos and elks experiencing joy; monkeys expressing anger; falcons seeming disconsolate; chickens becoming saddened; and pigs being terrified. Elephants may even understand—and be moved by—the concept of death. Indeed, scholars consider elephants the "poster species" for animal emotions. Studies indicate with a fair degree of certainty that they have intense experiences comparable to human feelings of joy, anger, love, exuberance, delight, compassion, sorrow, and grief.[18]

Even the lowly lab rat most likely feels. Experiments have shown that rats become agitated when seeing surgery performed on other rats and that when presented with a trapped lab-mate and a piece of chocolate, they will free their caged brethren before eating.[19] Panksepp even produced evidence that when tickled rats laugh—they emit ultrasonic chirps. Many of them clearly want to be tickled more, following researchers' hands and playfully nipping as in a game. "Every possible measure of whether they like it shows yes, they love it," he observed.[20]

Compassion in Our Fellow Creatures

The subject of animal empathy is dealt with in-depth in a fine book, *The Age of Empathy*, by renowned primatologist Frans de Waal of Emory University. He highlights not just the capacity but the inclination for non-human primates to be empathetic.

A chimpanzee called Yoni, investigated by Soviet-era primatologist Nadia Kohts, for example, demonstrated extreme concern and compassion for her. Kohts relates: "If I pretend to be crying, close my eyes and weep, Yoni immediately stops his play or any other activities, quickly runs over to me . . . from the most remote places in the house . . . from where I could not drive him down despite my persistent calls and entreaties. He hastily runs around me, as if looking for the offender; looking at my face, he tenderly takes my chin in his palm, lightly touches my face with his finger, as though trying to understand what is happening."[22]

This calls to mind the example of Weingarten's dog Harry. These animals are showing more than empathy—they're demonstrating *sympathy,* which not only encompasses an awareness of what someone else is feeling but the urge to act to alleviate the other's plight.[23]

Darwin illustrated this trait when he noted how a particular dog would never walk by a basket where a sick friend (a cat) lay without giving her a few licks with his tongue.[24] Many non-human animals evidence sympathy—and it's particularly striking when a member of one species acts to help a member of another. Apes have been known to save birds[25] and, in one case, a seal rescued an old dog that could barely keep its head above water in a river. According to an eyewitness, the seal "popped out of nowhere. He came behind [the dog] and actually pushed him. This dog would not have survived if it hadn't been for that seal."[26]

Equally compelling accounts of interspecies compassion are easy to find on the Web; an exemplary survey has been compiled by animal behaviorist and activist Marc Bekoff.[27] Stories abound of human swimmers being saved by dolphins or whales, or protected by them against sharks. Many other kinds of animals have gone to extraordinary lengths to rescue people or bring their plight to other people's attention. This honor roll includes creatures as diverse as a beluga whale, a Vietnamese potbellied pig, and a South American parrot.[28]

Perhaps the best-remembered case is that of Binti Jua, a female western lowland gorilla. In 1996, at the Brookfield Zoo outside Chicago, she likely saved the life of a three-year-old boy when he fell over a railing and plummeted down twenty-four feet into the gorilla enclosure. Binti Jua cradled his unconscious body and protected him from male gorillas that tried to get close. Then, carrying him along with her own infant, she gently handed him over to zookeepers at the habitat door.[29]

I have my own experience of animal loyalty and sympathy to relate. In the spring of 2002, my wife and I were planning a party to celebrate our daughter's second birthday. While carrying supplies into the house, I lost my footing on a flight of steps and landed in a painful heap. Our little Siamese cat Persephone, all nine pounds of her, appeared immediately and whirled around me in evident alarm. Having sprained my ankle (fortunately that's all it was), I was limping for several days afterward. Persephone's touching display of concern stayed with me for much longer.

Anyone who has lived with or observed animals for any length of time knows that they have distinct personalities. As with people, some of those personalities are truly memorable. Our Persephone was one such creature. I shall explain why—sharing an incident that points, in my estimation, to the universal and binding nature of emotion.

A Kitty Cat and the Uncanny

My wife and I have owned several cats and dogs over the years. One of them was painfully shy, another exuberant and playful. One I would characterize as a combination of laconic and sly. Another was resolute and dashing—the cat equivalent of Sean Connery or George Clooney. And then there was Persephone. She was sleek, elegant, fiercely intelligent and, may I say, discerning. My wife had gotten her as a kitten and the three of us quickly bonded. Later she became attached to our young daughter, Gabrielle, and vice versa.

Persephone was a jet-black Siamese, vocal, small (she probably never got above ten pounds), and remarkably demonstrative. There was rarely a doubt as to what she was thinking or feeling. Her posture, glance, and vocalizations continuously conveyed her state of mind. We could tell when she was annoyed, anxious, determined, or blissfully restful. Most of all, though, she was *loving*. Unlike some cats, she enjoyed and sought out our company. One example: Whenever I was doing yard work or even relaxing in the hammock, Persephone would seek me out to keep me company.

She was also highly perceptive—attuned to what the people around her were doing and feeling. I've lost count of the number of times we intended to take her to the vet, for example, taking care not to "tip our hand," only to realize she'd gone into hiding. In other cases she clearly knew when some family member was in distress. In a few other memorable instances she seemed to be able to communicate exactly what she was feeling through her eyes. I vividly recall two such cases where her expression instantly conveyed what a person in the same situation would have said.

At age fourteen, Persephone suffered a stroke. She recovered to a great extent but we lost her a year and a half later. In the days following her death, something happened that even now is stunning to me. I want to relate this since it pertains to the deep and mysterious nature of feeling.

In the immediate aftermath of Persephone's passing, our family was sorrowful but the person who was the most broken up was Gabrielle. She loved Persephone as much as anyone, had grown up with her, and the two often slept together on my daughter's bed. In that bed was another constant companion, Daddy Hoo Hoo (aka DDHH), Gabrielle's stuffed gorilla. Daddy Hoo Hoo was about Persephone's size and, also like our kitty, furry and black. Gabrielle had grabbed DDHH for comfort when I'd begun to bury Persephone, and she kept hold of him as we said a prayer in loving memory of our feline friend. Later, she went to bed and took DDHH with her.

The following morning, DDHH was apparently no longer in Gabrielle's bed. We thought he might have fallen out (a common occurrence), but there was no sign of him on the floor, in the bedsheets, between the bed and the wall, or anywhere else in our daughter's room. Over the next five days, my wife made it a point to scour the house in search of the missing gorilla. Gabrielle tried to remember where else she might conceivably have left him, and we checked all those places. Not a trace.

Several nights later, my wife was consoling Gabrielle at bedtime. She remarked that perhaps DDDH had accompanied Persephone to wherever it was she was bound. Gabrielle appeared sympathetic to the story line but made it clear that "I need him here with me."

The next morning, I went into our daughter's room to wake her for camp. I sat down on her bed and, once she'd awoken, noticed a stuffed gorilla on the floor just by my foot. Thinking it must have been a "relative" gorilla (Gabrielle owned a Mommy Hoo Hoo, Grandma Hoo Hoo, etc.), I gave it to her asking which other one it was. "Daddy Hoo Hoo!" she exclaimed, and indeed it was him. This seems truly bizarre because one of us would surely have seen the gorilla in a spot as obvious as next to the bed.

After I'd related his discovery to my wife, Bonnie, I gingerly inquired whether she might have decided, for some unknown reason, to put DDHH away for a few days. This seemed entirely uncalled for, as well as completely out of character for my wife. Yet I felt I had to pose the question because otherwise we were left with no logical way for DDHH to have disappeared. *I* certainly hadn't moved the gorilla. But Bonnie replied that, of course, she hadn't—she wouldn't have played with Gabrielle's emotions like that.

In thinking about this, I'm reminded of a term from parapsychology: *apports*. These are household objects said to disappear and reappear literally out of thin air in at least some poltergeist cases. Apports have a symbolic or emotional meaning for the people involved. In our case, while no poltergeist was present, perhaps DDHH symbolized Persephone. As such, his absence might have been a synonym for *her* absence; only after Gabrielle had made it clear that she needed him back did he reappear. Or maybe the "daddy" in Daddy Hoo Hoo resonated for me, the dad of the house, whose loving responsibility it was to take care of Persephone in her dotage and who felt as sorrowful over her passing as anyone.

In any event, we all breathed easier knowing DDHH was back. It provided, on the one hand, a kind of closure and, on the other hand, a hint of an ineffable mystery. But the puzzle may not be as baffling as it seems. What our family members felt for Persephone—and what she felt for us—is at the core of what all mammals, and perhaps other sentient creatures, have in common. (Science is disclosing that at least some bird and invertebrates may have the same capacities.)[30] The feelings that flow within us, I contend, connect us to one another in ways both tangible and intangible.

The Empathosphere

One of the few people I shared my Persephone story with around the time that it happened is veterinarian Michael Fox, author of the nationally syndicated column "The Animal Doctor."[31] Dr. Fox related his concept of the *empathosphere,* which he proposes to be "a universal realm of feeling that can transcend both space and time." The seemingly miraculous accounts of pets who traverse long distances to reunite with their owners he attributes to the empathosphere, suggesting that non-human animals are more empathic than people and partake of this natural realm of feeling more readily than human beings do.[32]

Dr. Fox's belief that other mammals feel things more intensely than we do is supported by a growing number of researchers. As we've seen, other mammals likely possess a purer form of awareness given that they don't filter their experiences though language, with all the cogitation that language lends itself to. Whereas a non-human animal is likely to feel everything "closer to the bone," we humans—at least we adults—are apt to explain our feelings to ourselves, or discount them in the course of business or within polite society.

The empathosphere has a counterpart in other terms. *Telesomatic* was coined by the late psychiatrist Berthold Schwarz (and popularized by author Larry Dossey). It refers to spontaneously feeling the pain of a loved one at a distance, without the conscious knowledge that the other person is suffering.[33] *Psychesphere* is a parallel concept of Bernard Beitman, a psychiatrist at the University of Virginia. He conceives of the psychesphere as "something like our atmosphere—around us and in dynamic flux with us. We breathe in oxygen and nitrogen and water vapors, and we breathe out carbon dioxide, nitrogen, and more water vapors. . . . Our thoughts and emotions contribute to the psychesphere and our thoughts and emotions are influenced by it."[34]

What I find so arresting about situations akin to what my daughter and my family experienced is their intimate connection with *feelings.* Here I'm talking not just about surface feelings or feelings that quickly pass but more profound feelings that relate to the bonds between people or the bonds between people and their pets. As Dossey points out, telesomatic events "almost always take place between people who share empathic, loving bonds—parents and children, spouses, siblings, lovers."[35] These experiences arise wholly unexpectedly and when they do, they can shake even a die-hard skeptic to the core. Such an example was offered recently by the author Michael Shermer, whose worldview (expressed in such books as *Why People Believe Weird Things*)[36] leaves no room for the anomalous. What happened to Shermer and his bride is so bizarre that it could only be chalked up to a sheer, one in a million chance of happening were it not for its conjunction with deep emotion.

In a nutshell, this is what transpired. Shortly after saying their wedding vows, Shermer and his new wife, Jennifer, walked to the back of their house to be alone for a few minutes. They heard a love song wafting through the air but had no idea where it could be coming from. The source turned out to be a 1970s transistor radio owned by Jennifer's deceased grandfather. He had been a father figure to her when she was growing up in Germany. On this, her wedding day, "being 9,000 kilometers from family, friends and home, Jennifer was feeling amiss and lonely. She wished her grandfather were there to give her away." Unaccountably, this ancient radio that Shermer had not been able to fix sprang to life from the back of a desk drawer.

As Shermer writes, "the eerie conjunction of these deeply evocative events gave [Jennifer] the distinct feeling that her grandfather was there and that the music was his gift of approval. . . . I have to admit, it rocked me back on my heels. . . . I savored the experience more than the explanation."[37] Feeling stupefied is the most genuine reaction one can have in a situation like this. It's exactly what my wife and I felt when our daughter's stuffed animal reappeared on the floor by her bed. That both these experiences took place in the wake of profound feelings and passages I take to be more than coincidental.

Furthermore, there's good reason to suppose that non-human animals play as much a role in the empathosphere or psychesphere as human beings do. As was referenced earlier, all mammals are remarkably similar emotionally—we come equipped with the same fundamental neurology and physiology. The variations among us are, as Darwin posited, differences in degree rather than kind. It's bad biology, therefore, to assume that a capability we possess another sentient creature does not.[38]

Spirituality in Other Species

A Dutch ethologist named Adriaan Kortlandt once observed a wild chimp in the Congo "gaze at a particularly beautiful sunset for a full 15 minutes, watching the changing colors" and forsaking his customary evening meal in the process.[39] What could be going through this animal's mind at a time like this? To legendary primatologist Jane Goodall, it seems contemplative. Since the chimpanzee's brain is so much like ours, "why wouldn't they also have feelings of some kind of spirituality? Which is, really, being amazed at things outside yourself."[40]

Speaking of amazement, here's a remarkable anecdote from de Waal:

On a cold December Sunday in 2005, a female humpback whale was spotted off the California coast, entangled in the nylon ropes used by crab fishermen. She was about 50 feet long. A rescue team was dispirited by the sheer amount of ropes, about twenty of them, some around the tail, one in the whale's mouth. The ropes were digging into the blubber, leaving cuts. The only way to free the whale was to dive under the surface to cut away the ropes. Divers spent about one hour doing so. It was a herculean job, obviously not without risk given the power of a whale's tail. The most remarkable part came when the whale realized it was free. Instead of leaving the scene, she hung around. The huge animal swam in a large circle, carefully approaching every diver separately. She nuzzled one, then moved on to the next, until she had touched them all. [One of them] described the experience: "It felt to me like it was thanking us, knowing that it was free and that we had helped it. . . . It seemed kind of affectionate, like a dog that's happy to see you. I never felt threatened."[41]

On the Web is a video account of a nearly identical rescue, which occurred on Valentine's Day 2011 in the Sea of Cortez. After a young humpback whale was freed of netting that had completely tied it up, "She slowly swam away but about 500 feet from our boat, she breached high into the air. . . . For the next hour, she provided us with an incredible full-surface display. We saw at least 40 breaches as well as tail lobs, tail slaps, and pectoral fin slaps. We all believed it was at least a show of pure joy, if not thanks. . . . It was an incredible experience that none of us will ever forget."[42]

For an animal to express joy and thankfulness at being alive is the accompaniment, in my view, to contemplating nature. Both have to do with connection—with other beings and with creation.

This sense of connectedness, though it may exist among all mammals, is evidenced plainly and poignantly by elephants. Consider the way African elephants that belong to the same family or group greet one another after a separation. They rush together, flapping their ears and spinning in circles, emitting a loud chorus of rumbles and roars. Researcher Joyce Poole, who's observed and written extensively about them, is convinced that "greeting elephants feel a deep sense of joy at being reunited with friends, and that their [vocalizations] express something like: 'Wow! It's simply fantastic to be with you again.'"[43]

Conversely, elephants seem to react sorrowfully to death. Poole, Andrea Turkalo, and other field researchers have recorded instances of the animals standing beside the body of a dead relative, touching it with their trunks, apparently trying to coax it back to life. Elephants will carry the tusks and bones of their departed kin great distances and may even try to cover them with dirt or leaves. They are also known to form funeral processions. According to Turkalo, "They seem to recognize death and it upsets them. It [brings] home how emotional these animals are."[44] (Apropos of a complex emotional life, elephants are known to suffer from the harrowing condition of PTSD.)[45] The title of a groundbreaking 1995 book on animal emotions—*When Elephants Weep*—captures our dawning realization of the feeling life of these magnificent creatures.[46]

Animals that express gratitude, that play (a joyful expression of aliveness), that contemplate nature, that react mournfully to the loss of family members or other close companions, or that save a fellow creature are all, in my view, demonstrating aspects of connectedness. In all cases, the capacity to feel and to express feeling (i.e., emote) are central. This connectedness—underpinned by emotion—is the core of spirituality. At its root, spirituality really is a matter of "fellow feeling."

What all creatures have in common, of course, is that none of them willed themselves into existence. Those animals that are sentient and have the capacities noted above are able to literally feel a part of something greater. It is as if each of us—dog, cat, whale, seal, mouse, pig, elephant, monkey, human—is ensouled in nature. Each of us, to varying degrees, knows we have an existence and can feel pleasure and pain, wonder and threat, happiness and dejection. We can and do show compassion for other living beings. In sum, it's the embodiment, in nature, of the call enunciated by one of the characters in E. M. Forster's novel *Howard's End*—"Only connect!" It is also the basis of the empathosphere or psychesphere, that source of mysterious coincidences that occasionally—at conjunctures of deep, if unacknowledged emotion—have us scratching our heads in bewilderment.

Feeling and Soufulness in Nature

The profound connection that sentient creatures share—with one another and with nature—is felt and expressed in different ways.

One example, an especially exuberant and heartfelt one, is depicted by primatologist Sue Savage-Rumbaugh. Her subject of study, a male bonobo named Kanzi, was reunited with his adoptive mother, Matata, after several months apart. In the author's words:

I . . . told [Kanzi] there was a *surprise* in the colony room. He began to vocalize in the way he does when expecting a favored food—"eeeh . . . eeeh . . . eeeh." I said, 'No food surprise. Matata surprise; Matata in colony room.' He looked stunned, stared at me intently, and then ran to the colony room door, gesturing urgently for me to open it. When mother and son saw each other, they emitted earsplitting shrieks of excitement and joy and rushed to the wire that separated them. They both pushed their hands through the wire, to touch the other as best they could. Witnessing this display of emotion, I hadn't the heart to keep them apart any longer, and opened the connecting door. Kanzi leapt into Matata's arms, and they screamed and hugged for fully five minutes, and then stepped back to gaze at each other in happiness. They then played like children, laughing all the time as only bonobos can.[47]

Then there's the sort of striking, all-encompassing unity with nature that people sometimes feel (a variety of which at least some non-human animals presumably feel themselves). Goodall related one such experience when she was observing chimpanzees in the Gombe forest:

Lost in the awe at the beauty around me, I must have slipped into a state of heightened awareness. It is hard—impossible, really—to put into words the moment of truth that suddenly came upon me then. . . . It seemed to me, as I struggled afterward to recall the experience, that self was utterly absent: I and the chimpanzees, the earth and trees and air, seemed to merge, to become one with the spirit power of life itself. The air was filled with a feathered symphony, the evensong of birds. I heard new frequencies in their music and also in the singing insects' voices—notes so high and sweet I was amazed. Never had I been so intensely aware of the shape, the color of the individual leaves, the varied patterns of the veins that made each one unique. Scents were clear as well, easily identifiable . . . the aromatic scent of young, crushed leaves was almost overpowering.[48]

Such experiences are likely to be experienced by children, by the way. The foremost collection of such experiences that I can recommend is a 1992 book by Edward Hoffman, *Visions of Innocence*.[49] It's entirely possible that children, whose apprehensions of nature are unclouded by preconceptions and whose language skill has not matured to the point where they immediately leap to "explain" something to themselves, have a propensity to become immersed in the wholeness of life more so than adults.[50]

These mystical or overpowering spiritual experiences have several things in common: they arise spontaneously, they confer a heightened form of sensation in which the experiencer perceives everything with an incredible vividness, they endow the person with an all-encompassing (if fleeting) sense of oneness with the natural world, and they can't be easily described in words.

Goodall has come to consider the concept of *soul* in context of this spiritual connection with creation. Perhaps, she suggests, if individual people have souls capable of experiencing such a connection, then non-human animals—specifically the chimps she's most familiar with—do as well.[51] But consider a slightly different view, voiced by the psychologist and theologian Malcolm Jeeves: one doesn't *have* a soul, one *is* a living soul.[52] In this scheme of things, as long as one is alive—as long as one is sensing and feeling—then one is ensouled in nature. One is part, in other words, of the empathosphere or psychesphere that fixes our affinity with one another.

Think for a moment of how we use the word *soul* in common parlance. We may speak of a "soulless" corporation. Or confide to a lover that we want them "body and soul." Or we describe a certain ballplayer as the "soul" of his team. Or listen to "soul music" that conveys an unmistakable mood and rhythm. In each case, we are associating soul with feeling. And not just any feeling, but deep feeling, core values, that which is vitally important or just plain *moves* us.

These are not mere figures of speech, but reflections of true meaning: what our soul (if we *are* one) identifies with. Neuroscientist

Antonio Damasio, whose books explore the foundations of consciousness, has commented that "feelings form the basis for what humans have described for millennia as the . . . soul or spirit."[53] Ultimately, we know ourselves—and others—through feeling. This is what Panksepp may have meant when he stated his belief that, in coming to understand the nature of other animals' feelings, "we will finally understand ourselves."[54]

With all of life's ups and downs and frequently scary unpredictability, we understandably wonder "What's it all about?" and "Why am I here?" While answers to such questions can never be certain, one thing is clear: We're all in this together. We may compete, we may exploit, we may threaten, intimidate, and even kill, but none of these elements of our animal nature trumps the fact that we share this planet and all its beauty and resources with myriad other species that *feel*. Our nature, then, also allows for compassion, gratitude, courage, wonder, awe, and the exultation of fellow feeling.

6

Unimagined Sensitivities
How Trauma and Death Trigger Extraordinary Perceptions

Thus far in this volume, we've explored the way that individual differences in emotional biology play out in conditions ranging from PTSD and alexithymia to synesthesia, autism, and savantism. We've examined how mirror senses and other manifestations of extreme empathy illuminate nonordinary ways of perceiving while drawing attention to the fundamental question of how one's self is constituted. We have considered that a kind of preconscious emotional resonance may be the wellspring from which genuinely anomalous perception can result. We've explored the salience of emotion to the development of child prodigies, to children who seem to remember past lives and, even more esoteric, to individuals who seem to possess psychic sensitivity. We have recognized the parallels in emotional biology between human beings and other animals. We have considered how emotional bonds between individuals—even across species—shed light on uncanny occurrences, and how the ability to feel and express feeling may undergird spirituality in general.

Now we shall take up a truly touchy subject: death. While it would seem to represent the end of sensitivity (since a dead animal is manifestly nonsensate), the phenomenon actually conjures up a fascinating range of accounts and experiences that are highly relevant to sensitivity, not just in humans but in many other animals. Death seems to be something of a trigger mechanism for emotion-laden sensitivity. In order to shed light on the many curious anecdotes attending death in human beings, it will be useful to explore what death seems to mean for certain other species—how they react to it and what forms of sensitivity are evidently prompted. We shall see that emotion is paramount but does not always require preexisting bonds between individuals. Often enough, sensitivity can seemingly be aroused by the undercurrents of feeling itself.

Let's start by looking at a few intriguing examples involving two highly perceptive and social species: elephants and dolphins.

Elephants' Recognition of Death

As documented by researchers Cynthia Moss, Joyce Poole, and Iain Douglas-Hamilton, African elephants appear to recognize death, most plainly among their own kind. Often, just after an individual has died, other elephants will touch it gently with their hind feet, then cover the body with dirt and sticks, and stand guard.[1] Elephants show a consistent interest in the carcasses and bones of their fellows, even if the bones have been long bleached by the sun. When elephants encounter their dead, Moss says, they "stop and become quiet and tense in a different way from anything I have seen in other situations. First they reach their trunks toward the body to smell it, and then they . . . begin to touch the bones, sometimes lifting them and turning them with their feet and trunks. They seem particularly interested in the head and tusks. They run their trunk tips along the tusks and lower jaw and feel in all the crevices and hollows in the skull. I would guess they are trying to recognize the individual."[2] Sometimes elephants will pick up the bones, carrying them for a distance before dropping them. "It is a haunting and touching sight," Moss says, "and I have no idea why they do it."[3]

One case in point is that of a young elephant's reaction to the jawbone of an adult female that Moss had collected in order to determine its age. A few weeks after this individual's death, her family came through the camp. Each member stopped to examine the jawbone and teeth but, after the others had moved on, the elephant's seven-year-old son stayed behind, stroking the jaw, turning it over and smelling it repeatedly. "I felt sure that he recognized it as his mother's," Moss writes.[4] Might he have been remembering her face, her voice, her scent, her touch? Might he have been feeling something akin to what a human child would feel upon remembering his or her recently deceased parent? Was it a feeling of melancholy, nostalgia, sorrow, or perhaps a different shade of feeling than what we humans can identify?[5]

Intriguingly, elephants sometimes act similarly around the bodies of people they either find dead or have killed. In these cases, the elephants have no family connection or emotional tie to the deceased. In at least one instance, though, an elephant is known to have mourned the death of an individual of an entirely different species—yet one it had a close bond with. This young orphaned elephant, who lived in a sanctuary in South Africa, shrieked and moaned when it discovered the buried remains of its companion, a rhinoceros, that poachers had killed for its horn.[6]

Elephants can appear similarly agitated at the imminent death of one of their own, and behave in a way that indicates grief. One well-documented case is that of a matriarch named Eleanor. Weakened by age, Eleanor kept collapsing. A fellow matriarch, Grace, repeatedly attempted to lift Eleanor onto her feet. Grace appeared distraught, her facial glands streaming with emotion. Grace stayed with Eleanor as night fell—and overnight, Eleanor died. Over the next several days, Eleanor's family members and others—including her closest friend, Maya—spent time with her body, nudging it and feeling and smelling it with their trunks.[7]

Even more remarkable stories crop up concerning these creatures' apparent awareness of trauma and death. In Zimbabwe, officials decided to reduce the elephant population by culling hundreds of them.

They used helicopters to herd them together and had marksmen on the ground shoot entire families. On the day the cull started, some eighty elephants living in a sanctuary ninety miles away disappeared—to be found days later, bunched together in the corner of the sanctuary farthest from the carnage.[8]

Another arresting tale is the following. It concerns the late Lawrence Anthony, a South African wildlife conservationist (and author of *The Elephant Whisperer*) who owned the Thula Thula reserve, a large animal sanctuary. He began taking in endangered elephants from all over the globe, and he gradually developed a friendship and a trust with these creatures. When Anthony passed away unexpectedly in 2012, twenty elephants that he had rescued and given asylum to—from separate herds—converged on his home, lingering there for two days. These elephants had suddenly decided to travel there after not having visited their benefactor's house for a year and a half. In the words of Anthony's brother-in-law, "The fact they all trooped up to his house the night he died could in some unfathomable way indicate they know he has gone, and accept it as all things that come to pass."[9]

How that might be begs explanation. The word *telepathy* was used by another renowned wildlife conservator, the late Dame Daphne Sheldrick, who led the Wildlife Trust over decades. Sheldrick said that the adult elephants her organization had rescued seemed to know when a new group of orphans was headed there by the way they would spontaneously come up from the bush, apparently ready to greet the arrivals.[10] While the elephants could, of course, be responding to unconsciously displayed human cues, the anecdotes we have been examining suggest the value of maintaining an open mind—recognizing that we don't know what we don't know.

Dolphins' Extraordinary Awareness

In another highly social and perceptive species—dolphins—the recognition of death takes a bizarre turn, as recounted by marine biologist

Denise Herzing. In this instance, Herzing's vessel approached a familiar group of dolphins that her team had been studying. "They greeted us but they acted very unusual," not coming within fifty feet of the boat. They refused invitations to bow-ride, also at odds with their typical behavior. Soon, someone discovered that one of the people aboard had died during a nap in his bunk. As the vessel headed back to port, "the dolphins came to the side of our boat, not riding the bow as usual but instead flanking us . . . in an aquatic escort." After the crew had attended to the sad business at hand and the boat returned to the area, "the dolphins greeted us normally, rode the bow, and frolicked like they normally did."[11]

Apart from this incident, Herzing has never noticed such peculiar behavior in her twenty-five years of studying dolphins. "Perhaps," speculates naturalist Carl Safina, "in a way we don't understand, dolphin sonar lets them scan inside a boat and somehow realize and communicate among one another that a man in a bunk has a heart that is still. Perhaps they detected that a human had died using another sensory system, one that we humans neither possess nor suspect."[12]

Whatever sensory apparatus may be involved, there is ample evidence that dolphins and killer whales possess a capacity impelling them to care for humans and, occasionally, other animals. Stories of these marine mammals guiding people to safety are legion. Several are presented in Safina's popular book *Beyond Words: What Animals Think and Feel*.[13] Killer whales are even known to have saved dogs that have errantly swum out to sea.[14] Orca researchers link such behavior to these creatures' penchant for learning quickly and, some say, telepathically. Researcher Alexandra Morton, for example, once asked a trainer to show her how one teaches a new behavior to a whale. They decided to teach a pair of captive killer whales, Orky and Corky, how to slap their dorsal fins on the water—a trick neither whale had ever demonstrated. They agreed to work on the trick with the whales the following week.

"Then something happened," Morton wrote, "that has made me

careful of my thoughts around whales ever since." Corky slapped her dorsal fin on the water's surface. She actually did it several times, then charged around the tank, exuberantly smacking the water with her dorsal fin. "That's whales for you," said the trainer, smiling. "They can read your mind. We trainers see this kind of stuff all the time."[15]

The same is often true of dolphins. Trainer Karen Pryor discovered that once she rewarded her charges specifically for doing something new, they would "think of things to do spontaneously that we could never have imagined." When two Hawaiian bottlenose dolphins got the signal to do something new, for example, they would swim to the center of the pool, circle underwater for a few seconds, then put on an acrobatic performance in perfect unison that was entirely unrehearsed. No one knows how they do it.[16]

Being Minded by a Whale

An orphaned orca, named Luna by the people he befriended, showed up in British Columbia's Nootka Sound in 2001, miles from where he'd been born. He immediately began interacting with the local boaters and fishermen, demonstrating that he was a social being who desired company first and foremost and a killer whale second. An example: Luna would stay alongside a docked boat for hours as the people on it were busy delivering supplies and equipment. When the people left, he would leave, too. Yet if one person remained aboard sleeping, Luna would often stay with the boat all night.[17]

Once Luna came alongside a different boat and played "a bit too energetically" with the emergency outboard engine. The skipper said, "Hey, Luna, could you leave that alone for a while?" Luna immediately backed away. "A sense washed over me," said the skipper, "that this orca was just as aware of living as I was: that he could perceive all the details that I could perceive, the feeling of atmosphere and sea, the texture of emotions. . . . This was overwhelming."[18]

People who have interacted with killer whales remark often upon their intelligence, awareness, and sense of presence. Of Luna, one person said, "he could look through his otherness at you." Another related that she saw something so astonishing and deep in them that it took her breath away.[19] That sense of communion is attested by researcher Howard Garrett, who states that he and his colleagues "felt tested and our intentions probed by the orcas, and that the orcas not only learned our limits and abilities but seemed to have shared their knowledge of us with their tank mates. . . . Each of us was deeply moved."[20]

Whale researcher Ken Balcombe relates that "When you lock eyes with them, you get the sense that they're looking at *you*. It's a steady gaze. And you feel it. Much more powerful than a dog looking at you. A dog might want your attention. The whales, it's a different feeling. It's more like they're searching inside you. . . . A lot transmits in a very brief time about the intent of both sides."[21]

This "search" function is perhaps illuminated by an experience told to Safina by a friend. She was snorkeling in Hawaii when several killer whales showed up. "I heard a very strong clinking sound, like metal on metal. . . . It was a very high vibrating sound that did not feel uncomfortable but it did feel incredibly strong! It went right through me. It was the strongest energy that I have ever felt. A wave of energy, like transmitting. It was like a portal opened."[22]

Safina suggests that the minds of whales and dolphins may have evolved to allow for the sharing of thoughts, intentions, and feelings—not just between them but between them and human beings, who possess a brain large enough to appreciate it. The capacity would be roughly akin to the way our language—our art and music and drama and dance—all serve to convey the feelings and intentions of human beings.[23] But with these marine mammals, the function would be innate—an immediate part of their bodies and minds—rather than being mediated through paper, the internet, sound systems, canvas or clay, stage or screen.

Low Wavelength Communication:
Infrasound

Elephants are land mammals and their means of communication and empathy are easier to identify than those of dolphins and whales. By virtue of their magnificent trunks, elephants simultaneously feel and smell. They also listen to their fellows' rumbles by feeling the vibrations created in the ground. Special receptors in their feet, called Pacinian corpuscles, allow them to do this. Biologist Caitlin O'Connell-Rodwell calls the elephant an "amazing infrasound detection machine."[24]

The ability is known to extend up to twenty-five miles.[25] It (or something like it) might extend considerably farther given the instance noted earlier of a group of elephants in Zimbabwe that retreated to a corner of their preserve that was farthest from a murderous "culling" of elephants taking place ninety miles away. "Elephants are able to detect distress calls over large distances and are fully aware when their fellows are being killed," asserts Moss.[26]

Such long-distance communication could be accomplished through infrasound, which has a wavelength less than the 20 Hz threshold that distinguishes human hearing. Infrasound can travel vast distances unimpeded by land, air, or water. Many animal species are capable of registering infrasound, among them elephants, hippos, giraffes, rhinos, alligators, and whales. It was naturalist Katy Payne of Cornell University who first intuited what might be happening based on her standing near an elephant cage at the zoo one day and feeling a peculiar "throb and flutter" in the air. It reminded her, she said, of the deep bass notes she experienced as a girl in church.[27]

Here is a moving account of infrasonic communication as noted by the late naturalist Lyall Watson. He was whale watching from the cliffs of the South African coast and wrote:

The sensation I was feeling on the clifftop was some sort of reverberation in the air itself. . . . The whale had submerged and I was still feeling something. The strange rhythm seemed now to be coming from behind me, from the land, so I turned to look across the gorge . . . where my heart stopped.

. . . Standing there in the shade of the tree was an elephant . . . staring out to sea! . . . A female with a left tusk broken off near the base. . . . I knew who she was, who she had to be. I recognized her from a color photograph put out by the Department of Water Affairs and Forestry under the title "The Last Remaining Knysna Elephant." This was the Matriarch herself.

. . . She was here because she no longer had anyone to talk to in the forest. She was standing here on the edge of the ocean because it was the next, nearest, and most powerful source of infrasound. The under-rumble of the surf would have been well within her range, a soothing balm for an animal used to being surrounded by low and comforting frequencies, by the lifesounds of a herd, and now this was the next-best thing.

. . . The throbbing was back in the air. I could feel it, and I began to understand why. The blue whale was on the surface again, pointed inshore, resting, her blowhole clearly visible. The Matriarch was here for the whale! The largest animal in the ocean and the largest living land animal were not more than a hundred yards apart, and I was convinced that they were communicating! In infrasound, in concert, sharing big brains and long lives, understanding the pain of high investment in a few precious offspring, aware of the importance and the pleasure of complex sociality, these rare and lovely great ladies were commiserating over the back fence of this rocky Cape shore, woman to woman, matriarch to matriarch, almost the last of their kind.[28]

Infrasound as Early Warning System

One might think that the penchant Payne and Watson have—to physically witness infrasound—is uncommon. Yet an experiment conducted in a concert hall in London in 2003 found that 62 percent of an audience of 750 people reported a variety of reactions to infrasound themselves. Many were physiological: shivers down the spine, a sense of going hot and cold, increased heart rate, headache, an "odd feeling in [the] stomach," and so on. Intriguingly, many of the reports conjured up emotion: feelings of anxiety, panic, excitement, or sorrow. One person volunteered "a sudden memory of emotional loss."[29]

It's conceivable that these physical and emotional messages are within the spectrum of what whales and elephants are conveying through infrasound. Indeed, many species seem to rely on such avenues for crisis communications. Consider that over the centuries a range of creatures—including insects, birds, and fish, as well as mammals—have been observed to become agitated before natural disasters.[30] A fairly recent example is that of the tsunami that devastated East Asia in 2004. Numerous survivors observed birds suddenly taking flight, elephants trumpeting and fleeing to higher ground, and dolphins moving out to sea. Furthermore, virtually no animal remains were found in the aftermath of the tsunami—in contrast to the roughly two hundred thousand human bodies.[31]

This evidence suggests that various species benefit from an infrasonic or similar early-warning capacity. Infrasonic waves are produced by many kinds of natural disturbances—volcanoes, earthquakes, tornadoes, avalanches, and hurricanes. The waves' arrival would precede the disturbance itself and give precious hours or minutes of notice. It's also possible that animals sense changes in air and water pressure or that they simply *hear* the warning signals (a voluminous wave, in the case of a tsunami) far more acutely than humans do. Interestingly, while human beings' ability to detect such cues is relatively paltry, the instruments we deploy may have the necessary sensitivity themselves. Infrasonic waves generated by the 2011 Tohoku earthquake in Japan were picked up by a satellite orbiting 255 km above the Earth—high but still at the edge of Earth's atmosphere.[32]

Another explanation may lie in animals' sensitivity to electromagnetic field variations. Motoji Ikeya, a geophysicist, found that certain animals—especially catfish—react to even minor changes in electromagnetic current. Ikeya developed his theory after noticing, immediately before the earthquake that devastated Kobe, Japan, in 1995, that "so many earthworms dug themselves up in my small garden."[33]

Electromagnetic Sensitivity

As I have elaborated upon in my book *The Spiritual Anatomy of Emotion*,[34] sensitivity has a biological and physiological aspect but also an emotional and energetic one. In human beings, all these aspects are intertwined. A person who is highly sensitive to her or his feelings—and to the feelings of others—is likely to be extra sensitive to her or his environment. This can include changes in the weather, changes in the emotional atmosphere of a place, and changes in the ambient electromagnetics. A similar encompassing sensitivity is likely to occur in at least some non-human animals—beginning with other mammals, whose bodies and brains are constituted quite similarly to those of human beings.

Consider the "strong feeling of energy" felt by Safina's friend when she went snorkeling in Hawaii and met up with several orcas. This is but one of numerous accounts that certain people—particularly women—are apt to present. Sometimes the occasion comes out of the blue; other times the person views it as characteristic of who she is. Below is a case in point. The woman who provided me with this account recognizes her sensitivity very well:

> I've been overly sensitive for as long as I can remember. . . . If someone walked into the room with a headache, I would get a headache. If they pulled their back, mine would begin aching the minute I made eye contact. . . . I was definitely more in tune with my environment and the feelings of others than almost everyone else I knew.

. . . I continue to be sensitive to the pain levels of others, including pets. I give all new meaning to the term "I feel your pain." I am also able to pick up the energies of my surroundings. For example, when we were looking for a new home, we found a great fixer upper that we really liked, but the moment I set foot inside, I could sense a heavy/angry atmosphere that practically took my breath away. . . . Sure enough, when we went down to the basement, the walls were peppered with fist-holes. I can also pick up on the vibes of places that have very happy or particularly peaceful atmospheres.

This person also suspected that she was sensitive to electricity. During a period when her symptoms flared up, she told me, "I was unable to touch a lamp without bursting the bulb and had been in three different buildings where the generators blew up in my presence within a two-week period."[35]

Connections between purported sensitivity to electricity and sensitivity to emotions were explored in a fascinating book by Michael Shallis, then a professor at Oxford University, in the 1980s.[36] Shallis invited the readers of two dozen different magazines to share any accounts of electrical sensitivity. He received hundreds of replies—80 percent of them from women. He subsequently interviewed many of the respondents, gathering much evidence linking electrical anomalies to strong and distressing feelings. One woman said that her problems with electricity began after her father died. Another stated that her bedroom light glowed, even when it was not turned on, during a time of great emotional upheaval. An especially striking anecdote (literally) involved a woman who said she'd walked out of her front door after an intense emotional experience, at which point a lightning bolt struck the pathway at her feet. Remarkably, 23 percent of Shallis's respondents claimed to have been struck by lightning.[37]

Electrical sensitivity among human beings is a highly controversial topic. Shallis himself concluded that electromagnetism—"the physical force most apparent to us at the level at which we perceive the material world"—may be the vehicle for life forces that, at present, we simply do not comprehend.[38]

Sensory Anticipation of Death?

Recall marine biologist Denise Herzing's account of a pod her team was familiar with acting strangely at the same time that a dead body was found on her boat—something neither she nor her crew knew at the time but perhaps the cetaceans, in some way, did. It's not too far-fetched to consider this report in the same way that we consider the extraordinary information-processing abilities of other animals. This includes bats that home in on objects far away in complete darkness, elephants that communicate with each other through low-frequency underground vibrations, and birds that seasonally migrate vast distances to precise locations.

Author Guy Murchie devoted some thought to this subject, identifying thirty-two discrete senses possessed by living creatures, which he divided into five major categories.[39] One of these he termed the *radiation senses,* which include sight (i.e., the eyes' sensitivity to visible light) but also a sensitivity to radiation other than visible light, a temperature sense, and a sensitivity to electric current as well as magnetism. Regarding the latter, so many different species have been found to possess an electromagnetic sense that, as one observer remarks, it would be more surprising to discover that human beings don't have a shred of this sensitivity than to discover that we do.[40] Clearly, though, other animals have it in spades. My suggestion is that beyond the five tried-and-true senses that we humans take for granted, some of the sensory capacities that are more highly developed in other creatures may be intimately connected with health, danger, and emotion generally.

We've already seen how elephants react to the death of their fellows—even ninety miles away. Closer to home, some dogs are able to anticipate when a person is about to suffer a seizure. Whether they do this through their remarkably keen smell, their attentiveness to the individual's body signals, or a combination of these or some other way isn't yet known.[41] Other dogs have been able to "smell" cancer in a patient before the medical diagnosis was made.[42] And in one of the most remarkable cases on record, a cat named Oscar who lives in the advanced dementia unit of a nursing home in Providence, Rhode Island, accurately anticipated the passing of about fifty patients over five years by choosing to curl up with them in their final hours. Oscar's track record is better than that of the trained professionals who work there. Oscar is not an especially friendly cat, so his lying next to a patient for hours at a time is out of character. But "he doesn't make too many mistakes," and his case was published in the prestigious *New England Journal of Medicine*.[43]

No one knows how Oscar selects the patients to keep company with. It's possible he picks up on telltale scents (a chemical released just before death, for example), notices how still certain patients are becoming, reads something into the behavior of the medical staff, or all of the above.[44]

What might be highly relevant here is the close connection between smell and emotion in the mammalian brain. Only two synapses separate the olfactory lobe from the amygdala, a part of the brain critical to the perception of feeling. This is why, in us humans, memories that are tinged with smell carry a greater wallop than memories triggered by our other senses.[45] Marcel Proust provided a lasting illustration of the relationship between smell, memory, and feeling when he made an aroma central to the childhood recollections of his narrator in the novel *Au Recherche du Temps Perdu (Reflecting on Times Past)*. This connection between feelings and smell plays out most poignantly in the experience some people (particularly women) have when they seem to smell the cologne, hair tonic, or aftershave of a departed husband or father.[46]

Anomalous Accounts Involving Dogs and Cats

Both cats and dogs are known to have strange reactions around death. Folklore is replete with examples of these pets refusing to stay in certain rooms where someone has died or where a deceased person used to live.[47] Pet owners sometimes relate that their cat or dog seems to know when a family member has died off the premises. A poodle, for instance, was said to have become frantic around the time its family's eldest son was seriously injured in a car accident. Another report suggested that a Siamese cat began to cry in distress at exactly the time that his German shepherd companion died on the operating table at a veterinary hospital.[48] Of course, we've all heard accounts of family pets that traversed long distances to faithfully return to owners from whom they had become separated. Painstakingly (and controversially), biologist Rupert Sheldrake compiled reports of dogs whose behavior suggested that they knew when their owners had decided to come home.[49]

If true, then it's possible that such abilities stem from these animals' living "closer to the bone." In other words, they apprehend feelings more directly and feel them more intensely than human beings do because, unlike us, they don't traffic in rumination and analysis. A critical factor may also be that our pets are essentially family members. We love and provide for them, they love and rely upon us, and emotional bonds form as the result.

The deeply felt nature of people-pet relations manifests in numerous anomalous reports. Many of the following were collected by author Raymond Bayless in a 1970 book, *Animal Ghosts*,[50] though several— including my own—are of more recent vintage:

- A couple had owned an Irish setter for nearly fifteen years when he died. Three days after they buried Red, the woman awoke from "a realistic dream of seeing Red running across hills" to hear a characteristic barking. Her husband, who had also awoken, heard the same; it sounded exactly like Red. On three more occasions the wife would awaken from dreams of Red to hear the barking, and her husband would also hear the sounds (though he had not been dreaming of Red). A short time later, they brought a German shepherd puppy into their home and from that day forward the mysterious barking ceased.[51]

- A husband and wife each "saw" a medium-sized house cat in their new home. In one case, it raced by the wife and darted into an adjacent room; in another, it sat by the refrigerator as if anticipating a noonday feeding. In both instances, the cat vanished after a few moments. At the time, neither spouse had spoken to the other about their sighting.[52]

- A woman whose dog had died "heard" him whining and crying all night long. This continued periodically over the next two months; her husband said that he, too, heard Butch barking loudly at the back door. A neighbor (who knew Butch was deceased but not about the alleged sounds) told the couple about a dream he'd had where the dog was crying at the door wanting to be let in. The owner further related that she would hear a floorboard outside the bedroom squeak in the same way, and at roughly the same time, as it had when Butch was alive and wanting to be let out in the morning.[53]

- A man woke from a nightmare involving a desperate struggle as if he were drowning, and felt an apprehensive sense of terror and despair. He then had a second dream involving his dog Bob, who seemed to be lying in water. The dog's body was subsequently found—he had been hit by a passing train while on a bridge that crossed over a body of water.[54]

- After Nellie, a miniature dachshund, died, her owner started hearing whimpers that sounded like those the dog used to make. Initially, the man brushed off the sounds but then his fiancée heard them, too.[55]

- A couple who had recently bought a house reported seeing a cat—with the wife attesting that she felt it jump on the bed. A neighbor told them about the previous owner's cat, which had been run over by a car shortly before they bought the house and apparently matched the description of their apparition.[56]

- A husband and wife started to "hear" their sixteen-year-old dog's squeaky toys shortly after he was euthanized. Then they found that the toys had somehow moved from a box near the back door and to a spot near the couch, which had been the dog's favorite spot.[57]
- A family's dog, Bandit, had to be put down. Soon afterward, the owner and her youngest child were startled to "see" their beloved pet bounding toward their backdoor. So real did it seem that the woman opened the door before remembering that Bandit was no longer with them.[58]
- This last is a personal anecdote. Many years ago, I was reading in bed late one night. At some point I got the feeling of a presence in the room, which seemed to be several feet in front of me. About this same time, my cat Dalton, who had been lying on the bed, looked in the same direction, jumped off and scooted underneath the bed. (He had never acted that way before—nor did he after.) After nearly a half hour the uncomfortable and oppressive feeling passed. As if on cue, Dalton reappeared from under the bed.[59]

Trauma:
The Seedbed of the Anomalous

Accounts of animal apparitions have a collective power, even if one is inclined to dismiss them as coming from questionable sources. What may be more compelling is an account found in a source completely unrelated to anything anomalous. Consider the following, which is drawn from a book by Alaska author and nature photographer Nick Jans. *A Wolf Called Romeo* is the story of a wolf that, for reasons that can only be guessed at—curiosity, perhaps, or loneliness—established a friendly relationship with the residents of Juneau, Alaska (and their numerous dogs). This relationship lasted from 2003 to 2009, when the wolf was shot by a pair of out-of-state hunters. One of the city's residents, Harry Robinson, and his black Lab mix, Brittain, had become very close with this wolf (nicknamed Romeo because of his evident search for either love or companionship). The three would often meet daily, walking, playing, and resting together in the wilderness off one of the well-known glacier trails. By 2009, they had spent hundreds of hours in each other's company. Brittain was Romeo's pseudo-mate/love interest, and Robinson his trusted friend/alpha male role model.[60]

In September 2009, however, Robinson had a nightmare. "I felt Romeo scream," he said. "I could hear it inside my head. He was in agony. I saw him turn to bite at his side, and at that moment, I know he'd been shot." The next day, Romeo did not appear as usual to greet him and Brittain. Although there had been times when the wolf went missing for days or even weeks, Robinson, mindful of his dream, suspected something wasn't right.[61]

Over the next few days, a similar dream came to Vic Walker, a local veterinarian who had developed his own connection with the wolf. Walker recounts: "Romeo was wounded. . . . He'd been shot in the jaw. The bone was totally shattered. Harry was there. He said, 'He's done'; I told him, 'No, no. I can fix this.'"[62] Neither man knew of the other man's dream until years later.

These dreams remind me of a quite different account I once came across, not involving animals but likewise involving a mournful death. This story is also a well-documented one. On the bitter cold morning of January 13, 1964, a B-52 bomber flying over western Maryland was buffeted by a tremendous storm and crashed. Four of the crew managed to eject. They endured freezing cold conditions and deep snow on the ground; two of the men managed to survive. Two, however did not. One of them, Tech. Sgt. Mel Wooten, twenty-seven, was severely wounded because, on ejecting, a piece of the broken tail of the plane blew into him. Writer David Wood recounts:

> The impact shattered his left thigh and gashed his head, chest and hands, but he came down alive in a flat meadow known around Salisbury, Pa., as the Dye Factory field. There, he collapsed in the

snow. Behind him, warmth and salvation lay 200 yards away, in a line of houses just beyond some railroad tracks. In front of Wooten, half a mile away, were the twinkling lights of town. He cut himself loose from his blood-stained orange chute and survival kit and began crawling toward the lights, not knowing that between him and town lay the ice-choked Casselman River.[63]

That same night, the wife of one of the Maryland men who would embark on a search for the crew members had a startling dream. The woman "jerked awake . . . breathing hard: In a nightmare, she had seen a young man wearing an orange jacket, lying in the Dye Factory field at the edge of the Casselman River. The man was injured, bleeding and holding out his arms."

I see no overt reason that people should make up such accounts. If it's notoriety they seek, they must know that any attention that comes their way for the suggestion of an ESP-like ability is bound to be offset by skepticism and ridicule. Instead I suggest that what we have here is an illustration of how searing trauma—experienced by a human being *or* another mammal possessing a similar neurobiology, similar capacity for emotion, and similar social nature—produces effects that are simultaneously physical, emotional, and spiritual.

Prodromal Dreaming

In the first of two books that I coauthored with Dr. Marc Micozzi, *The Spiritual Anatomy of Emotion*,[64] I discuss how a life-threatening emergency marshals the complete attention of body and mind—and propose that the energy involved may, in some cases, upend the normal convergence of space/time so that anomalous perceptions result. The dynamics frequently though not inevitably involve people or animals that have emotional ties to one another. When such bonds do not exist, the person or animal involved is likely to be highly sensitive, physically and/or emotionally.

This theory is elaborated upon in an intriguing book by Brandon Massullo, a therapist interested in abnormal experiences of emotion. He considers the possibility that "traumatic events trigger conscious and unconscious processes [that] seek to alleviate our distress or communicate it to others."[65] A person who is dying or facing the threat of death may—especially if the circumstance is sudden or unexpected—experience "a myriad of . . . volatile emotions" ranging from fear to sadness to regret to anger. The feelings may emanate, like a distress signal, to certain others.[66]

This capacity, I suggest, is akin to a phenomenon known as *prodromal dreaming,* a term used by the late dream researcher Robert Van de Castle. He observed that "dreams can be sensitive indicators of biochemical or physiological changes."[67] Such dreams have been noted by observers going back to antiquity. The renowned second-century Greek physician Galen mentioned the case of a man who dreamed his leg had turned to stone and whose leg developed paralysis a few days later.[68]

Van de Castle offers several more modern examples:[69]

- A man who dreamed of eating pizza and then his stomach breaking open the night before he actually experienced a perforated ulcer.
- A woman who dreamed of "wiggly, incandescent worms of all colors" crawling over her eyelids, who developed an inflamed retina two days later.
- A girl who dreamed of being shot in the left side of the head, who woke up with a severe migraine headache on that side.

It would seem that dreams can, at least in some people, function as a virtual x-ray. Given how entwined and continuous is the communication between our brain and body, it's not surprising that physiological information should come into our awareness during sleep. This is, after all, when the brain is most likely to retrieve and assess subliminal information.

Extraordinary Communication
of Distress

Could something like a prodromal dream be produced—as in the case of Romeo's friend Harry Robinson or the woman who dreamed of the dying airman, Mel Wooten—when *someone else* is undergoing a profound biological struggle? I should like to consider the possibility. There are certainly many accounts of waking instances of such "distress signals." Despite their seeming strangeness and intangibility, it's striking that they involve such palpable physicality. For example:

- A mother was writing a letter to her daughter when her right hand felt as though it were burning and she dropped the pen. Less than an hour later, she received a phone call relating that her daughter's right hand had been severely burned by acid in a laboratory accident.[70]
- A man felt himself choking inexplicably, only to learn later that his father had been choking at the same time thousands of miles away.[71]
- A man and his wife were attending a football game when the man got up and announced they had to return home because their son had been hurt. Once home, they discovered that the boy had shot a BB into his thumb, which would require emergency surgery.[72]
- A nurse received a call after midnight concerning a patient she had been seeing. The patient's daughter had already called 911. The nurse went to the patient's home and found her looking terribly ill, with low blood pressure, chest pains, and breathing difficulties. After the ambulance had left with the patient, the nurse returned home to try to sleep. She was suddenly awakened by "a violent jerk that went through my whole body." As she was trying to figure out what had happened, the phone rang. The patient's daughter was on the line, saying that her mother had just experienced cardiac arrest but that the doctor was able to "shock her back" to life.[73]

- A family living on a farm in upstate New York began their day's work, but all returned to the house later in the morning after experiencing a strange feeling. All eight family members felt an intense foreboding, each without being aware that the others felt the same. That day, in Michigan, a son in the family died in an accident.[74]
- A woman felt a pain in her chest and said her sister had been hurt. The woman later found out that her sister was in a fatal car accident at the same time; her chest had been crushed by the steering wheel.[75]
- A soldier was knocked unconscious by shell fragments. That same day, a continent away, his daughter, age two and a half, was playing on the family's kitchen floor. According to the man's wife, their toddler suddenly got up, said to her mother "Daddy's been hurt," and then went back to her toys.[76]

Strong Feelings Emanating in Space and Time

A pair of terms has been developed to categorize the "coincidental" felt experience of someone else's physical or emotion distress: *telesomatic* (*tele* as in distance, *somatic* as in body) and *clairsentience* (as in *clairvoyant* but with the emphasis on literally feeling another's pain).[77]

We can all appreciate, more prosaically, how such dynamics might register. Begin with the fact that the more vividly felt an experience is, the clearer the memory. Think where you were at the time of the Challenger space shuttle explosion . . . the 9/11 attacks . . . or (much more happily) when you either proposed or accepted an offer of marriage from your beloved. You probably remember a plethora of details that you wouldn't recall if the events weren't so stunning, thrilling, or meaningful.

Such memories are not merely cognitive; their strength owes to being simultaneously *visceral*. This, I propose, is the key—both to prodromal dreaming and telesomatic perceptions. The more significant the physical and emotional experience, the more likely it is to be transmitted to oneself and to others. In the case of a true emergency, when one's life is on the line (or perceived to be on the line), the nature of the distress may subvert the normal bounds of time and space.

The general concept is outlined by Shallis:

> Bodies do not stop at the skin but extend outwards into the space around them. Human senses reach out into the world, some farther than others, but even apart from the five senses man extends outwards. . . . When feeling happy and expansive I extend out in some way, I feel bigger. When I feel insecure I shrink down both psychologically and in the space around me. . . . If people extend in space why not in time as well? . . . When lives suddenly become involved in extreme drama and emotional tension then the extended selves may well reach out dramatically in space and time, and thereby be "detected" by people sufficiently aware of their own sensitivity to these things.[78]

We have now come full circle to where this exploration started: by alighting on the phenomenon of death. While death tends not to be welcomed by any animal, it is a natural and inescapable part of life. Along with its close relative, trauma, death may trigger unimagined forms of sensitivity in human beings as well as in other perceptive, feeling creatures. The evidence, seriously investigated, offers a fascinating pathway to new and exciting knowledge.

7

The Endurance of Emotion

Birthmarks and the "Remembered" Lives of Others

One of the most intrepid explorers of this or any other age was undoubtedly the late Ian Stevenson (1918–2007), whom we touched on briefly in chapter 4. He was Carlson Professor of Psychiatry at the University of Virginia and the founding director of its Division of Personality Studies. Over decades, Stevenson meticulously investigated thousands of cases where young children seemed to recall the life and/or death of someone else. While these were, in his words, "suggestive of reincarnation,"[1] he duly considered other possibilities—including fraud. Stevenson and his colleagues went to great lengths to see if the children's statements could be verified. They did so by tracking down such sources as birth and death certificates, hospital records, and reports of postmortem examinations.

His research brought to light intriguing evidence of birthmarks and physical deformities as well as intense interests and aversions corresponding to the lives and deaths of people who could be—and often were—identified. For instance, an individual's malformed fingers might be found to correspond to fingers that were severed in an accident occurring to another individual many years before; congenital constriction rings might be found to correlate with ropes that bound the legs or feet of an individual who'd been killed in a different place and time. A birthmark might bear close resemblance to a knife or gunshot wound suffered by a deceased person elsewhere.

While some of the birthmarks occurring on children who say they recall another person's life are ordinary moles, most are not. These are quite distinctive and strangely unusual. Here are a few examples:[2]

- A woman had three scar-like birthmarks running down the middle of her back. As a child, she said that she remembered the life of a woman who'd been killed when struck three times in the back with an axe.
- A boy with a malformed ear in addition to underdevelopment of the right side of his face said that he recalled the life of a man who had been killed by a shotgun blast at point-blank range. Records disclosed that a wounded man who fit the description of this individual had perished in the hospital from wounds sustained from a bullet that had penetrated the right side of his skull.
- A girl born without her lower right leg said that she remembered the life of a girl who was run over by a train. Eyewitnesses reported that the train in question had severed the girl's right leg before running over her trunk.

Such abnormalities didn't always relate to a death by homicide or accident: one man's deformed nail on his right big toe seemed to correspond to a chronic infection, in the same toe, that his uncle had suffered for some years before he died. Stevenson found that about 35 percent of children who claimed to remember another life have such birthmarks or birth defects.[3]

Phobias Corresponding to the Mode of Death

Another 36 percent of the children studied had phobias relating to the "remembered" cause of death.[4] A child afraid of the water might recall someone whose life had ended in drowning; a child preternaturally afraid of loud noises might remember another person who had been shot.

Still other children, Stevenson and his associates found, had strangely particular likes and dislikes—in clothing, food, and personal habits—that would be found to relate to individuals whose names, families, professions, and preferences were apparently "remembered." In such cases, the inordinate likes and dislikes and intense fears and interests were hard to attribute to experiences in the life of these very young children. Often these characteristics occurred before the child was able to speak. For example:

> A baby struggled so much against being bathed that it took 3 adults to hold her down for this. Also, before she could speak she had manifested (at the age of 6 months) a marked phobia of buses and cried when transported in one. The life she later described was that of a young girl . . . who . . . had been walking on a narrow road that crossed flooded paddy fields. A bus had come along, and this girl, stepping back to avoid it, had fallen into the flood water and drowned. . . . [Another] boy showed a marked fear of airplanes before he could even speak; when he saw or heard one, he would run to his mother and cower or hide under a bed. Later, he described the previous life of a man who had been killed in an airplane crash. . . .
>
> The subject of another case . . . showed a phobia of policemen when he was just beginning to speak at the age of one-and-a-half years. If he saw a policeman or police vehicle, he would say "Police" and run inside the house. When he was about 4 years old, he gave details of a previous life that corresponded closely to events in Sri Lanka in April 1971, when the police and army suppressed a serious insurgency during which they killed hundreds of the insurgents. . . .

Another child . . . was observed (at the age of 4) to cringe with fear whenever airplanes flew over. Her father asked what was frightening her, and she said that she was afraid the airplanes would shoot her. She gradually explained that she had been a Japanese soldier (presumably in World War II) and had been shot and killed by a strafing airplane. In addition to the phobia of airplanes, this child liked to play at being a soldier, and she was markedly masculine in her behavior; her refusal to wear girls' clothes eventually led to her being expelled from her school.[5]

Stevenson notes that, in investigating these cases, he "never learned about any traumatic experience the subjects had had since their birth that could account for the phobia. Also, there were no other members of the family with the same phobia whom the child might have imitated."[6]

Link with Violence or Trauma

Most of the cases Stevenson tracked down were found overseas, particularly in India, Pakistan, Sri Lanka, and Burma (now Myanmar)—places where a belief in reincarnation is prevalent. He pointed out, however, that cases of apparent past-life memories have been found in every country where they have been looked for, including the United States.[7]

The clearest and most persistent trend was the apparent memory of a traumatic death. Recall the example we saw in chapter 4, where toddler James Leininger began having nightmares of a fatal plane crash. He engaged in intense play where he slammed toy planes into his family's coffee table, drew hundreds of battle scenes involving planes, and gave information to his parents that turned out to fit the details of the death of U.S. Navy pilot James Huston, whose plane crashed and sank during the Battle of Iwo Jima in 1945.[8]

A thoughtful observer of many baffling phenomena, physician and author Larry Dossey has pointed out that although birthmarks and birth deformities are quite common, just 30 to 50 percent of birth defects can be explained medically or genetically. Moreover, he remarks, scientists "can't tell us why a birthmark occurs at a particular *place*. In contrast, reincarnation, if real, provides a reason *why* a particular defect or birthmark occurs in one individual and not another, *where* it occurs on the body, and the *shape* it takes."[9] While this is a valid observation, others have suggested that reincarnation—implying as it does that an entire personality has somehow been incorporated into a new body—need not be invoked. H. H. Jürgen Keil, a longtime Australian researcher into children with past-life memories, suggests a narrower—if still difficult to comprehend—concept of "thought bundles." Expressing something essential about a given individual at the time of death, these, he conjectures, somehow become attached to infants *in utero*. Later, the growing child and those around him assume incorrectly that she or he is the reincarnation of a previous person.[10]

Can the Heart Transplant Memories?

A different lens on the situation can be brought by a newer phenomenon—though it is equally perplexing. Some people who receive heart transplants profess to having memories of their donors' end of life experiences—not to mention intense, completely new likes or dislikes. Numerous accounts collected by the late psychologist Paul Pearsall and his colleagues Gary Schwartz and Linda Russek attest to the possibility that someone's essence needn't be implanted in a neonate in order for it to be conveyed—or reanimated if you will.

Here is a sampling of these remarkable stories. In each instance, information about the donor and recipient was verified by family or friends, with the striking personality changes noted in the recipients having *preceded* any contact with the donor's family or friends.

- A seven-month-old boy received the heart of a sixteen-month-old boy who had drowned. Four years later, the recipient met the donor's mother. "When [he] first saw me, he ran to me and pushed his nose against me and rubbed and rubbed it. It was exactly what we did with [our son]. . . . When he hugged me, I could feel my son. I mean I could feel him, not just symbolically. He was there. I felt his energy." The recipient's mother reported that her son acted much differently in the presence of the donor's mother: "He is very, very shy, but he went over to her just like he used to run to me when he was a baby. When he whispered 'It's okay, mama,' I broke down." Similarly, when the families went to church together, her son "let go of my hand and ran right to [the donor's father]. He climbed on his lap, hugged him and said 'Daddy.' We were flabbergasted. How could he have known him? Why did he call him dad? He never did things like that. He would never let go of my hand in church and run to a stranger. When I asked him why he did it, he said he didn't. He said [the donor] did and he went with him."[11]

- A white foundry worker received the heart of a black teenager who'd been killed in a drive-by shooting. The recipient was amazed: "I used to hate classical music, but now I love it. So I know it's not my new heart, because a black guy from the 'hood wouldn't be into that." However, according to the donor's mother, "Our son was walking to violin class when he was hit. . . . He died right there on the street, hugging his violin case. He loved music and the teachers said he had a real thing for it."[12]

- "When I got my new heart, two things happened to me. First, almost every night, and still sometimes now, I actually feel the [auto] accident my donor had. I can feel the impact in my chest. . . . Also, I hate red meat now. I can't stand it. I was McDonald's biggest money maker, but now red meat makes me throw up."[13]

- A college professor received the heart of a police officer shot while attempting to arrest a drug dealer. The recipient remarked, "A few weeks after I got my heart, I began to have dreams. I would see a flash of light right in my face and my face gets real, real hot. It actually burns."[14]

- A middle-aged [man] received the heart of a fourteen-year-old girl with anorexic/bulimic tendencies. He commented, "I feel like a teenager. I actually feel giddy. . . . I have this annoying tendency to giggle that drives my wife nuts. And there's something about food. I don't know what it is. I get hungry, but after I eat I often feel nauseated and [think] that it would help if I could throw up."[15]

- "I never really was all that interested in sex. I never really thought about it much. Don't get me wrong, my husband and I had a sex life, but it was not a big part of our life. Now, I tire my husband out. . . . When I told my psychiatrist about this, she said it was a reaction to my medications and my healthier body. Then I found out that my donor was a young college girl who worked as a topless dancer and in an out-call service. I think I got her sexual drive, and my husband agrees."[16]

- "I never told anyone at first, but I thought having a woman's heart would make me gay. Since my surgery [though], I've been hornier than ever and women seem to look even more erotic and sensual. . . . I think I've got a woman's way of thinking about sex now." This man's wife concurs: "He's a much better lover . . . he just knows my body as well as I do. He wants to cuddle, hold and take a lot of time. . . . And one more thing, he loves to go to museums. He would never, absolutely never, do that. Now he [goes] every week. Sometimes he stands for minutes and looks at a painting without talking."[17]

- A nine-year-old boy received the heart of a three-year-old girl who, tragically, had drowned in her family's pool. The boy's mother reported: "The one thing I notice most is that [her son] is now deathly afraid of the water. He loved it before. We live on a lake and he won't go into the backyard. He keeps closing and locking the back door. He says he's afraid of the water and doesn't know why."[18]

- A five-year-old boy received the heart of a three-year-old boy who had fallen from an apartment window. The recipient took to calling his donor Timmy, saying "He's just a little kid. He's a little brother about half my age. He got hurt bad when he fell down. He likes Power Rangers a lot, I think, just like I used to. I don't like them anymore, though." In fact, the donor's name was Thomas though his family called him Tim. Even more striking, according to the recipient's mother, was that their family had only recently learned that Tim "fell trying to reach a Power Ranger toy that had fallen from the ledge of the window. [Our son] won't even touch his Power Rangers anymore."[19]

- A girl, age eight, received the heart of another little girl who had been murdered. She started screaming at night about her dreams of the man who had killed her donor. She told her mother she knew who it was. After several sessions with a psychiatrist, the latter "could not deny the reality of what this child was telling [her]." The mother and the psychiatrist together decided to call the police. Using the descriptions provided by the little girl, the murderer was found and convicted. "The time, the weapon, the place, the clothes he wore, what the little girl he killed had said to him . . . everything [she] reported was completely accurate."[20]

As regards dreams, a number of years ago I came across a fascinating account myself. A man in his fifties had received the heart of a college student who had gotten drunk at a sorority party and died from the fall down a flight of stairs. For three nights following the transplant, the man had dreams of falling down stairs. Then his nightmares stopped, and the recipient had no further symptoms that appeared to be connected to the donor.[21]

Here is one final curious anecdote:

- A female heart recipient found herself becoming more energetic, more assertive, and more flirtatious. She started "admiring shorter, rounder, blonder women, where before she had admired tall, dark, slender ones. Being propositioned by a lesbian made her wonder what signals she was giving out." (She knew that her heart had come from a man.) She developed a taste for chicken nuggets and green peppers. Five months after the operation, she said she dreamed of a young man named Tim. Tracking down the donor's family, it turned out that his name was just that. "And he'd had chicken nuggets under his jacket when he died. He loved green peppers. He was incredibly energetic. He had a short blond girlfriend."[22]

A New Hypothesis

In the aggregate, these accounts suggest that the heart (and perhaps other organs as well) carries within it a memory of the person from whom it came. One must presume, of course, that Pearsall's subjects (seventy-three heart transplant patients and their families, plus eighteen donor families) were not being deceitful.[23] The paucity of such cases—just 6 percent of heart transplant recipients according to one study[24]—indicates the phenomenon is not widespread, in any event. But the many similarities with cases "suggestive of reincarnation" imply that reincarnation as it's typically thought of—in other words, someone reborn in an entirely new individual—is off base, or at least incomplete. Seemingly the transplant of a highly significant organ, the heart, into an already living person can do the trick (whatever the "trick" might be).

Stepping into a more skeptical mode, we ought to consider the fact that the transplant process is inherently stressful, with psychiatric symptoms arising in up to half of transplantees.[25] Depression is common, and so is survivor guilt. As one person has commented: "Imagine: a hospital has agreed, at least in principle, to rip the heart and lungs out of your body and replace them with the heart and lungs of somebody who has just died. And for this you're being congratulated?"[26] Most powerfully, the heart retains age-old symbolic associations that make swapping this organ with anyone else's extremely problematic. For millennia, the heart has been regarded as the source of courage, wisdom, love, and even identity. So it should not be surprising that many recipients wonder "Who am I now?" in the aftermath of their surgery. How much of their "old self," their unique set of likes and dislikes, their cumulative life experience is still with them? And how much might be conveyed from their now deceased donor? Are they still themselves—or some sort of strange, new amalgam?

All things considered, the explanation I wish to advance for these extraordinary cases begins with the recognition that they're just that—extraordinary. Hearkening back to the question explored at the outset of this book—who becomes afflicted with PTSD, what kind of PTSD, and *why?*—we must consider the personality of he or she who is dying, the circumstances of that death, and the personality of the individual who suddenly begins to manifest memories or traits quite like the deceased, or whose dreams seem to intensively concern the deceased. We must also consider the concept of emotional energy—the way our bodies' cells convert the energy of food and light into palpable, biochemical energy that literally animates us for the business of living. Such business can range anywhere from getting up in the morning to seeing a difficult project through . . . from laughing uproariously or crying sorrowfully to quietly assessing a situation . . . and from tackling some new challenge to recollecting an endearing memory.

My hypothesis is that the person who has died had a surplus, a profusion of such animate energy essentially frozen at the time of death because there was something meaningful that he or she wanted to express or to resolve but couldn't, or because a torrent of energy was marshaled to survive a life-or-death situation but couldn't be discharged. It's possible, returning to the immensely useful concept of Boundaries, that the person dying was of a thick-boundary constitution, that he or she wasn't in the habit of recognizing or acting on feelings anyway.

Relevant Personality Concepts

I further posit that the person having memories or dreams associated with the deceased, or who appears to take on wholly new traits, likes, or dislikes, is of a thin-boundary constitution. In such case, he or she would be natively more open to new possibilities, new feelings, and new experiences—and more conversant with emotion in general.

This latter proposition is borne out by Pearsall, who found the heart transplant patients he interviewed seemed to have numerous personality traits in common, which he took the trouble to catalog. He referred to these individuals as "cardio-sensitive."[27] Their characteristics are precisely those of the thin-boundary person. For a start, nearly all cardio-sensitives are female. Most reported an active fantasy life prior to their transplant; they are adept at conjuring up visual imagery. They are hyperalert to their environment. Many have allergies. Long before their transplant surgery, most reported extensive dreaming and interest in the significance of their dreams. Most say they are highly sensual and aware of their body (and many are athletes, musicians, or dancers). They're often described by family members and friends as being "psychic" or "very sensitive," and are said to have showed this sensitivity long before their illness was diagnosed and their eventual transplant.

A concept that parallels Boundaries, known as *transliminality,* is also applicable here. Proposed by the eminent psychologist William James (who termed it *subliminal consciousness*), the idea has recently been refined and refreshed by the late Australian psychologist Michael Thalbourne and his colleague Peter Delin. They define transliminality as the tendency for psychological material to cross thresholds in or out of consciousness. People who display a high degree of transliminality "might . . . be expected to have erupt into consciousness, from the pre-conscious, experiences that we variously know . . . as psychic, mystical, and creative." On the other hand, "persons low in transliminality would be expected to . . . rarely if ever report [such] experiences."[28]

Interestingly, there's evidence that highly transliminal people are more likely to be synesthetes.[29] This would make sense if we suppose that synesthesia reflects more extensive neural interconnectivity—not only across brain regions but hierarchically, from preconscious glimmers of sensation through to fully conscious awareness of feelings and thoughts.

Energy Marshaled, Energy Constrained

If these concepts—boundaries and transliminality—shed light on the types of individuals likely to be the prime actors in such extraordinary circumstances, what of the energy dynamics taking place within the mind and body of the person confronting prospective death? Recall the tally of Dr. Jim Tucker—who ably carries on Stevenson's work at the University of Virginia—that 70 percent of the approximately 2,500 cases investigated to date involve a child who recalled a violent death.[30]

We need to envision a scenario where a great deal of energy is marshaled for the emergency but the individual is prevented from discharging it because he or she is literally overcome, either by fear or by a superior force (whether human or natural). James Huston, we learned, couldn't get out of his plane, which, having been hit by Japanese fire, exploded, crashed into the water, and quickly sank.

Two analogies have been suggested. The first is to imagine flooring the accelerator of your car and simultaneously stomping on the brake. "The difference between the inner racing . . . and the outer immobility . . . creates a forceful turbulence similar to a tornado." The second analogy is to imagine that you're having sex with your partner and are on the verge of climax when suddenly, some outside force stops you. "Now, multiply that feeling of withholding by one hundred, and you may come close to the amount of energy aroused by a life-threatening experience."[31]

The latter comparison seems especially apt since, during orgasm, one's heart rate more than doubles[32] (and we have been focusing quite a bit on heart transplants). Accelerated heart rate is a sure indicator that energy production is being boosted—as is faster respiration, the tensing of muscles, higher blood pressure, and increased sweating. All of these are signs of sympathetic nervous system activation. While sex is not a fearful activity (at least not when it's voluntary), various aspects of sympathetic nervous activity are called into play. We saw in chapter 4 that when faced with a significant threat, many more aspects of the sympathetic nervous system are switched on. These include:

- Riveting of all senses on the perceived danger
- Cessation of movement in order to concentrate and lay low
- Widening of the eyes and dilation of the pupils
- Diversion of blood from the skin to the muscles in order to facilitate fight or flight
- Suppression of appetite and the production of saliva (causing dry mouth)
- Relaxation of the gut and bladder (causing butterflies or even, if stressed enough, wetting or soiling one's pants)

Within the brain, activity increases in limbic structures such as the hypothalamus and amygdala, which register and process emotion. The pituitary gland is signaled to release a hormone called ACTH. Carried to the adrenal glands, ACTH causes the hormones adrenaline, noradrenaline, and cortisol to be released. This brain-based stress response system, as noted earlier, is called the hypothalamic-pituitary-adrenal (HPA) axis. Its effect is to speed up one's thinking and reactivity, mobilize bodily energy, and suppress immune activity. The function of cortisol is especially noteworthy in this regard. Once in the bloodstream it prompts the liver to release glucose, a substance vital to rapid exercise, and acts to release fat, an excellent source of fuel for the body. It also acts inside the cell nucleus, instructing select genes to increase or decrease their activity. So the impact of cortisol is quite wide-ranging, going to the core of cellular activity and the body's ability to marshal the energy it needs to respond to a threat.

All of the foregoing is analogous to the individual flooring the accelerator or coming to a climax during sex. Now consider that because the person is suddenly overtaken or overwhelmed—either by human violence or the force of nature—that flow of energy comes to a screeching halt. There's no real opportunity to fight or flee, just an enforced and permanent immobilization—outwardly, anyway. But what happens *internally* to that vortex of energy? I suggest that the stage can be set for the sort of anomalous conveyance of experience and personality that we have been considering. Death, after all, is the ultimate form of dissociation. And dissociation from the felt sense, as we have seen repeatedly, appears to be the prompt for all manner of strangeness.

Experimental Evidence

Several intriguing pieces of evidence exist for the scenario I'm suggesting. First is a pair of studies indicating that as the moment of death approaches, brain activity surges briefly—and may even continue for a time after the heart stops and blood flow ceases. The researchers in both cases were surprised at the high levels of activity. Though one of the studies (a terribly inhumane one) was performed on rats, it suggests that "at near-death, many known electrical signatures of consciousness exceed levels found in the waking state."[33]

The other study, far less objectionable given that it was done on human volunteers, demonstrates that, for many people, the final seconds of life bring a pronounced spike in neural activity "consistent with the wide awake state."[34] These findings offer evidence of a window where we are capable of—even inclined to—gather strength before the end. How much more intense this process must be in the throes of a trauma. While it may not be possible to experimentally assess the emotional energy mustered to meet a profound crisis, we can at least imagine a parallel.

A further, provocative piece of evidence comes from a 2004 study done by biochemist Richard Myers, then at Stanford University, and colleagues. They were studying the preserved brain tissue of people affected during their lives by depression, bipolar disorder, and schizophrenia. In searching for the genes that might underlie these conditions, they noticed that the patterns of active genes fell into two distinct groups, depending on how the patients had died. "The statistics were screaming at us," related Myers. "It was pretty remarkable." What emerged was that the individuals who had endured prolonged deaths, over hours or days, showed one pattern of genetic activation. Those who had died suddenly showed another. Myers's team suggested that during a prolonged illness or coma the dying brain runs on low energy.[35]

I find this discovery highly noteworthy for two reasons. First, it seems that when the brain senses it's dying, certain genes switch on. Cellular processes are affected, perhaps throughout the organism. If there were something meaningful that the person wanted to express or to resolve, an effort could at least be made toward that end. However, in the case of a sudden demise, such processing would be short-circuited. Bodily energy would not "peter out" but might remain trapped, as I have speculated.

Second, the Stanford finding has a stunning *epigenetic* implication. Epigenetics is the study of how lived experience affects gene expression. In chapter 4 we surveyed the remarkable evidence that fearful experiences may effectively "program" infants—even two generations removed—to be more anxious, reactive, and environmentally sensitive. I introduced the possibility that just as human beings retain a vivid memory of events that are emotionally meaningful, traumatic experiences might, in certain circumstances, "imprint" upon others distant in time and space. Though the mechanism is far from clear, there is plenty of circumstantial evidence to support it.

The Importance of What Is "Heart Felt"

The fact that epigenetics can describe the echoes of fear being transmitted across generations makes a more anomalous mechanism plausible, in my humble opinion. So does the field of psychoneuroimmunology, which over the past thirty years has overturned long-accepted doctrines that the mind and the body are separate, that the immune system and the nervous system don't communicate, and that one's emotional state has no bearing on health. We now know that what we feel fundamentally affects what we think. We also know that the brain is not a dictator over the rest of the body but rather an important player in a highly coordinated troupe, and that hormones, peptides, and other "informa- tion substances" coursing throughout the body constitute a veritable psychosomatic network. Psychoneuroimmunology has shown that the human being is effectively a unified *bodymind.*

Within this framework, I submit, feelings are both energetic and of fundamental importance. I have stressed that feeling flow can best be envisioned as a stream in continuous motion. Its sources are all the cells that, together, transform food and oxygen into the body's energy; its course is nerve fiber and the bloodstream itself; its tributaries are our muscles, organs, and skin.

In this conception, the heart is inevitably the most important organ. It can be viewed as a central pump as well as a checkpoint for the flow of feeling. Indeed, neuropeptide receptors have been located in the heart, providing a means of instantaneous communication with the brain. Its atrium produces a hormone (known as ANF) that affects several parts of the brain as well as the pituitary and pineal glands.[36] Ongoing research suggests this communication is electromagnetic as well, with the heart's electromagnetic output changing in tandem with the state of bodily feeling. Thus, the traditional view of the heart as harboring its own, distinctive intelligence is not merely metaphorical— it is increasingly backed up by science.[37]

Our typical gestures and expressions are consistent with this under- standing. We put our hands over our hearts (not our heads) when tak- ing a pledge, for example. We observe that someone's "heart doesn't seem to be in it" or that a rejection left a friend "heartbroken." We're "heartened" by good news, our heart "skips a beat" when we're excited, and we're urged to "take heart" when we're feeling down. Such expres- sions, I submit, have their basis in bodymind reality.

Role of the Immune System

From a consideration of the heart, let's return to one particularly inter- esting consequence of activity within the brain's HPA axis. We saw that once the threat response system has been triggered, immune activity is damped down while reserves of energy are being called up. The primary function of the immune system, of course, is to distinguish self from nonself, friendly cells from enemy. The fact that one's immune function is suppressed during an emergency suggests a temporary blurring of distinctions between self and other. A biological opening might conceivably be presented for the conveyance of someone else's memories, experiences, and personality traits.

If this strikes you as far-fetched, consider the following real-life illustration. Drawn from the *Archives of Internal Medicine,* it concerns an Australian man whose transplanted liver came from a fifteen-year-old boy who had died from an allergic reaction to peanuts. The boy's allergy was never officially diagnosed, so the doctors involved were unaware of it. The day after the man returned home from the hospital, he ate a handful of cashews—and shortly afterward had a life-threatening allergic reaction. He recovered, but tests showed that he had developed an allergy to cashews, peanuts, and sesame seeds—the same allergies his donor had.[38]

This account is revealing precisely because there is nothing paranormal about it. All we have is a life-or-death drama stemming from an allergy, but an allergy that came from *someone else.* Perhaps, under certain circumstances, something even more extraordinary could be transferred, something even more emblematic of the self that is "other" to the transplant recipient.

There are other permutations of the immune system worth noting. Time and again, people have demonstrated an uncanny ability to manifest, under duress or through hypnosis, the same physical insults suffered years before at the hands of another. We saw numerous examples of such psychosomatic plasticity in chapter 2. While women are typically involved in these instances, men are surely not excluded. One man (whose case was published in a reputable medical journal) manifested "an extraordinarily faithful repetition" of an earlier incident wherein he had been hospitalized for sleepwalking, with his hands tied behind his back for his protection during sleep. Later on, his right forearm developed indentations resembling rope marks.[39]

Pain Has Power

Such cases abound. They typically occur in people who have experienced some type of trauma. In people who are devout Catholics, for example, stigmata will sometimes appear corresponding to the wounds Jesus is believed to have suffered when being nailed to the cross.[40] All of this demonstrates the capacity of certain people (who, as I've speculated, are highly empathetic/thin-boundary) to not only manifest their own pain in extraordinary ways but to register the pain of others in a similar fashion. These are people who resonate with another's injury, illness, or distress to an extent that amazes and baffles the rest of us.

Pain—and even more so the resonance of physical and emotional trauma—serves as a potent reminder of the necessity of survival and healing. We always wish to escape that which plagues us, especially if it was life-threatening, or perceived as such, in its original incarnation. Pain, and especially the consequences of trauma, inevitably reminds us of our vulnerability, perhaps even our mortality. We cannot grow, we cannot learn, we cannot create meaning—all of which is central to the business of being human—if we are existentially threatened.

This must be why the bodymind *remembers* so keenly, or at least harbors the capacity to do so. It is stunning to consider how someone under duress or under hypnosis could spontaneously manifest hives, bruises, welts, rope marks, or stigmata on highly specific areas of the body, with the skin just a few millimeters away being unaffected.[41] The term *body haunting* has been invoked to describe such cases, wherein a person's intense emotional experience is somehow encoded and recreated many years after the original episode.[42] In the aggregate, these examples point to legitimate—if insufficiently understood—biological processes, along with the sheer power of feelings.

Speaking of the term *haunting,* it's remarkable how often ghosts are said to be reenacting something traumatic. Far from being inexplicably spooky, the process may be identical to what we examined in chapter 1, when low-reactive/thick-boundary people develop PTSD. Their felt sense becomes dissociated and they end up feeling numb—at a distance from their customary reality. The people so afflicted may even replay the traumatic situation, seeking presumably to be free of it.

For example, in the early morning hours every July 5, a certain Vietnam veteran would simulate the circumstances surrounding his buddy's death in a rice paddy. He would do this by staging robberies—but with only a finger in his pocket as his gun. The man would remain at the scene, the police would arrive, and he would be taken into custody. A psychiatrist at the local VA hospital, being conversant with PTSD, realized that the vet "had orchestrated the cast of characters needed to play the role of the Viet Cong. . . . Once he became aware of his feelings and the role the original event had played in driving his compulsion, the man was able to stop reenacting this tragic incident."[43]

Some instances of accident-proneness may be viewed as fitting this pattern,[44] and the compulsively repeated play of traumatized children certainly does.[45] Such incessant and often bizarre reenactments have been called "the most intriguing and complex symptom of trauma," demonstrating the need to "resolve a deep emotional scar."[46] I suggest that ghosts—energetic vestiges of the bodymind—are doing exactly the same thing. They go on performing the same actions year after year, generation after generation, because they are neither mindful (in a literal sense) nor able to transmute the feelings engendered by the original trauma into any sort of conscious resolution. One further curious note is that people may go cold, clammy, or pale when severely stressed or frightened—and ghosts down the centuries not only appear as white but supposedly cause a chill when they appear. (Readers interested in this subject matter are referred to my earlier book with Dr. Marc Micozzi, *The Spiritual Anatomy of Emotion.*)[47]

Willpower Summoned to Survive

One final aspect of personality needs to be appraised if we're to develop anything like a satisfactory picture of why birthmarks or birth deformities might be associated with an infant who later recalls the life of someone else. Or why a heart transplant recipient (or a young child, for that matter) would seemingly manifest the habits and intense interests of someone who's deceased, not to mention have phobias or nightmares relating to the death of that person. This final dimension is what I'll call the strength of one's personality—the vigor, the propensity to fight against adversity, and the will to assert oneself.

We recognize this quality (or lack of it) from everyday experience. I'm talking less about an opportunist or a bully and more about someone with courage or steely determination or "fire in the belly." Someone who can be counted upon to stick up for her- or himself, to willingly meet a difficult challenge, to rally the troops, or just plain fight. Such a person doesn't have to be outgoing or even outwardly energetic, but they do need to be someone whom you can count on in an emergency, who has essential determination and, in the immortal words of Tom Petty, "won't back down." Perhaps, in shorthand, someone with a survival instinct.

Individuals such as this, it occurs to me, are inevitably the protagonists of films by Michael Mann. Whether it's Daniel Day-Lewis in *Last of the Mohicans,* Tom Cruise in *Collateral,* or James Caan in *Thief,* Mann's central characters are pushed to the brink, only to summon extraordinary strength of will to prevail. Another good example from pop culture is Captain Kirk of *Star Trek.* An episode from the original series illustrates this well. Spock is attempting a mind meld with Kirk in order to "retrieve" him from memory loss. Kirk recoils from the meld, forcefully wishing to retain the new identity he's assumed. Spock, shaken, believes the mind meld has failed, remarking with some understatement, "His mind . . . He is an extremely dynamic individual."[48] This quality of mind, of dynamic feeling flow, is what I'm alluding to.

One particular—and particularly unusual—birthmark case will convey this strength of will, and suggest its essential role where anomalies arising from trauma are concerned. The case was investigated and written up by past-life researchers Keil and Tucker.[49] It concerns a Burmese subject who from birth had very strange deformities thought by his family to relate to the accidental death of his mother's first husband, a military airman. At the age of twenty, he had died after parachuting out of a plane during a night exercise, landing in a pond, and drowning. His wife went on to marry again and bear a son, who was born prematurely, with odd birthmarks and deformities. These included, on one leg, a mark that appeared as three rope-like rings, and hands that were not fully formed, with some of the fingers fused together.

Between the ages of three and five, this child would often talk about having come from the sky. He would say that he had been tangled up in ropes and then died in a pond. His parents had not shared with him any information about his mother's first husband and the man's untimely demise. Could the rope-like birthmark on this young boy's leg have "conveyed" through the trauma of a prior life? Yet how does one explain the fact that the boy's hands had such strange deformities? There was no indication, from witnesses later questioned, that the parachutist's hands had been damaged in any discernible way in the accident. There is a rare physiological condition known as cadaveric spasm that might explain this strange situation. Cadaveric spasm is a form of muscle stiffening known to occur in rapid deaths marked by extreme emotional intensity. In the case of a drowning victim, the person might clutch at whatever was at hand to try and save themselves—reeds, for instance, or in the case we are illustrating here, the ropes of a parachute. If cadaveric spasm occurred as the victim attempted to free himself from entanglement, the constriction of the man's hands would suggest a correlation with the congenital deformities of the young boy's hands.[50]

In this I am reminded of the B-52 crewman we met in the last chapter, who ejected from his stricken bomber in the middle of a freezing cold night over western Maryland. Severely injured, he crawled toward the lights of town, not knowing they were on the other side of an icy river. He died in a snowy field, his orange jacket around him. That same night, a woman who lived in the area had a nightmare apparently about this young man, seeing him in her mind's eye as he lay expiring.

In each of these instances—as well as James Leininger's "recollection" of James Huston—we have a sudden and overwhelming emergency, a person unable to escape but also someone, I would surmise, expending all of his might to survive. The vortex of emotional energy generated in such a circumstance . . . the concerns that might have occurred to them in their last moments . . . and their sheer willpower combine, in my estimation, to produce a veritable "snapshot" conveyed to another. That "other" could, for unknown reasons, be a woman sleeping at that very moment miles away, a child related or completely unrelated to the traumatized individual, or the recipient of that person's heart.

The Primacy of Meaning and Movement

The tendency of some people to ponder or even just alight on a subject that has emotional meaning—even when facing a mortal threat—is illustrated by this anecdote. A nurse, age fifty, was flying in a plane that suddenly lost an engine. Over those next turbulent moments of uncertainty, she recollected, "All I could think about was my garage. How I hadn't cleaned it, and how messy it would be when someone came in and saw it. It's crazy what you think about."[51] Why, indeed, would her mind—or anyone's mind—be drawn to such a comparatively trivial issue during a crisis? Perhaps because it represented some kind of a lingering, emotionally resonant concern that she wished to resolve, if at all possible, in what could have been construed as her final moments.

Emotion, I submit, is ultimately about meaning. We worry over, feel guilty about, become angered by, or are thrilled about matters that are invariably meaningful to us. The converse is also true: if it doesn't matter much, we won't bother to feel something about it, nor will we express that feeling to someone else. And the more something matters, the stronger we'll feel—even if it's something comparatively trivial. (We don't always realize how an apparently minor "something" may be connected with another matter we *do* care deeply about.)

The neurologist Pierre Gloor postulated that the brain's limbic region is where all sensations, all perceptions must be "tagged" with some sort of feeling if they are to be consciously experienced or recalled.[52] His insight has been highlighted and expanded upon by University of Southern California neuroscientist Antonio Damasio in the title of his popular book *The Feeling of What Happens*. Damasio explains the role of feeling in the context of the whole human body. He shows that it's the brain's job to sort through sensory input, determine what is paramount, what should be acted upon, what should be ignored, and what should be filed away. The limbic circuitry is involved in sifting through such inputs and assigning shades of feeling to them. The type and degree of feeling equates to the current and remembered meaning for the individual.[53]

The writer Aldous Huxley (*Brave New World*) must have known as much, as he took this insight a step further. "Experience is not what happens to you," he observed, "it's what you do with what happens to you." Everyone, naturally and fundamentally, seeks to understand what life is about, to construct meaning, to make sense of it all. Feeling, and its outward expression from the body—encompassed in the very word *emotion*—is central to that process. E-motion alludes to movement, the self *becoming,* not merely being. Life is constantly in flux and, as long as we are alive, so are we.[54]

This is why, I strongly suspect, anomalies arise in situations where people are overwhelmed and unable to escape. It is not in the nature of any animal to be confined, restricted, or immobilized. Parapsychologist Nandor Fodor recognized something similar through his investigations of alleged psychic phenomena from the 1930s to the 1960s. Late in his life, he singled out the feeling of anguish as having a presumed connection with many of the strange circumstances he'd looked into.[55] The Latin root of the word *anguish,* it so happens, is *angustia,* meaning "straightness, narrowness, or constriction." The lesson I take away is that bodily energy and feeling-tinged preoccupations caught or constricted within the bodymind lead to trouble.

People aren't things; we are animate. If a person's natural dynamism is thwarted—especially through the enforced immobility of an overwhelming crisis—there would seem to be no further opportunity for meaning. An individual trapped in such a situation, especially someone who is thick-boundary and/or possessing tremendous willpower or courage, may effectively impart the essentials of his or her bodily and emotional experience to someone else removed in space and time. In this conception, one is not being reborn but instead managing to convey what is most characteristic and most intensively *felt* to some new "home"—at least for a time. This is the somatic, psychological, existential, and mind-bendingly human explanation I proffer for bizarre birthmarks and inexplicable deformities, as well as for unaccountable phobias and the sudden, enigmatic likes and dislikes that we have surveyed.

A Universe Conducive to Emotion

I will close with a surmise about the perpetually astonishing universe in which we live. Based on all the evidence—some of which is very strange evidence indeed—it seems to me that emotion is both fundamental to sentient life as we know it and a property toward which the universe is favorably disposed. We have spoken of the psychesphere or empathosphere, a pair of names for a hypothetical realm of feeling so thoroughly pervasive that it transcends both space and time. There is likely a third name for this realm: C. G. Jung's *unus mundus,* from which he supposed synchronicities sprung. It should be clear by now that feeling is ground zero for all our sensibilities, all our perceptions, memories, dreams, and insights. Furthermore, as we've surveyed throughout this book, what we feel—especially feelings that are deep or intense—has the capacity to bridge what is physical, mental, and spiritual. It follows that what we partake in when we feel something deeply is indeed overarching. In that broad sense, I suggest, the universe is conducive to emotion.

It's impossible to prove this with a theorem because feelings are neither a fact that can be objectively weighed nor continuously present for communal inspection. They are insubstantial and never stand still. Like a breeze, we only sense their action on us and gather what has changed in their wake. More often than not, emotion takes us unaware.

This state of affairs points to yet another, almost insurmountable barrier to our fully understanding the nature of the world in which we are ensouled. Our conscious faculties, housed in the cerebral cortex, are the highly evolved tip of a very large iceberg. What is available to us— the raw material of feeling and thought—is repeatedly filtered before we become cognizant of it. Indeed, everything processed through our sensory apparatus and our nervous systems is reduced and crystallized. What we ultimately take for reality are slivers of that reality, wavelengths of the entire spectrum that we end up focusing upon.[56] Most of what we're about—including the primal activity within our cells, the flow of blood, the circulation of hormones and neurotransmitters, the function of our organs, and the "friend or foe" activity of our immune system—happens completely below the threshold of consciousness. Yet it is of overriding importance. If these operations cease, we will die.

In the same way, the stuff of feelings is elemental and preconscious. People who are highly transliminal may stand the best chance of accessing it. Yet even here, I suggest, the forces at work are difficult if not impossible to discern. Like the wind, their effects are seen in passing. Two propositions seem like a fair bet, though. The first is that feelings can endure and be conveyed beyond anything we can conventionally explain. The second is that human beings—and other sentient creatures as well—are connected by emotion in a more than human, more than temporal, and more than strictly physical world.

Conclusion

I am fond of aphorisms—especially from great scientists, those who embody a particular combination of verve and humility. In spite of what they have boldly discovered, their outlooks tend to be tempered with a healthy dose of modesty, even reverence for all there is still to be found out and understood:

> *Not only is the universe stranger than we imagine, it is stranger than we* can *imagine.*
> BRITISH BIOLOGIST J. B. S. HALDANE OR
> BRITISH ASTRONOMER SIR ARTHUR EDDINGTON
> (THE STATEMENT IS ATTRIBUTED TO BOTH)

> *Sit down before fact as a little child, be prepared to give up every conceived notion, follow humbly wherever and whatever abysses nature leads, or you will learn nothing.*
> T. H. HUXLEY

> *I believe there is no source of deception in the investigation of nature which can compare with a fixed belief that certain kinds of phenomena are impossible.*
> WILLIAM JAMES

Often, the biggest impediment to scientific progress is not what we don't know but what we know.

ROBERT SAPOLSKY

You either hug the coast or head for blue water.

EDWARD O. WILSON

The last quotation is the most recent, and I like how Wilson, even in his eighties, urges a spirit of enterprise and exploration.

My intent has been for the same spirit to imbue this book. I should like to close with word of an interesting experiment, suggestive of one of the themes I have emphasized and illustrative of the "blue water" that holds so much promise.

The experiment, a collaboration between researchers at Durham University and University College London, found that people who hear phantom voices have an enhanced ability to detect meaningful speech patterns in ambiguous sounds. Here's how it worked. Participants listened to a set of disguised sounds, known as sine-wave speech, while they were having an MRI brain scan. Sine-wave speech has been described as sounding a bit like birdsong. Usually the sounds can be understood only when people are told to listen for sounds akin to speech or if they've been trained to decode sine-wave speech. Once it can be recognized, listeners are able to make out simple sentences such as "The boy ran down the path" or "The clown had a funny face."

In the experiment, many of the listeners recognized the hidden speech before being told it was there. On average, they tended to notice it earlier than other participants who had no history of hearing voices. The listeners showed distinct neural responses when they heard the sine-wave speech versus sounds that contained nothing hidden. The bottom line: some people are especially adept at gathering meaning from sound. They may constitute up to 15 percent of the population.[1]

This 2017 experiment, I should note, contained just a few participants (nineteen total) and has not yet been replicated. But it suggests that hearing voices need not necessarily be tied to psychosis. Indeed, an authority on the subject, Charles Fernyhough of Durham University, suggests that 1 percent of people have "more complex and extended voice hearing experiences in the absence of any need for psychiatric care."[2] Fernyhough and others advocate the concept of a *continuum of experience* along which certain people are apt to hear voices while others have other exceptional experiences. The continuum spans the gamut from completely healthy individuals to those who are schizophrenic or otherwise emotionally or mentally ill.[3]

The question then becomes: Could some portion of the population discern meaningful information that is encoded—just as the sine-wave speech was—in environmental stimuli that most other people won't apprehend? My guess is yes, and that thin-boundary people are the most likely candidates. If this is correct, it opens up the possibility that many phenomena that science tends to dismiss outright (apparitional perceptions, apparently telepathic or precognitive dreams, forms of waking ESP) may have a validity both in the manner in which they're perceived and in the external environment *through* which they're perceived. Since we are beings primed to generate, take in, and act upon emotion, it stands to reason that we are primed (some of us, anyway) to perceive messages that are emotionally resonant. Our neural and physiological apparatus certainly seems suited to a wide emotional repertoire. The same is true for our mammalian cousins and perhaps other creatures as well.

This brings us back to the original concept of wonder that opened this book. If our senses can be attuned to unanticipated influences, should not our intellects be open to them as well? Would we not benefit from putting aside the preconception that something or other is impossible? Surely the marvelous things that humans have accomplished—and continue to accomplish, technologically, in ever-surpassing fashion—should convince us that nothing is out of the question. We do ourselves a grave injustice by arbitrarily limiting our concept of what life is about, what emotions are for, and how we may be connected—in ways strange, fantastic, unforeseen, astounding, bewildering, stupendous, and ultimately meaningful—to one another and to nature, which has spawned us.

The last word here goes to journalist and animal advocate Charles Siebert. "Our human gaze has been misdirected," he points out. "We look heavenward for deliverance when deliverance comes from looking down and back into the biology from whence we came and that great symphony we're part of."[4] Perhaps emotion, in all its bodily glory and tumult, is the fundamental binding force in a more than human, more than temporal, and more than merely physical world.

Acknowledgments

Not a single idea or argument advanced in this book developed in a vacuum. I have many people to thank for offering a sounding board, constructive criticism, and, often enough, praise and encouragement that boosted my confidence. While not all of them agreed with my premises or my inferences from the evidence, collectively their reactions convinced me that the concepts had legs and were sufficiently supported rhetorically. In many cases they didn't know me from Adam when I first reached out, so I appreciate their graciousness all the more.

I wish to thank David Henry Feldman, Dean Radin, Jim Tucker, Rupert Sheldrake, Eric Leskowitz, Christine Simmonds-Moore (who did me the honor of writing the Foreword), Joanne Ruthsatz, Darold Treffert, Scott Barry Kaufman, Allan Schore, Emma Young, Maureen Seaberg, C. C. Hart, Marc Bekoff, Michael Fox, Nick Jans, Dave Abram, Jeff Kripal, John Horgan, Jonathan Balcombe, Frans de Waal, and Carl Safina. I want to provide a special shout-out to Stan Krippner and Larry Dossey, whose vast knowledge and encouragement over many years means more than they know. I also wish to thank Sy Montgomery, who lights up minds with her writing (both the minds of readers and the animals minds she sheds light on) and conveys extraordinary grace and energy in her every communication.

Sadly, several pioneering researchers passed from the scene since my last book was published in 2011—indeed, since I began my research and writing in the mid-1990s. Principal among them is Ernest Hartmann, father of the Boundaries concept. I will never forget the thrill of receiving his first message on my voice mail and then speaking with him, listening carefully to parse his Austrian-inflected English. We had many more phone and email conversations, and I got to meet him near where he lived in Newton, Massachusetts. Ernest was truly a scholar and a gentleman, a scientist and a poet. His research and writing on the subject of dreams and, later in his career, on thick and thin boundaries, has opened a remarkable door on human nature. I hope that the direction of my own work might please him and succeed in (as he elegantly stated) "extending the boundaries of Boundaries."

I likewise lament the passing of William Roll, who did as much as anyone to extend our knowledge of the poltergeist—a singularly strange phenomenon addressed in my first book, *The Spiritual Anatomy of Emotion*. I had the pleasure of sitting with Bill one afternoon in his living room in Villa Rica, Georgia, and receiving all manner of wonderful advice. His suggestions led directly to my environmental sensitivity survey and my first published paper. Bill's energy, enthusiasm, and childlike sense of wonder find, I hope, some reflection in the aims and tenor of this book.

It's important to acknowledge two men—Oliver Sacks and Jaak Panksepp—who pushed boundaries themselves so substantively and successfully in their own work. In taking the inner lives of his subjects seriously, and writing about them in such a penetrating manner, Sacks humanized the "exceptions" of everyone he profiled. While not as well-known to the public, Panksepp put the field of affective neuroscience on his shoulders and, furthermore, demonstrated that humans and other mammals have much the same capacity for feeling. I am privileged to have corresponded with both these men; their spirit, I hope, permeates this work.

I also value the key contributions of Marc Micozzi, medical editor and coauthor of my previous books. Marc's capacious knowledge and iconoclastic outlook are infectious and have helped propel this further endeavor.

I thank my agent, John White, for his wise counsel and tenacity in moving this project toward publication. At Inner Traditions, I deeply appreciate the opportunity to again work with Jon Graham on the acquisitions side, Kelly Bowen on the business side, the superb editorial quartet of Patricia Rydle, Jennie Marx, Eliza Homick, and Anne Dillon, special projects person extraordinaire Erica Robinson, and John Hays and Manzanita Carpenter Sanz in marketing.

Some related work of mine was published by *Aeon* and I thank editor Pam Weintraub. Similarly, I wish to thank John Steele and Brian Gallagher of Nautilus for publishing my essay there, as well as Michael Lemonick at *Scientific American*. Appreciation likewise goes to Patrick Huyghe of *Edge Science* and Tara MacIsaac, then of the *Epoch Times*. My psychologist friend Roy Wilensky closely reviewed chapter 1 of this book; I'm grateful for his suggestions relating to the explanations of trauma and PTSD.

April Barrett at the Jung Society of Washington has planned three events at which I've spoken. In addition to her being a pleasure to work with, I'll not forget her kind comment that were C. G. Jung alive today, he would be interested in the themes I'm exploring.

On the home front, my wife Bonnie Wald provides constant support, love, and encouragement. She is truly a "woman of valor" (to borrow a phrase from Proverbs): lovely, patient, and kind, with an internal strength that has enabled her to put up with me for many years. "Her value is far above jewels," and I treasure her as a partner and helpmate. My kids Gabrielle and Bradley have grown up at the same time as my thinking on this book's subjects has itself matured; they are a joy to behold as their unique talents and interests assert themselves. My mother, Helene Jawer, is a kind and sensitive soul herself who continues to inspire me with her gentleness combined with strength of character.

Last but not least, I would never have written the portions of this book concerning non-human animals if not for my family's experience with our own domestic critters. Chief among them are doggies Olivia and Daisy (both snoozing as I write this), and late, great kitty cats Persephone, Sally, Chauncey, Petey, and Dalton (aka His Beastliness). Each has—or had—a distinctive personality that is either active in our lives or abides in our memory. The more I learn about our animal friends, the more I appreciate their affection, funny habits, and endearing qualities.

If I have left anyone out of these acknowledgments who should have been credited, please know that the omission was inadvertent.

Notes

Introduction. At the Confluence of Science and Wonder

1. Adams, *Salmon of Doubt,* 132 (emphasis original).
2. Donald Kalsched, interviewed by David Van Nuys, Shrink Rap Radio, Episode 416, "Trauma and the Soul," August 14, 2014.
3. Michael Shermer, "Do Anomalies Prove the Existence of God?," posted on the Michael Shermer website on May 12, 2018. Originally published on the Slate website in 2015.

Chapter 1. PTSD

1. Association for Psychological Science, "Embattled Childhoods May Be the Real Trauma for Soldiers with PTSD," posted on the MedicalXpress website on November 19, 2012; Aarhus University, "War Is Not Necessarily the Cause of Post-Traumatic Stress Disorder," posted on the ScienceDaily website on August 17, 2012.
2. Stein et al., "Dissociation in Posttraumatic Stress Disorder"; Steuwe et al., "Evidence for a Dissociative Subtype of PTSD"; Lanius et al., "Emotion Modulation in PTSD"; Wolf et al., "A Latent Class Analysis of Dissociation and Posttraumatic Stress Disorder"; Wolf and Miller, "Scientists Discover Dissociative Subtype of Post-Traumatic Stress Disorder," posted on the MedicalXpress website on July 2, 2012.

3. Fontenelle et al., "Towards a Post-Traumatic Subtype of Obsessive–Compulsive Disorder"; Rodrigues, "Compulsions Can Follow Trauma"; Matthew Tull, "The Link between PTSD and OCD," posted on the Verywell Mind website, last updated November 24, 2019.

4. Hughes, "Stress."

5. Sidran Institute, "What Is Post-Traumatic Stress Disorder (PTSD)?," PDF posted on the Sidran Institute website.

6. Elaine K. Howley, "Statistics on PTSD in Veterans," posted on the US News & World Report website on January 28, 2019.

7. Matthew Tull, "An Overview of Post-Traumatic Stress Disorder," posted on the Verywell Mind website, last updated June 24, 2019.

8. Martin, *Healing Mind*; Goleman and Gurin, *Mind/Body Medicine*; latest evidence linked at the Your Emotional Type website, the "Chronic Conditions" page in the "Illness and Healing" section.

9. Wolf et al., "The Dissociative Subtype of PTSD."

10. Lanius et al., "Emotion Modulation in PTSD."

11. Craig, "Interoception."

12. Craig, "Interoception."

13. Lanius et al., "Emotion Modulation in PTSD."

14. Hölzel et al., "Mindfulness Practice Leads to Increases in Regional Brain Gray Matter Density"; Lazar et al., "Meditation Experience Is Associated with Increased Cortical Thickness."

15. Lanius et al., "Emotion Modulation in PTSD"; Frewen and Lanius, "Toward a Psychobiology of Posttraumatic Self-Dysregulation."

16. Muller, "When a Patient Has No Story to Tell."

17. MacClaren, "Emotional Disorder and the Mind-Body Problem."

18. Frewen and Lanius, "Toward a Psychobiology of Posttraumatic Self-Dysregulation."

19. Frewen et al., "Clinical and Neural Correlates of Alexithymia in Posttraumatic Stress Disorder."

20. McDougall, *Theaters of the Body,* 94, 169, 175–76.

21. Warren Zevon, "Ain't that Pretty at All," on *The Envoy* (LP) (Los Angeles and New York: Elektra/Asylum Records, 1982).

22. Sternberg, *Balance Within.*

23. Hartmann, *Boundaries in the Mind,* 4–7.

24. Kline and Rausch, "Olfactory Precipitants of Flashback."

25. Jawer and Micozzi, *Your Emotional Type,* 47.

26. Jawer and Micozzi, *Your Emotional Type,* 64.

27. Ader, quoted by Pisano in "Mind-Body Connection."

28. Goleman, *Emotional Intelligence,* 14–25.

29. Gershon, *Second Brain,* xiii; H. Brown, "The *Other* Brain," D5.

30. Maté, "The Healing Force Within."

31. Vedantam, "Variation in One Gene," A1; Dobbs, "The Science of Success."

32. O'Connor, *Undoing Perpetual Stress,* 330–32.

33. McCrae and Costa, "Conceptions and Correlates of Openness to Experience."

34. Dan Cossins, "Personality Predicts Placebo Effect," posted on The Scientist website on November 16, 2012.

35. Wurzman and Giordano, "Differential Susceptibility to Plasticity."

36. Wurzman and Giordano, "Differential Susceptibility to Plasticity."

Chapter 2. Mirror Senses

1. Osborn and Derbyshire, "Pain Sensation Evoked by Observing Injury in Others"; Body in Mind, "Stuart Derbyshire on I Feel Your Pain," posted on the Body in Mind website on January 9, 2010.

2. Banissy and Ward, "Mirror-Touch Synesthesia Is Linked with Empathy."

3. Salinas, *Mirror Touch,* 202–3.

4. Cytowic, *Man Who Tasted Shapes.*

5. Cytowic, "Synesthesia: Phenomenology and Neuropsychology."

6. Milán et al., "Auras in Mysticism and Synaesthesia."

7. Terhune, "The Incidence and Determinants of Visual Phenomenology."

8. Maureen Seaberg, "In Search of Wonder," posted on the *Psychology Today* website on May 15, 2012.

9. Simmonds-Moore, "An Interpretive Phenomenological Analysis Exploring Synesthesia," 303–27.

10. Cytowic and Eagleman, *Wednesday Is Indigo Blue,* 160–61.

11. Cytowic and Eagleman, *Wednesday Is Indigo Blue,* 159.

12. Cytowic and Eagleman, *Wednesday Is Indigo Blue,* 157.

13. Cytowic and Eagleman, *Wednesday Is Indigo Blue,* 157.

14. Cutsforth, "The Role of Emotion in a Synesthetic Subject."

15. Cytowic, *Synesthesia,* 50–51.

16. Ward, "Emotionally Mediated Synesthesia."

17. Ramachandran et al., "Colored Halos around Faces."

18. Cytowic and Eagleman, *Wednesday Is Indigo Blue,* 104; D'Andrade and Egan, "The Colors of Emotion."

19. Pam Frost Gorder, "At First Blush, You Look Happy—Or Sad, or Angry," *Ohio State News,* posted on the Ohio State University website on March 19, 2008.

20. Pam Frost Gorder, "At First Blush, You Look Happy—Or Sad, or Angry," *Ohio State News,* posted on the Ohio State University website on March 19, 2008.

21. Kreskin, *Secrets of the Amazing Kreskin,* 145.

22. Personal interview with Kreskin, April 5, 2005.

23. Maureen Seaberg, "Nurse Literally Feels Your Pain," posted on the *Psychology Today* website on October 1, 2015.

24. Banissy et al., "Enhanced Sensory Perception in Synesthesia."

25. Carol Crane interviewed on *The Diane Rehm Show,* National Public Radio (WAMU-FM), March 6, 2000; Cytowic and Eagleman, *Wednesday Is Indigo Blue,* 102.

26. Appellation coined by the author and researcher Elaine Aron, see the Highly Sensitive Person website.

27. Terhune et al., "The Induction of Synaesthesia in Non-Synaesthetes."

28. Glisky et al., "Absorption, Openness to Experience, and Hypnotizability."

29. Cardeña and Terhune, "Hypnotizability, Personality Traits."

30. Luke and Terhune, "The Induction of Synaesthesia with Chemical Agents."

31. Atwater, *Beyond the Light,* 129–32, 239–47.

32. Bonenfant, "A Comparative Study of Near-Death Experience."

33. P. M. H. Atwater, "Physiological Aftereffects of Near-Death States," PDF posted on the PMH Atwater website, http://pmhatwater.com/resources/PDFs/Articles/C-Aftereffects-Percentages-3.pdf.

34. Greyson, "Increase in Psychic Phenomena"; Sutherland, "Psychic Phenomena."

35. Atwater, *Beyond the Light,* 135–41; Ring, *Heading Toward Omega,* 236–37.

36. Jawer with Micozzi, *Spiritual Anatomy of Emotion.*

37. P. M. H. Atwater, "Electrical Sensitivity: A 2012 Update," PDF posted on the PMH Atwater website, http://pmhatwater.com/resources/PDFs/Articles/Electrical-Sensitivity-Update.pdf.

38. Nouri and Holden, "Electromagnetic Aftereffects."

39. Sacks, "A Bolt from the Blue."

40. Tony Cicoria, search on YouTube for "Lightning Sonata performance at Mozart House," posted November 7, 2013.

41. Roach, *Spook,* 204.

42. Personal interview with Tony Cicoria, April 20, 2018.

43. Tony Cicoria profiled in a story on WNYW, Fox 5-New York. Search on YouTube for "Struck by Lightning: What Is It Like?," posted on September 14, 2015.

44. Sacks, "A Bolt from the Blue."

45. Hartmann, *Boundaries: A New Way,* 6.

46. Cytowic and Eagleman, *Wednesday Is Indigo Blue,* 152–53.

47. Cytowic and Eagleman, *Wednesday Is Indigo Blue,* 153–54.

48. Cytowic and Eagleman, *Wednesday Is Indigo Blue,* 154.

49. Jawer and Micozzi, *Your Emotional Type,* 8–9.

50. G. Brown, *Energy of Life,* 15–35.

51. *American Heritage Dictionary,* 428.

52. Jawer and Micozzi, *Your Emotional Type,* 23.

53. Hartmann, *Boundaries in the Mind,* 4–7.

54. Thalbourne et al., "Transliminality, Brain Function, and Synesthesia"; Hartmann, *Boundaries: A New Way,* 11, 161.

55. American Migraine Foundation, "Migraine and Aura," posted on the American Migraine Foundation website on April 23, 2016.

56. Mark W. Green, neurologist quoted in "How Can Stress Cause Headaches?," posted on the ShareCare website.

57. Lance, *Migraines and Other Headaches,* 57.

58. Lance, *Migraines and Other Headaches,* 89.

59. Stephen Appel, "Notes on the Psychosomatic Element of Migraine," posted on the National Council of Psychotherapists (UK) website.

60. Sacks, *Migraine.*

61. Stephen Appel, "Notes on the Psychosomatic Element of Migraine," posted on the National Council of Psychotherapists (UK) website.

62. Dychtwald, *Bodymind,* xii.

63. Gershon, *Second Brain,* xiii.

64. Gershon, *Second Brain,* xiii.

65. Chris Woolston, "Gut Feelings: The Surprising Link between Mood and Digestion," posted on the Consumer HealthDay website, last updated January 1, 2020.

66. Michael John Coleman and Terri Miller Burchfield, "Migraines: Myth

vs. Reality," Migraine Awareness Group: A National Understanding for Migraineurs, posted on the Migraines.org website.

67. Melissa Conrad Stöppler, "Abdominal Migraine in Children," posted on the MedicineNet website; "What Are Abdominal Migraines?," posted on the WebMD website.

68. Goadsby, "The Vascular Theory of Migraine"; "Pathophysiology of Migraine," posted on the Migraine website.

69. "11 Reasons Why Migraines Are in the Gut," posted on the Migraine Key website; Douglas Richards and David McMillin, "Migraine: A Complementary Medicine Approach," lecture at the Meridian Institute on February 18, 1996, posted on the Meridian Institute website.

70. Levine with Frederick, *Waking the Tiger,* 68–70.

71. Craig, "Interoception."

72. Barrett et al., "Interoceptive Sensitivity and Self-Reports"; Wiens, "Interoception in Emotional Experience"; Herbert et al., "Interoceptive Sensitivity and Emotion Processing."

73. Terasawa et al., "Interoceptive Sensitivity Predicts"; Ainley et al., "Heartfelt Imitation."

74. Schneider et al., "Emotional Intelligence and Autonomic Self-Perception."

75. Katkin, "Blood, Sweat, and Tears"; Ainley and Tsakiris, "Body Conscious?"

76. Katkin, "Blood, Sweat, and Tears."

77. Irwin, "Childhood Antecedents."

78. Fraser, *Voices of Time,* 254–55.

79. A. Brown, "The Déjà Vu Illusion."

80. Tim Newman, "Déjà Vu: Reexperiencing the Unexplained," posted on the Medical News Today website on June 14, 2017.

81. Cleary et al., "Familiarity from the Configuration of Objects."

82. Melzack, "Phantom Limbs"; de Roos et al., "Treatment of Chronic Phantom Limb Pain."

83. Leskowitz, "Phantom Pain."

84. Fitzgibbon et al., "Shared Pain."

85. Thomson, "We Feel Your Pain."

86. Levine and Frederick, *Waking the Tiger,* 53–54.

87. Levine and Frederick, *Waking the Tiger,* 54.

88. Heller, *Too Loud, Too Bright, Too Fast, Too Tight,* 3; Bergman and Escalona, "Unusual Sensitivities."

89. Heller, *Too Loud, Too Bright, Too Fast, Too Tight,* 9, 146–47.

90. Goller at al., "Mirror-Touch Synesthesia."

91. Flor et al., "Phantom Limb Pain."

92. Hanley et al., "Preamputation Pain and Acute Pain."

93. J. Katz, "Psychophysiological Contributions."

94. "Alternative Treatments for Migraines and Headaches," posted on the WebMD website; Stokes and Lappin, "Neurofeedback and Biofeedback with 37 Migraineurs"; Newberg et al., "Cerebral Blood Flow Effects of Pain and Acupuncture."

95. Weiss et al., "On the Interaction of Self-Regulation."

96. "How Trauma Lodges in the Body," Krista Tippett's interview with Bessel van der Kolk, posted on the On Being website on March 9, 2017.

97. De Roos et al., "Treatment of Chronic Phantom Limb Pain."

98. Bradbrook, "Acupuncture Treatment of Phantom Limb Pain"; Jacob and Niemtzow, "Treatment of Phantom Limb Pain"; Leskowitz, "Phantom Limb Pain Treated."

99. Leskowitz, "Energy Medicine Perspectives."

100. Michael Banissy, "Some People with Synesthesia Feel Other People's Sensations of Touch—Painful and Pleasurable," posted on the Conversation website on May 21, 2018.

101. Seaberg, "Meet the Nurse."

102. Seaberg, "Meet the Nurse."

103. Torrence, "Experience."

104. Arnold, "'I Literally Feel Your Pain.'"

105. Mirror-Touch Synesthesia: Pain & Empathy, Synesthesia Test, February 2013, and later available at www.synesthesiatest.org/blog/mirror-touch-synesthesia; "I Feel Your Pain, I REALLY Do: Synesthesia for Another's Pain," posted on the Neurocritic blog, November 14, 2009, and later available at http://neurocritic.blogspot.com/2009/11/i-feel-your-pain-i-really-do.html.

106. Costandi, "Reflecting on Mirror Neurons."

107. Jarrett, "A Calm Look."

108. Torrence, "Experience."

109. Maureen Seaberg, "Bearing Witness to Mirror Touch Synesthesia," posted on the Psychology Today website on May 10, 2018.

110. Banissy et al., "Prevalence, Characteristics." For more evidence that automatic imitation is linked to self/other confusion, see Ainley et al., "Heartfelt Imitation."

111. Michael Banissy, "Some People with Synesthesia Feel Other People's

Sensations of Touch—Painful and Pleasurable," posted on the Conversation website on May 21, 2018.

112. Michael Banissy, "Some People with Synesthesia Feel Other People's Sensations of Touch—Painful and Pleasurable," posted on The Conversation website on May 21, 2018.

113. Hartmann, *Boundaries in the Mind,* 4–7, 34, 72, 225.

114. Hartmann, *Boundaries in the Mind,* 233, 241.

115. Hartmann, *Boundaries in the Mind,* 236.

116. Moseley et al., "Psychologically Induced Cooling"; Sadibolova and Longo, "Seeing the Body Produces"; Kammers et al., "Feeling Numb."

117. Wilson and Barber, "Fantasy-Prone Personality."

118. Dienstfrey, "The Aware Mind."

119. Bufalari et al., "Atypical Touch Perception."

120. "Philosophy in the Flesh: A Talk with George Lakoff," interview from March 9, 1999, posted on the Edge website.

121. Ackerman, *A Natural History of the Senses,* xix.

122. Jawer and Micozzi, *Your Emotional Type.*

123. Dienstfrey, "The Aware Mind."

124. Windbridge Institute, "Hematological and Psychophysiological Correlates of Anomalous Information Reception in Mediums," posted on the Bial Foundation website on September 22, 2015.

125. Barnsley et al., "The Rubber Hand Illusion Increases Histamine Reactivity in the Real Arm."

126. Damasio, *Feeling of What Happens,* 50.

127. Motz, *Hands of Life,* 101.

128. Motz, *Hands of Life,* 102.

129. Motz, *Hands of Life,* 103.

130. Motz, *Hands of Life,* 103.

131. Gershon, *Second Brain,* xiii.

132. Derbyshire et al., "Feeling the Pain of Others," 107.

133. Body in Mind, "Stuart Derbyshire on I Feel Your Pain," posted on the Body in Mind website on January 9, 2010.

134. Stony Brook University News, "Sensitive? Emotional? Empathetic? It Could be in Your Genes," posted on the Stony Brook University News website on June 23, 2014.

135. Aron, *Highly Sensitive Person,* 14–15.

136. Kagan and Snidman, "Temperament and a Religious Perspective."

137. Ramachandran and Rogers-Ramachandran, "Hey, Is That Me Over There?"; University College of London, "First Out-of-Body Experience Induced in Laboratory Setting," posted on the ScienceDaily website on August 24, 2007; Daniel Engber, "The Out-of-Body Electric," posted on the Slate website on August 23, 2007.

138. Blanke et al., "Linking Out-of-Body Experience and Self Processing to Mental Own-Body Imagery at the Temporoparietal Junction."

139. Hoffman, *Visions of Innocence.*

140. Daniel Engber, "The Out-of-Body Electric," posted on the Slate website on August 23, 2007.

141. Blanke and Arzy, "Out-of-Body Experience."

142. E. Young, "Researchers Have Identified."

143. Grosso, "Some Varieties."

144. Tsakiris, "The Multisensory Basis of the Self."

145. Damasio, "Mental Self."

146. Mirjam Guesgen, "Animal Pain Is About Communication, Not Just Feeling," *Aeon* digital magazine, posted on June 15, 2018.

147. Schultz, *Awakening Intuition,* 76.

148. Cytowic and Eagleman, *Wednesday Is Indigo Blue,* 246.

149. Grosso, "Some Varieties."

Chapter 3. The Resonance of Perception

1. Williams, *Nobody Nowhere,* 188.

2. Williams, *Nobody Nowhere,* 6–7, 15.

3. Williams, *Nobody Nowhere,* 3–4, 45.

4. Williams, *Nobody Nowhere,* 43.

5. Williams, *Nobody Nowhere,* 59.

6. Williams, *Nobody Nowhere,* 207.

7. Williams, *Nobody Nowhere,* 35–36, 138.

8. Williams, *Nobody Nowhere,* 158–61.

9. Williams, *Autism and Sensing,* 14–16.

10. Williams, *Autism and Sensing,* 11.

11. Williams, *Autism and Sensing,* 37.

12. Williams, *Autism and Sensing,* 36.

13. Wilson and Barber, "The Fantasy-Prone Personality."

14. Wilson and Barber, "The Fantasy-Prone Personality."

15. Maia Szalavitz, "The Boy Whose Brain Could Unlock Autism," posted on the Matter website on December 11, 2013.

16. Williams, *Autism and Sensing,* 59.

17. Williams, *Autism and Sensing,* 55.

18. Williams, *Autism and Sensing,* 56.

19. Williams, *Autism and Sensing,* 61.

20. Aron, *Highly Sensitive Child,* 4.

21. Grandin and Johnson, *Animals in Translation,* 67.

22. Williams, *Autism and Sensing,* 40–42.

23. "Why Streep Plays It Safe," *The Week,* People section, August 13, 2004, 10.

24. Joe Blevins, "I Am the President: The Rise and Fall of David Frye," posted on the Vulture website on December 8, 2015.

25. Williams, *Autism and Sensing,* 64.

26. Williams, *Autism and Sensing,* 36, 41.

27. Parra, "On the Edge of the Anomalous Experience"; Simmonds-Moore and Moore, "Exploring How Gender Role"; Rabeyron and Watt, "Paranormal Experiences"; Thalbourne and Maltby, "Transliminality, Thin Boundaries"; Parra and Argibay, "The Boundary Construct"; Parra, "Thin Boundary and Transliminality."

28. Hartmann, Harrison, and Zborowski, "Boundaries in the Mind."

29. Kreitz et al, "Some See It, Some Don't."

30. Goldhill, "Open-Minded People."

31. Ro et al., "Extrageniculate Mediation."

32. Grandin and Johnson, *Animals in Translation,* 65.

33. Williams, *Autism and Sensing,* 63.

34. Williams, *Autism and Sensing,* 37.

35. Williams, *Autism and Sensing,* 37.

36. Grandin and Johnson, *Animals in Translation,* 63.

37. Williams, *Autism and Sensing,* 36.

38. Williams, *Autism and Sensing,* 60.

39. Williams, *Autism and Sensing,* 34–35.

40. Ross and Joshi, "Paranormal Experiences"; Irwin, "Origins and Functions"; Irwin, "Childhood Antecedents"; Terr, "Childhood Traumas."

41. Irwin, "Parapsychological Phenomena."

42. Terr, "Childhood Traumas."

43. Bergman and Escalona, "Unusual Sensitivities."

44. Ring, *Omega Project,* 146.

45. Grosso, "Some Varieties."

46. Grosso, "Some Varieties."

47. Grosso, "Some Varieties."

48. Sabom, *Recollections of Death,* 161.

49. Williams, *Autism and Sensing,* 52.

50. Williams, *Autism and Sensing,* 53.

51. Williams, *Autism and Sensing,* 59.

52. Williams, *Autism and Sensing,* 94.

53. Pearsall, *Heart's Code,* 29.

54. Pearsall, *Heart's Code,* 29.

55. Maia Szalavitz, "The Boy Whose Brain Could Unlock Autism," posted on the Matter website on December 11, 2013.

56. Moody and Perry, *Reunions,* 145.

57. Gernsbacher, "Autism without Borders."

58. Williams, *Autism and Sensing,* 61.

59. de Saint Exupéry, *Little Prince.*

60. Shermer, "Demon-Haunted Brain."

Chapter 4. Unspooling the Thread

1. Jawer with Micozzi, *Spiritual Anatomy of Emotion,* 283–316.

2. Carol Crane, "Synesthesia" interview on *The Diane Rehm Show,* National Public Radio, March 6, 2000.

3. Hughes, "Sound and Touch Collide."

4. Hughes, "Sound and Touch Collide."

5. Shruti Ravindran, "A Circus of the Senses," *Aeon* digital magazine, posted on January 20, 2015.

6. Baron-Cohen, "Is There a Normal Phase of Synaesthesia in Development?"

7. University of Cambridge, "Synesthesia Is More Common in Autism," posted on the ScienceDaily website on November 19, 2013.

8. Brenda Goodman, "Study Probes Why Kids with Autism are Oversensitive to Touch, Noise," posted on the HealthDay website on May 14, 2014.

9. Hornik, "For Some, Pain Is Orange."

10. A previous study turned up almost identical findings: Harmon, "Autism Might Slow Brain's Ability to Integrate Input from Multiple Senses."

11. Smith and Gouze, *Sensory-Sensitive Child.*

12. Eide and Eide, *Mislabeled Child,* 256; Miller et al., "Quantitative Physiologic Evaluation."

13. Smith and Gouze, *Sensory-Sensitive Child,* 32–3.

14. Heller, *Too Loud, Too Bright, Too Fast, Too Tight.*

15. Personal communication with the late Jane Koomar, occupational therapist, December 21, 2007.

16. Richard Zwolinski, "Whole-Body Strategies for Autism with Dr. Martha Herbert," posted on the PsychCentral website, September 13, 2012.

17. Maia Szalavitz, "The Boy Whose Brain Could Unlock Autism," posted on the Matter website on December 11, 2013.

18. Maia Szalavitz, "The Boy Whose Brain Could Unlock Autism," posted on the Matter website on December 11, 2013.

19. Brenda Goodman, "Study Probes Why Kids with Autism are Oversensitive to Touch, Noise," posted on the HealthDay website on May 14, 2014.

20. Maia Szalavitz, "The Boy Whose Brain Could Unlock Autism," posted on the Matter website on December 11, 2013.

21. Rachel Cohen-Rottenberg, "The 'Intense World Syndrome' Theory of Autism," posted on the Shift Journal website on June 3, 2011; "Theory Finds that Individuals with Asperger's Syndrome Don't Lack Empathy," posted on the Seventh Voice website on November 16, 2013.

22. Francis and Kaufer, "Beyond Nature vs. Nurture."

23. Careaga et al., "Immune Dysfunction in Autism."

24. Peshava, "Autism's Origins"; Connors et al., "The Prenatal Environment."

25. Yong, "Maternal Antibodies Linked to Autism"; Connors, "The Prenatal Environment."

26. Braunschweig et al. "Autism-Specific Maternal Antibodies."

27. Anthes, "Are Immune System Molecules Brain Builders—and Destroyers?"

28. Personal communication with Lisa Boulanger, May 5, 2014.

29. Kuehn, "Scientists Probe Immune System's Role."

30. Bruce Goldman, "Neuroinflammation, Microglia, and Brain Health in the Balance," posted on the Scope [Stanford Medicine] website on January 10, 2013; Hughes, "Microglia."

31. Vargas et al., "Neuroglial Activation and Neuroinflammation."

32. Pardo et al., "Immunity, Neuroglia and Neuroinflammation in Autism."

33. Schwartz and Bilbo, "Sex, Glia, and Development."

34. Neimark, "Autism."

35. Grandin and Johnson, *Animals in Translation.*

36. Grandin and Johnson, *Animals in Translation,* 65.

37. "Poor Recognition of 'Self' Found in High Functioning People with Autism," posted on the Medical Xpress website on February 6, 2008.

38. "Children of Parents in Technical Jobs at Higher Risk for Autism," posted on the ScienceDaily website on May 15, 2014.

39. Hartmann et al., "Boundaries in the Mind: Past Research and Future Directions."

40. Johnson, "A Genius Explains."

41. Johnson, "A Genius Explains."

42. Scott Barry Kaufman, "Where Do Savant Skills Come From?," posted on the *Scientific American* website, *Beautiful Minds* blog on February 25, 2014.

43. "Savant Life," interview with Daniel Tammet, on the *To the Best of Our Knowledge* program on Wisconsin Public Radio on November 6, 2012.

44. Daniel Tammet, "Different Ways of Knowing," TED lecture, Long Beach, California, March 2011; "Savant Life," interview with Daniel Tammet, on the *To the Best of Our Knowledge* program on Wisconsin Public Radio on November 6, 2012.

45. "Savant Life," interview with Daniel Tammet, on the *To the Best of Our Knowledge* program on Wisconsin Public Radio on November 6, 2012.

46. Smith, "Can Synesthesia in Autism Lead to Savantism?"

47. Darold Treffert, "Savant Syndrome 2013—Myths and Realities," posted on the Agnesian Healthcare website on April 25, 2017.

48. "Darold Treffert on Extraordinary Brains," interview by Jim Fleming on the *To the Best of Our Knowledge* program on Wisconsin Public Radio on October 30, 2012.

49. "Darold Treffert on Extraordinary Brains," interview by Jim Fleming on the *To the Best of Our Knowledge* program on Wisconsin Public Radio on October 30, 2012.

50. Darold Treffert, "Savant Syndrome 2013—Myths and Realities," posted on the Agnesian Healthcare website on April 25, 2017.

51. Scott Barry Kaufman, "Where Do Savant Skills Come From?," posted on the *Scientific American* website, *Beautiful Minds* blog on February 25, 2014.

52. Darold Treffert, "Savant Syndrome 2013—Myths and Realities," posted on the Agnesian Healthcare website on April 25, 2017.

53. Cerebral lateralization theory, proposed by Norman Geschwind and Albert Galaburda, summarized in Treffert, "Savant Syndrome."

54. Darold Treffert, "The 'Acquired' Savant: 'Accidental' Genius," posted on the Agnesian Healthcare website on April 25, 2017.

55. Sacks, "A Bolt from the Blue"; *Expressions: The Art & Soul of the Southern Tier,* television program profiling Tony Cicoria on WSKG-TV, Binghamton, N.Y., broadcast on September 11, 2008.

56. Darold Treffert, "The 'Acquired' Savant: 'Accidental' Genius," posted on the Agnesian Healthcare website on April 25, 2017.

57. Darold Treffert, "Is There a Little 'Rain Man' in Each of Us?," posted on the Agnesian Healthcare website on April 25, 2017.

58. Darold Treffert, "'Ancestral' or 'Genetic' Memory: Factory Installed Software," posted on the Agnesian Healthcare website on April 25, 2017.

59. Darold Treffert, "Alonzo Clemons," posted on the Agnesian Healthcare website on April 25, 2017.

60. Cahalan, "From Mullet to Math Genius after a Concussion"; Neal Karlinsky and Meredith Frost, "Real 'Beautiful Mind': College Dropout Becomes Mathematical Genius After Mugging," posted on the *ABC News* website on April 27, 2012.

61. Darold Treffert, "'Ancestral' or 'Genetic' Memory: Factory Installed Software," posted on the Agnesian Healthcare website on April 25, 2017.

62. Scott Barry Kaufman, "Where Do Savant Skills Come From?," posted on the *Scientific American* website, *Beautiful Minds* blog on February 25, 2014.

63. Scott Barry Kaufman, "The Mind of the Prodigy," posted on the *Scientific American* website, *Beautiful Minds* blog on February 10, 2014.

64. Ruthsatz and Urbach, "Child Prodigy."

65. Scott Barry Kaufman, "The Mind of the Prodigy," posted on the *Scientific American* website, *Beautiful Minds* blog on February 10, 2014.

66. Smith, "Anxiety about Certain Things Can Be Hereditary."

67. Arielle Duhaime-Ross, "Sperm Can Pass Trauma Symptoms through Generations, Study Finds," posted on the Verge website on April 13, 2014; Gaisler-Salomon, "Inheriting Stress."

68. Callaway, "Fearful Memories Haunt Mouse Descendants."

69. Jovanovic et al., "Childhood Abuse"; Jovanovic et al., "Physiological Markers."

70. Nathanielsz, *Life in the Womb,* 24.

71. Maia Szalavitz, "The Boy Whose Brain Could Unlock Autism," posted on the Matter website on December 11, 2013.

72. Maia Szalavitz, "The Boy Whose Brain Could Unlock Autism," posted on the Matter website on December 11, 2013.

73. Annemarie Roeper, "The Emotional Needs of the Gifted Child," originally posted on the Supporting Emotional Needs of the Gifted website and reposted on the Education Oasis website.

74. Kerri Smith, "Genes Influence Emotional Memory," posted on the Bioedonline website on August 6, 2007.

75. Feldman, *Nature's Gambit,* 200.

76. Personal communications: Joanne Rutsatz of Ohio State University, June 14, 2014; Linda Silverman of the Gifted Development Center, July 18, 2014.

77. Personal interview with Joanne Rutsatz of Ohio State University, June 14, 2014.

78. Personal interview with Joanne Rutsatz of Ohio State University, June 14, 2014.

79. Janet Epping, "Autoimmune Genes Linked to Preeclampsia," posted on the Medical News Today website on February 15, 2011.

80. Catherine Paddock, "Air Traffic Pollution Linked to Increased Risk of Preeclampsia and Preterm Birth in Southern California Study," posted on the Medical News Today website on June 26, 2009.

81. Mann et al., "Pre-eclampsia, Birth Weight, and Autism Spectrum Disorders"; Walker et al., "The Role of Preeclampsia."

82. Belluck, "Study Ties Autism Risk to Creases in Placenta"; Weintraub, "A Newborn's Placenta May Reveal Autism Risk."

83. Dave Ghose, "Raising a Boy Wonder," posted on the Columbus Monthly website on February 6, 2014.

84. Joy Navan, "Touching the Mystery: Spiritually Gifted Children," posted on the Supporting Emotional Needs of the Gifted website on September 13, 2012.

85. Personal interview with Dr. Joanne Ruthsatz of Ohio State University, June 5, 2014.

86. Joy Navan, "Touching the Mystery: Spiritually Gifted Children," posted on the Supporting Emotional Needs of the Gifted website on September 13, 2012.

87. Linda Silverman, "The Moral Sensitivity of Gifted Children and the Evolution of Society," posted on the Supporting Emotional Needs of the Gifted website on September 14, 2011.

88. Personal correspondence, July 9, 2014, with Susan Daniels, Summit Center for the Gifted, Talented, and Creative.

89. Mooney, "Plastic within the Great Pacific Garbage Patch."

90. Gibson, "Change in Greta's Life."

91. Joy Navan, "Touching the Mystery: Spiritually Gifted Children," posted on the Supporting Emotional Needs of the Gifted website on September 13, 2012.

92. Linda Silverman, "The Moral Sensitivity of Gifted Children and the Evolution of Society," posted on the Supporting Emotional Needs of the Gifted website on September 14, 2011.

93. Michael Piechowski, quoted in Linda Silverman, "The Moral Sensitivity of Gifted Children and the Evolution of Society," posted on the Supporting Emotional Needs of the Gifted website on September 14, 2011.

94. Feldman, *Nature's Gambit,* 193.

95. Pearce, *Evolution's End,* 8–9.

96. Joy Navan, "Touching the Mystery: Spiritually Gifted Children," posted on the Supporting Emotional Needs of the Gifted website on September 13, 2012.

97. Feldman, *Nature's Gambit,* 195–96.

98. "Darold Treffert on Extraordinary Brains," interview by Jim Fleming on the *To the Best of Our Knowledge* program on Wisconsin Public Radio on October 30, 2012.

99. Cahalan, "From Mullet to Math Genius after a Concussion."

100. Scott Barry Kaufman, "Where Do Savant Skills Come From?," posted on the *Scientific American* website, *Beautiful Minds* blog on February 25, 2014.

101. Dossey, "Savants."

102. Cahalan, "From Mullet to Math Genius after a Concussion."

103. Stillman, *Soul of Autism.*

104. Williams, *Autism and Sensing.*

105. Rimland, "Savant Capabilities of Autistic Children."

106. Personal communication with Darold Treffert, May 4, 2014.

107. Hennacy Powell, "Autistics, Savants and Psi."

108. Jawer with Micozzi, *Spiritual Anatomy of Emotion.*

109. Chalmers, "An Interview with Matthew Manning."

110. Chalmers, "An Interview with Matthew Manning."

111. Chalmers, "An Interview with Matthew Manning."

112. Chalmers, "An Interview with Matthew Manning."

113. Ehrenwald, *ESP Experience,* 188.

114. "My Healing Journey: Matthew Manning," interview by Iain McNay for ConsciousTV, posted on YouTube on March 20, 2009.

115. Psychologist Peter Bander, originally quoted in Manning, *Link,* and then by Ehrenwald, *ESP Experience,* 185.

116. Manning, *Link,* 25.

117. Tucker, *Return to Life.*

118. "Dr. Jim Tucker Compiles Database of Past Life Memories (#239)," interview by Alex Tsakiris, posted on the Skeptiko website on February 25, 2014.

119. Lyons, "The Science of Reincarnation."

120. "Dr. Jim Tucker Compiles Database of Past Life Memories (#239)," interview by Alex Tsakiris, posted on the Skeptiko website on February 25, 2014.

121. Lyons, "The Science of Reincarnation."

122. Rufus, "Book Review: Return to Life."

123. Lyons, "The Science of Reincarnation."

124. Feldman, *Nature's Gambit,* 169; Leslie Kay Sword, "Emotional Intensity in Gifted Children," posted on the Supporting Emotional Needs of the Gifted website on September 14, 2011.

125. Daniel Strudwick, "Jim B. Tucker Tells Stories of Children Who Believe They Are Reincarnated in New Book 'Return to Life,'" posted on the News.com.au website on November 26, 2013.

126. "The Boy Who Lived Before," October Films documentary, aired on Channel 5 (UK) on September 18, 2006.

127. Blake, *Marriage of Heaven and Hell.*

128. *American Heritage Dictionary of the English Language,* 554.

129. Hillman, *Soul's Code,* 8–11.

130. Buten, *Through the Glass Wall.*

131. Katz, "Descartes' Carton—On Plausibility."

Chapter 5. Living Closer to the Bone

1. Weingarten, "Something About Harry."

2. Bekoff, *Emotional Lives of Animals,* 16.

3. Panksepp, "The Chemistry of Caring," 59.

4. Masson and McCarthy, *When Elephants Weep,* xiii.

5. Masson and McCarthy, *When Elephants Weep,* 222.

6. Krutch, *Great Chain of Life,* 106.

7. Krutch, *Best of Two Worlds,* 92–94.

8. Masson and McCarthy, *When Elephants Weep,* 223.

9. "The Science of Emotions: Jaak Panksepp at TEDx Rainier," TEDx Talks, posted on January 13, 2014.

10. Bekoff, *Emotional Lives of Animals,* 15.

11. Bekoff, *Emotional Lives of Animals,* 16.

12. Bekoff, *Emotional Lives of Animals,* 130.

13. Brandon Keim, "Being a Sandpiper," *Aeon* digital magazine, posted on July 2, 2013.

14. Goleman, *Emotional Intelligence,* 9.

15. Goleman, *Emotional Intelligence,* 10

16. Bekoff, *Emotional Lives of Animals,* 18.

17. "Profile: Irene Pepperberg & Alex," *NOVA* program, on the PBS website, posted on February 9, 2011.

18. Sources: dolphins, dogs, wolves, horses, chimpanzees—Bekoff, *Emotional Lives of Animals,* 7, 93–95, 104; baboons—Smuts, "Child of Mine," 151–53; sea lions—Bekoff, "The Emotional Lives of Animals"; parrots—"'Alex and Me': The Hidden World of Animal Minds," *Fresh Air* program on National Public Radio, aired November 12, 2008; rhinos—Bekoff, *Emotional Lives of Animals,* 113; elks—Bekoff, *Smile of a Dolphin,* 114; dogs—Bekoff, *Emotional Lives of Animals,* 9, 32, 56; monkeys—Bekoff, *Emotional Lives of Animals,* 11; falcons—Bekoff, *Emotional Lives of Animals,* 91; chickens—"The Science of Emotions: Jaak Panksepp at TEDxRainier," TEDx Talks, posted on January 13, 2014; pigs—Bekoff, *Emotional Lives of Animals,* 229; elephants—Bekoff, *Emotional Lives of Animals,* 41, 95–96; Masson and McCarthy, *When Elephants Weep,* xiv, 190; Wise, *Drawing the Line,* 164–65.

19. Brandon Keim, "Being a Sandpiper," *Aeon* digital magazine, posted on July 2, 2013; Marc Bekoff, "Empathetic Rats Save Drowning Pals Rather than Eat Chocolate," posted on the *Psychology Today* website on May 13, 2015.

20. Amanda Onion, "Studies Show Rats Enjoy Tickling," posted on the *ABC News* website on March 31, 2005; Bates, "Tickling Rats for Science."

21. "The Science of Emotions: Jaak Panksepp at TEDxRainier," TEDx Talks, posted on January 13, 2014.

22. De Waal, *Age of Empathy,* 86.

23. De Waal, *Age of Empathy,* quoting psychologist Lauren Wispé, 88.

24. De Waal, *Age of Empathy,* 92.
25. Account by de Waal, cited in Mark Rowlands, "Kindness of Beasts," *Aeon* digital magazine, posted on October 24, 2012.
26. De Waal, *Age of Empathy,* 129.
27. Bekoff, "The Emotional Lives of Animals."
28. Jessica Kinnison, "5 More Life-Saving Animals: Filippo the Dolphin, Binti Jua the Gorilla, and More," posted on the Gimundo website on February 23, 2012.
29. King, "What Binti Jua Knew."
30. Royte, "The Caged Bird Speaks"; Barbara J. King, "In 'Soul of an Octopus,' an Invertebrate Steals Our Hearts," posted on the *Cosmos & Culture* blog on the National Public Radio website on June 25, 2015.
31. Michael W. Fox, "Animal Doctor" column on the *Washington Post* website, accessed May 22, 2019.
32. Fox, "The Nature of Compassion," 178.
33. Examples of telesomatic events in Dossey, *Healing Beyond the Body,* 253–54; and Dossey, *Reinventing Medicine,* 93–94, 136–37.
34. Tara MacIsaac, "Feeling Another's Distress at a Distance: A Seemingly Psychic Connection," posted on the *Epoch Times* website on July 22, 2014.
35. Dossey, *Healing Beyond the Body,* 254.
36. Shermer, *Why People Believe Weird Things.*
37. Shermer, "Anomalous Events."
38. Marc Bekoff, "Animal Minds and the Foible of Human Exceptionalism," posted on the *Huffington Post* website on August 5, 2011; Mark Rowlands, "The Kindness of Beasts," *Aeon* digital magazine, posted on October 24, 2012.
39. Kortlandt, "Chimpanzees in the Wild," cited in Harrod, "The Case for Chimpanzee Religion"; Bill Wallauer, "Chimpanzee Central—Waterfall Displays," posted on the Jane Goodall Institute website.
40. Keim, "Chimps and the Zen of Falling Water," *Nautilus* digital magazine, posted on June 29, 2015.
41. De Waal, *Age of Empathy,* 129–30.
42. Fishbach, "Saving Valentina."
43. Tangley, "Natural Passions."
44. Andrea Turkalo, quoted in "The Secret Language of Elephants," *60 Minutes* program on *CBS News,* January 1, 2010.

45. Bradshaw, et al., "Elephant Breakdown," 807; Siebert, "An Elephant Crackup?"

46. Masson and McCarthy, *When Elephants Weep.*

47. Savage-Rumbaugh, *Kanzi,* 143–44.

48. Goodall, *Reason for Hope,* 173–74.

49. Hoffman, *Visions of Innocence.*

50. Pearce, *Magical Child;* Watson, *Lifetide,* 336–37.

51. "Jane Goodall on Chimpanzees, Language and the Soul," interview with Steve Graydanus, posted on DecentFilms.com.

52. Jeeves, "Neuroscience and the Soul."

53. Damasio, *Descartes' Error,* xvi.

54. "The Science of Emotions: Jaak Panksepp at TEDx Rainier," TEDx Talks, posted on January 13, 2014.

Chapter 6. Unimagined Sensitivities

1. Morell, *Animal Wise,* 148.

2. Morell, *Animal Wise,* 149.

3. Morell, *Animal Wise,* 149.

4. Morell, *Animal Wise,* 149.

5. Masson and McCarthy, *When Elephants Weep,* 96.

6. Morell, *Animal Wise,* 148.

7. Safina, *Beyond Words,* 69; Morell, *Animal Wise,* 149.

8. Safina, *Beyond Words,* 92.

9. Safina, *Beyond Words,* 92; "Update: Elephants who Appeared to Mourn their Human Friend Remain Protected," posted on the Canadian Broadcasting Corporation website on July 25, 2012.

10. Safina, *Beyond Words,* 93.

11. Safina, *Beyond Words,* 363–64.

12. Safina, *Beyond Words,* 364.

13. Safina, *Beyond Words,* 352–53.

14. Safina, *Beyond Words,* 355.

15. Safina, *Beyond Words,* 356.

16. Safina, *Beyond Words,* 363.

17. Safina, *Beyond Words,* 360.

18. Safina, *Beyond Words,* 361.

19. Safina, *Beyond Words,* 358–59.

20. Safina, *Beyond Words,* 357.

21. Safina, *Beyond Words,* 351.

22. Safina, *Beyond Words,* 353.

23. Safina, *Beyond Words,* 362.

24. O'Connell-Rodwell, quoted in "Can Animals Predict Disaster?," *Nature* television program aired on PBS on May 13, 2008.

25. "Eyewitness Accounts: Gehan De Silva Wijeyeratne," posted on the *Nature* program website (PBS) on June 3, 2008.

26. Safina, *Beyond Words,* 92.

27. Payne, *Silent Thunder,* 20–21; "In the Presence of Whales and Elephants," interview with Katy Payne, *On Being* with Krista Tippett program on National Public Radio, August 13, 2015.

28. Watson, *Elephantoms,* 207.

29. Jonathan Amos, "Organ Music Instills Religious Feelings," *BBC News Online,* posted September 8, 2003.

30. David Jay Brown and Rupert Sheldrake, "Unusual Animal Behavior Prior to Earthquakes: A Survey in Northwest California," posted on the Animals and Earthquakes website; Mott, Maryann, "Can Animals Sense Earthquakes?," posted on National Geographic website on November 11, 2003.

31. "Can Animals Predict Disaster?," *Nature* television program aired on PBS May 13, 2008; "Tall Tales or True?," *Nature* television program aired on PBS on June 3, 2008.

32. Jonathan Amos, "Japan Quake Heard at Edge of Space," *BBC News Online,* posted on March 10, 2013.

33. David Jay Brown and Rupert Sheldrake, "Unusual Animal Behavior Prior to Earthquakes: A Survey in Northwest California," posted on the Animals and Earthquakes website.

34. Jawer with Micozzi, *Spiritual Anatomy of Emotion.*

35. Personal correspondence, October 18, 2004.

36. Shallis, *Electric Connection.*

37. Shallis, *Electric Connection,* 32–33.

38. Shallis, *Electric Connection,* 263.

39. Murchie, *Seven Mysteries of Life,* 178–80.

40. Robin Baker, University of Manchester, as quoted by Bauer, *Science or Pseudoscience,* 130.

41. Grandin and Johnson, *Animals in Translation,* 288.

42. Tyberg and Frishman, "Animal Assisted Therapy."

43. Dosa, "A Day in the Life of Oscar the Cat"; "Cat Plays Furry Grim Reaper at Nursing Home," *Associated Press,* July 27, 2007.

44. Kathleen Doheny, "Cat's 'Sixth Sense': Predicting Death?," posted on the WebMD website on July 26, 2007.

45. Watson, *Jacobson's Organ,* 180–81.

46. Moody and Perry, *Reunions,* 137–38; Joann Austin, "Weird NJ: The Ghost of the Old Bernardsville Library," *Asbury Park Press,* November 15, 2015.

47. Storr, *Will Storr vs. The Supernatural,* 206–7, 210–11; Kowalski, *Souls of Animals,* 44.

48. Fox, "The Nature of Compassion," 178.

49. Sheldrake, *Dogs That Know.*

50. Bayliss, *Animal Ghosts.*

51. Bayliss, *Animal Ghosts,* 123.

52. "Animal Apparitions," posted on the ParaResearchers of Ontario website.

53. Bayliss, *Animal Ghosts,* 103–4.

54. Bayliss, *Animal Ghosts,* 43.

55. Vickie Snow, "Pet Ghosts: Animal Encounters from Beyond the Grave," October 1, 2006, Daily Southtown section of the *Chicago Tribune,* posted on the Mind Power News website.

56. Vickie Snow, "Pet Ghosts: Animal Encounters from Beyond the Grave," October 1, 2006, Daily Southtown section of the *Chicago Tribune,* posted on the Mind Power News website.

57. Vickie Snow, "Pet Ghosts: Animal Encounters from Beyond the Grave," October 1, 2006, Daily Southtown section of the *Chicago Tribune,* posted on the Mind Power News website.

58. "Animal Apparitions," posted on the ParaResearchers of Ontario website.

59. Jawer with Micozzi, *Spiritual Anatomy of Emotion,* 210–11.

60. Jans, *A Wolf Called Romeo,* 157–58.

61. Jans, *A Wolf Called Romeo,* 201.

62. Jans, *A Wolf Called Romeo,* 202.

63. Wood, "Bomber Down."

64. Jawer with Micozzi, *Spiritual Anatomy of Emotion.*

65. Massullo, *Ghost Studies,* 64.

66. Massullo, *Ghost Studies,* 108.

67. Van de Castle, *Our Dreaming Mind,* xix.

68. Van de Castle, *Our Dreaming Mind,* 364.

69. Van de Castle, *Our Dreaming Mind,* 368–69.

70. Dossey, *Healing Beyond the Body,* 253.

71. Tara MacIsaac, "Feeling Another's Distress at a Distance," posted on the *Epoch Times* website on July 22, 2014; "Connecting with Coincidence," interview with Bernard Beitman, aired on *Coast to Coast AM* on July 21, 2019.

72. Dossey, *Healing Beyond the Body,* 253–54.

73. Dossey, *Reinventing Medicine,* 136–37.

74. Dossey, *Healing Beyond the Body,* 254.

75. Dossey, *Healing Beyond the Body,* 254.

76. Burkeman, "Spooky! Messages from the Beyond."

77. Dossey, *Healing Beyond the Body,* 253; Schulz, *Awakening Intuition,* 75.

78. Shallis, *On Time,* 174–75.

Chapter 7. The Endurance of Emotion

1. Stevenson, *Twenty Cases Suggestive of Reincarnation.*

2. Stevenson, "Birthmarks and Birth Defects."

3. Stevenson, "Birthmarks and Birth Defects."

4. Cook et al., "A Review and Analysis of 'Unsolved' Cases of the Reincarnation Type."

5. Stevenson, "Phobias in Children."

6. Stevenson, "Phobias in Children."

7. Stevenson, "Phobias in Children."

8. Tucker, "The Case of James Leininger."

9. Dossey, "Birthmarks and Reincarnation" (italics original).

10. Keil, "Questions of the Reincarnation Type."

11. Pearsall at al., "Changes in Heart Transplant Recipients."

12. Pearsall at al., "Changes in Heart Transplant Recipients."

13. Pearsall at al., "Changes in Heart Transplant Recipients."

14. Pearsall at al., "Changes in Heart Transplant Recipients."

15. Pearsall at al., "Changes in Heart Transplant Recipients."

16. Pearsall, *Heart's Code,* 89.

17. Pearsall at al., "Changes in Heart Transplant Recipients."

18. Pearsall at al., "Changes in Heart Transplant Recipients."

19. Pearsall at al., "Changes in Heart Transplant Recipients."

20. Pearsall, *Heart's Code,* 7.

21. Personal correspondence, August 3, 2001, with Bruce Greyson, Department of Psychiatric Medicine, University of Virginia Health System.

22. L. Young, *Book of the Heart,* 95–97.

23. Pearsall, *Heart's Code,* 8.

24. Bunzel et al., "Does Changing the Heart Mean Changing Personality?"

25. L. Young, *Book of the Heart,* 93.

26. L. Young, *Book of the Heart,* 90.

27. Pearsall, *Heart's Code,* 95–97.

28. Thalbourne, "Transliminality: A Review."

29. Thalbourne et al., "Transliminality, Brain Function, and Synesthesia."

30. "Dr. Jim Tucker Compiles Database of Past Life Memories (#239)," interview by Alex Tsakiris, posted on the Skeptiko website on February 25, 2014.

31. Levine with Frederick, *Waking the Tiger,* 20.

32, Pearsall, *Heart's Code,* 179.

33. University of Michigan Health System, "Electrical Signatures of Consciousness in the Dying Brain," posted on the ScienceDaily website on August 12, 2013.

34. Baker, "Dying Patients Study Reveals 'Brain Surge' in Final Moments of Life."

35. "Dying Leaves Its Mark in the Brain," posted on *The Guardian* website on February 4, 2004.

36. Pearce, *Evolution's End,* 104.

37. "Science of the Heart: Exploring the Role of the Heart in Human Performance," posted on the HeartMath Institute website.

38. Phan et al., "Passive Transfer of Nut Allergy."

39. Robert Moody, "Bodily Changes During Abreaction."

40. Whitlock and Hynes, "Religious Stigmatization."

41. Taylor, *Natural History of the Mind,* 143.

42. Motz, *Hands of Life,* 104.

43. Levine with Frederick, *Waking the Tiger,* 182.

44. Levine with Frederick, *Waking the Tiger,* 183–84.

45. Levine with Frederick, *Waking the Tiger,* 260–61.

46. Levine with Frederick, *Waking the Tiger,* 183–84.

47. Jawer with Micozzi, *Spiritual Anatomy of Emotion.*

48. "The Paradise Syndrome," *Star Trek,* episode 58, broadcast October 4, 1968.

49. Keil and Tucker, "An Unusual Case."

50. Keil and Tucker, "An Unusual Case."

51. Benedict Carey, "The Afterlife of Near-Death," posted on the *New York Times* website on January 18, 2009.

52. Gloor et al., "The Role of Limbic Systems."

53. Damasio, *Feeling of What Happens*.

54. Kegan, *Evolving Self,* 7–8.

55. Spraggett, "Nandor Fodor: Analyst of the Unexplained."

56. Darling, *Soul Search,* 158.

Conclusion

1. "People Who 'Hear Voices' Can Detect Hidden Speech," posted on the University College of London website on August 21, 2017.

2. Charles Fernyhough, "What Kinds of People Hear Voices?," posted on the *Psychology Today* website, the *Voices Within* blog, on June 28, 2014.

3. K. Sheikh, "Do You Hear What I Hear? Auditory Hallucinations Yield Clues to Perception."

4. "Charles Siebert on Translating Nature's Symphony," *When We Talk about Animals,* episode 8, Yale University podcast, January 28, 2019.

Bibliography

Ackerman, Diane. *A Natural History of the Senses*. New York: Random House, 1990.

Adams, Douglas. *The Salmon of Doubt*. New York: Ballantine, 2003.

Ader, Robert, quoted by Marina Pisano in "Mind-Body Connection." *San Antonio News-Express*, March 21, 2004, Life section, 1.

American Heritage Dictionary of the English Language. Edited by William Morris. Boston: Houghton Mifflin, 1981.

Ainley, Vivien, Marcel Brass, and Manos Tsakiris. "Heartfelt Imitation: High Interoceptive Awareness Is Linked to Greater Automatic Imitation." *Neuropsychologia* 60, no. 1 (July 2014): 21–28.

Ainley, Vivien, Lara Maister, and Manos Tsakiris. "Heartfelt Empathy? No Association between Interoceptive Awareness, Questionnaire Measures of Empathy, Reading the Mind in the Eyes Task or the Director Task." *Frontiers in Psychology* 6, Article 554 (May 2015).

Ainley, Vivien, and Manos Tsakiris. "Body Conscious? Interoceptive Awareness, Measured by Heartbeat Perception, Is Negatively Correlated with Self-Objectification." *PLOS One,* February 6, 2013.

Anthes, Emily. "Are Immune System Molecules Brain Builders—and Destroyers?" *Scientific American,* March 3, 2008.

Arnold, Nick. "'I Literally Feel Your Pain': What Life's Like with Mirror-Touch Synesthesia." *BBC Health and Wellbeing,* September 1, 2017.

Aron, Elaine. *The Highly Sensitive Child: Helping Our Children Thrive When the World Overwhelms Them*. New York: Broadway Books, 2002.

———. *The Highly Sensitive Person: How to Thrive When the World Overwhelms You.* New York: Carol Publishing Group, 1996.

Atwater, P. M. H. *Beyond the Light: What Isn't Being Said About Near-Death Experience.* New York: Birch Lane Press, 1994.

Baker, Jordan. "Dying Patients Study Reveals 'Brain Surge' in Final Moments of Life." *Daily Telegraph* [New South Wales, Australia], June 4, 2017.

Banissy, Michael J., Roi Cohen Kadosh, Gerrit W. Maus, Vincent Walsh, and Jamie Ward. "Prevalence, Characteristics and a Neurocognitive Model of Mirror-Touch Synesthesia." *Experimental Brain Research* 198, nos. 2–3 (September 2009): 261–72.

Banissy, Michael J., Vincent Walsh, and Jamie Ward. "Enhanced Sensory Perception in Synesthesia." *Experimental Brain Research* 196, no. 4: 565–71.

Banissy, Michael J., and Jamie Ward. "Mirror-Touch Synesthesia Is Linked with Empathy." *Nature Neuroscience* 10, no. 7 (July 2007): 815–16.

Barnsley, N., J. H. McAuley, R. Mohan, A. Dey, P. Thomas, and G. I. Moseley. "The Rubber Hand Illusion Increases Histamine Reactivity in the Real Arm." *Current Biology* 21, no. 23 (December 2011): R945–46.

Baron-Cohen, Simon. "Is There a Normal Phase of Synaesthesia in Development?" *Psyche* 2, no. 27 (June 1996). Republished by the Association for the Scientific Study of Consciousness.

Barrett, Lisa Feldman, Karen S. Quigley, Eliza Bliss-Moreau, and Keith R. Aronson. "Interoceptive Sensitivity and Self-Reports of Emotional Experience." *Journal of Personality and Social Psychology* 87, no. 5 (November 2004): 684–97.

Bates, Mary. "Tickling Rats for Science." *Wired,* September 9, 2013.

Bauer, Henry H. *Science or Pseudoscience.* Urbana and Chicago, Ill.: University of Chicago Press, 2001.

Bayliss, Raymond. *Animal Ghosts.* New York: University Books, 1970.

Bekoff, Marc. "The Emotional Lives of Animals." *YES! Magazine,* March 2, 2011.

———. *The Emotional Lives of Animals.* Novato, Calif.: New World Library, 2007.

———, ed. *The Smile of a Dolphin: Remarkable Accounts of Animal Emotions.* New York: Discovery Books, 2000.

Belluck, Pam. "Study Ties Autism Risk to Creases in Placenta." *New York Times,* April 25, 2013.

Bergman, Paul, and Sibylle K. Escalona. "Unusual Sensitivities in Very Young Children." *The Psychoanalytic Study of the Child* 3, no. 4 (1949): 333–52.

Blake, William. *The Marriage of Heaven and Hell.* 1790.

Blanke, Olaf, and Shahar Arzy. "The Out-of-Body Experience: Disturbed Self-Processing at the Temporo-Parietal Junction." *The Neuroscientist* 11, no. 1 (February 2005): 16–24.

Blanke, Olaf, Christine Mohr, Christophe M. Michel, Alvaro Pascual-Leone, Peter Brugger, Margitta Seeck, Theodor Landis, and Gregor Thut. "Linking Out-of-Body Experience and Self Processing to Mental Own-Body Imagery at the Temporoparietal Junction." *Journal of Neuroscience* 15, no. 3 (January 19, 2005): 550–57.

Bonenfant, Richard J. "A Comparative Study of Near-Death Experience and Non-Near-Death Experience Outcomes in 56 Survivors of Clinical Death." *Journal of Near-Death Studies* 22, no. 3 (Spring 2004): 155–78.

Bradbrook, David. "Acupuncture Treatment of Phantom Limb Pain and Phantom Limb Sensation in Amputees." *Acupuncture in Medicine* 22, no. 2 (June 2004): 93–97.

Bradshaw, G. A., Allan N. Schore, Janine L. Brown, Joyce H. Poole, and Cynthia J. Moss. "Elephant Breakdown." *Nature* 433 (Feb. 24, 2005).

Braunschweig, D., P. Krakowiak, P. Duncanson, R. Boyce, R. L. Hansen, P. Ashwood, I. Hertz-Picciotto, I. N. Pessah, and J. Van de Water. "Autism-Specific Maternal Autoantibodies Recognize Critical Proteins in Developing Brain." *Translational Psychiatry* 3, e277 (2013).

Brown, Alan S. "The Déjà Vu Illusion." *Current Directions in Psychological Science* 13, no. 6 (December 2004): 256–59.

Brown, Guy. *The Energy of Life.* New York: The Free Press, 1999.

Brown, Harriett. "The *Other* Brain, the One with Butterflies, Also Deals with Many Woes." *New York Times,* August 23, 2005, D5.

Bufalari, Ilaria, Guiseppina Porciello, and Salvatore Maria Aglioti. "Atypical Touch Perception in MTS May Derive from an Abnormally Plastic Self-Representation." *Cognitive Neuroscience* 6, nos. 2–3 (June 2015): 139–40.

Bunzel, B., S. Schmidl-Mohl, A. Grundböck, and G. Wollenek. "Does Changing the Heart Mean Changing Personality? A Retrospective Inquiry on 47 Heart Transplant Patients." *Quality of Life Research* 1, no. 4 (August 1992): 251–56.

Burkeman, Oliver. "Spooky! Messages from the Beyond or Just Coincidence?" *The Guardian,* June 17, 2016.

Buten, Howard. *Through the Glass Wall.* New York: Bantam Books, 2004.

Cahalan, Susannah. "From Mullet to Math Genius After a Concussion." *New York Post,* April 20, 2014.

Callaway, Ewen. "Fearful Memories Haunt Mouse Descendants." *Nature,* December 1, 2013.

Cardeña, Etzel, and Devin B. Terhune. "Hypnotizability, Personality Traits, and the Propensity to Experience Alterations of Consciousness." *Psychology of Consciousness: Theory, Research, and Practice* 1 (2014): 292–307.

Careaga, Milo, Judy Van de Water, and Paul Ashwood. "Immune Dysfunction in Autism: A Pathway to Treatment." *Neurotherapeutics* 7 (July 2010): 283–92.

Chabris, Christopher, and Daniel Simons. *The Invisible Gorilla: and Other Ways Our Intuitions Deceive Us.* New York: Crown, 2010.

Chalmers, Robert. "An Interview with Matthew Manning: Poltergeist Boy." *British GQ,* May 8, 2014.

Cleary, Anne M., Alan S. Brown, Benjamin D. Sawyer, Jason S. Nomi, Adaeze C. Ajoku, and Anthony J. Ryals. "Familiarity from the Configuration of Objects in 3-Dimensional Space and Its Relation to Déjà Vu: A Virtual Reality Investigation." *Consciousness and Cognition* 21, no. 2 (June 2012): 969–75.

Connors, Susan L., Carlos A. Pardo, and Andrew W. Zimmerman. "The Prenatal Environment and Neuroinflammation in Autism." *Autism Advocate,* 5th edition, Autism Society, 2006.

Cook, Emily Williams, Satwant Pasricha, Godwin Samararatne, U Win Muang, and Ian Stevenson. "A Review and Analysis of 'Unsolved' Cases of the Reincarnation Type: II. A Comparison of Features of Solved and Unsolved Cases." *Journal of the American Society for Psychical Research* 77 (1983): 115–35.

Costandi, Mo. "Reflecting on Mirror Neurons." *The Guardian,* August 23, 2013.

Craig, A. D. "Interoception: The Sense of the Physiological Condition of the Body." *Current Opinion on Neurobiology* 13 (2003): 500–505.

Cutsforth, T. D. "The Role of Emotion in a Synesthetic Subject." *American Journal of Psychology* 36 (1925): 527–43.

Cytowic, Richard. *The Man Who Tasted Shapes.* New York: Jeremy P. Tarcher/ Putnam, 1993.

———. "Synesthesia: Phenomenology and Neuropsychology: A Review of Current Literature." *Psyche* 2, no. 10 (July 1995).

———. *Synesthesia: A Union of the Senses.* New York: Springer, 1999.

Cytowic, Richard E., and David M. Eagleman. *Wednesday Is Indigo Blue: Discovering the Brain of Synesthesia*. Cambridge, Mass.: The MIT Press, 2009.

Damasio, Antonio R. *Descartes' Error: Emotion, Reason and the Human Brain*. New York: G. P. Putnam's Sons, 1994.

————. *The Feeling of What Happens: Body and Emotion in the Making of Consciousness*. New York: Harcourt, Brace & Co., 1999.

————. "Mental Self: The Person Within." *Nature* 423, no. 227 (May 15, 2003).

D'Andrade, R., and M. Egan. "The Colors of Emotion." *American Ethologist* 1 (February 1974): 49–63.

Darling, David. *Soul Search: A Scientist Explores the Afterlife*. New York: Villard Books, 1995.

Derbyshire, Stuart W. G., Jody Osborn, and Steven Brown. "Feeling the Pain of Others Is Associated with Self-Other Confusion and Prior Pain Experience." *Frontiers in Human Neuroscience* 7, article 470 (August 2013): 1–7.

de Roos, Carlijn, A. C. Veenstra, Ad de Jongh, Margien Den Hollander-Gijsman, Nic J. A. van der Wee, F. G. Zitman, and Yonda van Rood. "Treatment of Chronic Phantom Limb Pain Using a Trauma-Focused Psychological Approach." *Pain Research and Management* 15, no. 2 (March/April 2010): 65–71.

Deroy, Ophelia, ed. *Sensory Blending: On Synaesthesia and Other Phenomena*. Oxford, UK: Oxford University Press, 2017.

de Saint Exupéry, Antoine. *The Little Prince*. Translated by Richard Howard. New York: Houghton Mifflin Harcourt, 2000.

de Waal, Frans. *The Age of Empathy: Nature's Lessons for a Kinder Society*. Toronto: McClelland & Stewart, 2009.

Dienstfrey, Harris. "The Aware Mind." *Noetic Sciences Review* 21 (1992).

Dobbs, David. "The Science of Success." *The Atlantic,* December 2009.

Dosa, David M. "A Day in the Life of Oscar the Cat." *New England Journal of Medicine* 357, no. 4 (July 26, 2007): 328–32.

Dossey, Larry. "Birthmarks and Reincarnation." *Explore* 11, no. 1 (January–February 2015): 1–4.

————. *Healing Beyond the Body*. Boston: Shambhala, 2001.

————. *Reinventing Medicine*. New York: HarperSanFrancisco, 1999.

————. "Savants: What They Can Teach Us." *Explore: The Journal of Science and Healing* 8, no. 4 (July 2012): 213–17.

Dychtwald, Ken. *Bodymind*. Los Angeles: Jeremy P. Tarcher, 1977.

Ehrenwald, Jan. *The ESP Experience: A Psychiatric Validation*. New York: Basic Books, 1978.

Eide, Brock, and Fernette Eide. *The Mislabeled Child*. New York: Penguin, 2005.

Feldman, David Henry. *Nature's Gambit: Child Prodigies and the Development of Human Potential*. New York: Basic Books, 1986.

Fishbach, Michael. "Saving Valentina: A Humpback's Tale." Video produced by Great Whale Conservancy, 2011.

Fitzgibbon, Bernadette M., Melita J. Giummarra, Nellie Georgiou-Karistianis, Peter G. Enticott, and John L. Bradshaw. "Shared Pain: From Empathy to Synaesthesia." *Neuroscience and Biobehavioral Reviews* 34, no. 4 (March 2010): 500–512.

Flor, Herta, Lone Nikolajsen, and Troels Staehelin Jensen. "Phantom Limb Pain: A Case of Maladaptive CNS Plasticity?" *Nature Reviews Neuroscience* 7, no. 11 (November 2006): 873–81.

Fontenelle, L. F., L. Cocchi, B. J. Harrison, R. G. Shavitt, M. Conceição do Rosário, Y. A. Ferrão, and M. A. de Mathis, et al. "Towards a Post-Traumatic Subtype of Obsessive–Compulsive Disorder." *Journal of Anxiety Disorders* 26, no. 2 (March 2012): 377–83.

Fox, Michael W. "The Nature of Compassion." In *The Smile of a Dolphin*, edited by Marc Bekoff. New York: Discovery Books, 2000.

Francis, Darlene, and Daniela Kaufer. "Beyond Nature vs. Nurture." *The Scientist*, Oct. 1, 2011.

Fraser, J. T., ed. *The Voices of Time*. New York: George Brazillier Inc., 1966.

Frewen, P. A., and R. A. Lanius. "Toward a Psychobiology of Posttraumatic Self-Dysregulation." *Annals of the New York Academy of Sciences* 1071 (2006): 110–24.

Frewen, P. A., R. A. Lanius, D. J. A. Dozois, W. J. Neufeld, C. Pain, J. W. Hopper, and M. Densmore. "Clinical and Neural Correlates of Alexithymia in Posttraumatic Stress Disorder." *Journal of Abnormal Psychology* 117, no. 1 (2008): 171–81.

Gaisler-Salomon, Inna. "Inheriting Stress." *New York Times*, March 7, 2014.

Gernsbacher, Morton Ann. "Autism without Borders." *Nature Medicine* 14, no. 3 (2008): 241.

Gershon, Michael. *The Second Brain: The Scientific Basis of Gut Instinct*. New York: HarperCollins, 1998.

Geschwind, Norman, and Albert M. Galaburda. *Cerebral Dominance: The Biological Functions.* Cambridge, Mass.: Harvard University Press, 1988.

Gibson, Caitlin. "The Change in Greta's Life." *Washington Post*, March 17, 2020, C1.

Glisky, Martha L., Douglas J. Tataryn, Betsey A. Tobias, John F. Kihlstrom, and Kevin M. McConkey. "Absorption, Openness to Experience, and Hypnotizability." *Journal of Personality and Social Psychology* 60, no. 2 (February 1991): 263–72.

Gloor, Pierre, André Olivier, Luis F. Quesney, Frederick Andermann, and Sandra Horowitz. "The Role of Limbic Systems in Experiential Phenomena of Temporal Lobe Epilepsy." *Annals of Neurology* 12, no. 2 (August 1982): 129–44.

Goadsby, Peter J. "The Vascular Theory of Migraine—A Great Story Wrecked by the Facts." *Brain* 132, no. 1 (January 2009): 6–7.

Goldhill, Olivia. "Open-Minded People Have a Different Visual Perception of Reality." *Quartz,* June 4, 2017.

Goleman, Daniel. *Emotional Intelligence: Why It Can Matter More than IQ.* New York: Bantam Books, 1995.

Goleman, Daniel, and Joel Gurin, eds. *Mind/Body Medicine: How to Use Your Mind for Better Health.* Yonkers, N.Y.: Consumers Union, 1993.

Goller, Aviva I., Kerrie Richards, Steven Novak, and Jamie Ward. "Mirror-Touch Synesthesia in the Phantom Limbs of Amputees." *Cortex* 49, no. 1 (January 2013): 243–51.

Goodall, Jane. *Reason for Hope: A Spiritual Journey.* New York: Warner, 2000.

Grandin, Temple, and Catherine Johnson. *Animals in Translation.* New York: Scribner, 2005.

Greyson, Bruce. "Increase in Psychic Phenomena Following Near-Death Experiences." *Theta* 11, no. 2 (Summer 1983): 26-29.

Grosso, Michael. "Some Varieties of Out-of-Body Experience." In *Mind Beyond the Body: The Mystery of ESP Projection,* edited by D. Scott Rogo, 52–69. New York: Penguin Books, 1978.

Hanley, Marisol A., Mark P. Jensen, Douglas G. Smith, Dawn M. Ehde, W. Thomas Edwards, and Lawrence R. Robinson. "Preamputation Pain and Acute Pain Predict Chronic Pain After Lower Extremity Amputation." *The Journal of Pain* 8, no. 2 (February 2007): 102–9.

Harmon, Katherine. "Autism Might Slow Brain's Ability to Integrate Input from Multiple Senses." *Scientific American,* August 21, 2010.

Harrod, James B. "The Case for Chimpanzee Religion." *Journal for the Study of Religion Nature and Culture* 8, no. 1 (June 2014): 8–45.

Hartmann, Ernest. *Boundaries: A New Way to Look at the World.* Summerland, Calif.: CIRCC EverPress, 2011.

———. *Boundaries in the Mind: A New Dimension of Personality.* New York: Basic Books, 1991.

Hartmann, Ernest, Robert Harrison, and Michael Zborowski. "Boundaries in the Mind: Past Research and Future Directions." *North American Journal of Psychology* 3 (June 2001): 347–68.

Heller, Sharon. *Too Loud, Too Bright, Too Fast, Too Tight.* New York: Harper Collins, 2002.

Hennacy Powell, Diane. "Autistics, Savants and Psi: A Radical Theory of Mind." *Edge Science* 23 (September 2015): 12–18.

Herbert, Beate M., Olga Pollatos, and Rainer Schandry. "Interoceptive Sensitivity and Emotion Processing: An EEG Study." *International Journal of Psychophysiology* 65, no. 3 (September 2007): 214–27.

Hillman, James. *The Soul's Code.* New York: Random House, 1996.

Hoffman, Edward. *Visions of Innocence.* Boston and London: Shambhala, 1992.

Hölzel, Britta K., James Carmody, Mark Vangel, Christina Congolton, Sita M. Yerramsetti, Tim Gard, and Sara W. Lazar. "Mindfulness Practice Leads to Increases in Regional Brain Gray Matter Density." *Psychiatry Research: Neuroimaging* 191, no. 1 (January 30, 2011): 36-43.

Hornik, Susan. "For Some, Pain Is Orange." *Smithsonian,* February 2001, 48–56.

Hughes, Virginia. "Microglia: The Constant Gardeners." *Nature* 30 (May 2012).

———. "Sound and Touch Collide." *Nautilus* digital magazine, February 6, 2014.

———. "Stress: The Roots of Resilience." *Nature* 490 (October 11, 2012): 165–67.

Irwin, Harvey J. "Childhood Antecedents of Out-of-Body and Déjà Vu Experiences." *Journal of the American Society for Psychical Research* 90, no. 3 (July 1996): 157–72.

———. "Origins and Functions of Paranormal Belief: The Role of Childhood Trauma and Interpersonal Control." *Journal of the American Society for Psychical Research* 86, no. 3 (1992): 199–208.

———. "Parapsychological Phenomena and the Absorption Domain." *Journal of the American Society for Psychical Research* 79, no. 1 (1985): 1–11.

Jacob, Michael Bradley, and Richard C. Niemtzow. "Treatment of Phantom Limb Pain with Laser and Needle Auricular Acupuncture: A Case Report." *Medical Acupuncture* 23, no. 1 (March 2011): 57–60.

Jans, Nick. *A Wolf Called Romeo.* Boston/New York: Houghton Mifflin Harcourt, 2014.

Jarrett, Christian. "A Calm Look at the Most Hyped Concept in Neuroscience—Mirror Neurons." *Wired,* December 13, 2013.

Jawer, Michael A., and Marc S. Micozzi. *Your Emotional Type.* Rochester, Vt.: Healing Arts Press, 2011.

Jawer, Michael A., with Marc S. Micozzi. *The Spiritual Anatomy of Emotion.* Rochester, Vt.: Park Street Press, 2009.

Jeeves, Malcolm, "Neuroscience and the Soul." Forum cosponsored by the Woodstock Theological Center and the Georgetown University Center for the Study of Science and Religion. *Woodstock Report,* no. 53 (March 1998).

Johnson, Richard. "A Genius Explains." *The Guardian,* February 11, 2005.

Jovanovic, Tanja, N. Q. Blanding, S. D. Norrholm, E. Duncan, B. Bradley, and K. J. Ressler. "Childhood Abuse Is Associated with Increased Startle Reactivity in Adulthood." *Depression and Anxiety* 26, no. 11: 1018–26.

Jovanovic, Tanja, A. Smith, A. Kamkwalala, J. Poole, T. Samples, S. D. Norrholm, K. J. Ressler, and B. Bradley. "Physiological Markers of Anxiety Are Increased in Children of Abused Mothers." *Journal of Child Psychological and Psychiatry* 52, no. 8: 844–52.

Kagan, Jerome, and Nancy Snidman. "Temperament and a Religious Perspective." *APS Observer* 18, no. 10 (October 2005).

Kammers, Marjolein P. M., Katy Rose, and Patrick Haggard. "Feeling Numb: Temperature, but Not Thermal Pain, Modulates Feeling of Body Ownership." *Neuropsychologia* 49, no. 5 (April 2011): 1316–21.

Katkin, Edward S. "Blood, Sweat, and Tears: Individual Differences in Autonomic Self-Perception." *Psychophysiology* 22, no. 2 (March 1985): 125–37.

Katz, David L. "Descartes' Carton—On Plausibility." *Explore: The Journal of Science and Healing* 6, no. 5 (September/October 2010): 288–89.

Katz, Joel. "Psychophysiological Contributions to Phantom Limbs." *Canadian Journal of Psychiatry* 37, no. 5 (July 1992): 282–98.

Kegan, Robert. *The Evolving Self.* Cambridge, Mass.: Harvard University Press, 1982.

Keil, H. H. Jürgen. "Questions of the Reincarnation Type." *Journal of Scientific Exploration* 24, no. 1 (Spring 2010): 79–99.

Keil, H. H. Jürgen, and Jim B. Tucker. "An Unusual Case Thought to be Linked to a Person Who Had Previously Died." *Psychological Reports* 87 (2000): 1067–74.

King, Barbara J. "What Binti Jua Knew." *Washington Post*, August 15, 2008.

Kline, Neil A., and Jeffrey Rausch. "Olfactory Precipitants of Flashback in Posttraumatic Stress Disorder: Case Reports." *Journal of Clinical Psychiatry* 67 (9) (September 1985): 383–84.

Kortlandt, Adriann. "Chimpanzees in the Wild." *Scientific American* 206 (May 1962): 128–38.

Kowalski, Gary. *The Souls of Animals*. Novato, Calif.: New World Library, 1991.

Kreitz, Carina, Robert Schnuerch, Henning Gibbons, and Daniel Memmert. "Some See It, Some Don't: Exploring the Relation between Inattentional Blindness and Personality Factors." *PLOS One,* May 26, 2015.

Kreskin. *Secrets of the Amazing Kreskin*. Buffalo, N.Y.: Prometheus Books, 1991.

Krutch, Joseph Wood. *The Best of Two Worlds*. New York: William Sloan Associates, 1950.

———. *The Great Chain of Life*. Boston: Houghton Mifflin, 1956.

Kuehn, Bridget M. "Scientists Probe Immune System's Role in Brain Function and Neurological Disease." *Journal of the American Medical Association* 299, no. 6: 619–20.

Lance, James W. *Migraines and Other Headaches*. East Roseville, New South Wales, Australia: Simon and Schuster, 1998.

Lanius, R. A., E. Vermetten, R. J. Loewenstein, et al. "Emotion Modulation in PTSD: Clinical and Neurobiological Evidence for a Dissociative Subtype." *American Journal of Psychiatry* 167, no. 6 (June 2010): 640–47.

Lazar, Sara W., Catherine E. Kerr, Rachel H. Wasserman, et al. "Meditation Experience is Associated with Increased Cortical Thickness." *NeuroReport* 16, no. 17 (November 28, 2005): 1893-97.

Leskowitz, Eric. "Energy Medicine Perspectives on Phantom-Limb Pain." *Alternative and Complementary Therapies* 15, no. 2 (April 2009): 59–63.

———. "Phantom Limb Pain Treated with Therapeutic Touch: A Case Report." *Archives of Physical Medicine and Rehabilitation* 81, no. 4 (April 2000): 522–24.

———. "Phantom Pain: Subtle Energy Perspectives." *Subtle Energies and Energy Medicine* 8, no. 2 (2001): 125–52.

Levine, Peter, with Ann Frederick. *Waking the Tiger, Healing Trauma.* Berkeley, Calif.: North Atlantic Books, 1997.

Luke, David P., and Devin B. Terhune. "The Induction of Synaesthesia with Chemical Agents: A Systematic Review." *Frontiers in Psychology* 4 (October 2013): Article 753 (pages 1–12).

Lyons, Sean. "The Science of Reincarnation." *University of Virginia Magazine,* Winter 2013.

MacClaren, Kym. "Emotional Disorder and the Mind-Body Problem: A Case Study of Alexithymia." *Chiasmi International: Trilingual Studies Concerning Merleau-Ponty's Thought* 8 (2007): 139–55.

Mann, J. R., S. McDermott, H. Bao J. Hardin, and A. Gregg. "Pre-eclampsia, Birth Weight, and Autism Spectrum Disorders." *Journal of Autism and Developmental Disorders* 40, no. 5 (May 2010): 548–54.

Manning, Matthew. *The Link.* New York: Holt, Reinhart and Winston, 1975.

Martin, Paul. *The Healing Mind: The Vital Links between Brain and Behavior, Immunity and Disease.* New York: St. Martin's Press, 1997.

Masson, Jeffrey Moussaieff, and Susan McCarthy. *When Elephants Weep.* New York: Delacorte Press, 1995.

Massullo, Brandon. *The Ghost Studies.* Wayne, N. J.: New Page Books, 2017.

Maté, Gabor. "The Healing Force Within." *Vancouver Sun,* April 8, 2003.

McCrae, Robert R., and Paul T. Costa. "Conceptions and Correlates of Openness to Experience." In *Handbook of Personality Psychology,* edited by R. Hogan, J. A. Johnson, and S. R. Briggs, 825–47. Orlando, Fla.: Academic Press, 1997.

McDougall, Joyce. *Theaters of the Body: A Psychoanalytic Approach to Psychosomatic Illness.* New York: Norton, 1989.

Melzack, Ronald. "Phantom Limbs." *Scientific American* 266, no. 4 (April 1992): 120–26. Available online at the *Scientific American* website (updated 2006).

Milán, E. G., O. Iborra, M. Hochel, M. A. Rodríguez Artacho, L. C. Delgado-Pastor, E. Salazar, and A. González-Hernández. "Auras in Mysticism and Synaesthesia: A Comparison." *Consciousness and Cognition* 21, no. 1 (March 2012): 258–68.

Miller, L.J., S. Schoen, J. Coll, B. Brett-Green, and M. Real. (2005). "Quantitative Physiologic Evaluation of Sensory Processing in Children with Autism Spectrum Disorders: A Final Report for Cure Autism Now," February 2005.

Moody, Raymond, and Paul Perry. *Reunions: Visionary Encounters with Departed Loved Ones.* New York: Villard Books, 1993.

Moody, Robert L. "Bodily Changes During Abreaction." *Lancet* 248, no. 6435 (December 28, 1946): 934–35.

Mooney, Chris. "Plastic within the Great Pacific Garbage Patch Is 'Increasing Exponentially,' Scientists Find." *Washington Post,* March 22, 2018.

Morell, Virginia. *Animal Wise: The Thoughts and Emotions of Our Fellow Creatures.* New York: Crown, 2013.

Moseley, G. Lorimer, Nick Olthof, Annemeike Venema, Sanneke Don, Marijke Wijers, Alberto Gallace, and Charles Spence. "Psychologically Induced Cooling of a Specific Body Part Caused by the Illusory Ownership of an Artificial Counterpart." *Proceedings of the National Academy of Sciences* 105, no. 35 (September 2, 2008): 13169–73.

Motz, Julie. *Hands of Life.* New York: Bantam Books, 1998.

Muller, René. "When a Patient Has No Story to Tell: Alexithymia." *Psychiatric Times* 17 (July 2000): 71–72.

Murchie, Guy. *The Seven Mysteries of Life.* Boston: Houghton Mifflin Co., 1978.

Nathanielsz, Peter W. *Life in the Womb: The Origin of Health and Disease.* Ithaca, N.Y.: Promethean Press, 1999.

Neimark, Jill. "Autism: It's Not Just in the Head." *Discover,* April 2007, 33–38, 75.

Newberg Andrew B., Patrick J. Lariccia, Bruce Y. Lee, John T. Farrar, Lorna Lee, and Abass Alavi. "Cerebral Blood Flow Effects of Pain and Acupuncture: A Preliminary Single-Photon Emission Computed Tomography Imaging Study. *Journal of Neuroimaging* 15, no. 1 (January 2005): 43–49.

Nouri, Farnoosh (Faith), and Janice Miner Holden. "Electromagnetic Aftereffects of Near-Death Experiences." *Journal of Near-Death Studies* 27, no. 2 (Winter 2008): 83–109.

O'Connor, Richard. *Undoing Perpetual Stress.* New York: Berkley Books, 2005.

Osborn, Jody, and Stuart W. G. Derbyshire. "Pain Sensation Evoked by Observing Injury in Others." *Pain* 148, no. 2 (February 2010): 268–74.

Panksepp, Jaak. "The Chemistry of Caring." In *The Smile of a Dolphin: Remarkable Accounts of Animal Emotions,* edited by Marc Bekoff. New York: Discovery Books, 2000.

Pardo, Carlos A., Diana L. Vargas, and Andrew W. Zimmerman. "Immunity, Neuroglia and Neuroinflammation in Autism." *International Review of Psychiatry* 17, no. 6 (December 2005): 485–95.

Parra, Alejandro. "On the Edge of the Anomalous Experience: Out of Body

Experiences, Transliminality and 'Thin' Boundaries." *International Journal of Neurology Research* 1, no. 1 (January 2015): 8–13.

———. "Thin Boundary and Transliminality in Relation with Apparitional Experiences and Sense of Presence." *Pensamiento Psicológico* 15, no. 1 (January–June 2017): 103–14.

Parra, Alejandro, and Juan Carlos Argibay. "The Boundary Construct and Anomalous Experiences in Psychics." *Journal of the Society for Psychical Research* 80, no. 1 (January 2016).

Payne, Katy. *Silent Thunder: In the Presence of Elephants*. New York: Simon & Schuster, 1998.

Pearce, Joseph Chilton. *Evolution's End: Claiming the Potential of Our Intelligence*. New York: HarperSanFrancisco, 1992.

———. *Magical Child: Rediscovering Nature's Plan for Our Children*. New York: Bantam Books, 1977.

Pearsall, Paul. *The Heart's Code*. New York: Broadway Books, 1998.

Pearsall, Paul, Gary E. R. Schwartz, and Linda G. S. Russek. "Changes in Heart Transplant Recipients that Parallel the Personalities of their Donors." *Journal of Near-Death Studies* 20, no. 3 (Spring 2002): 191–206.

Peshava, Katerina. "Autism's Origins: Mother's Antibody Production May Affect Fetal Brain." *The Gazette* [Johns Hopkins University] 37, no. 24 (March 3, 2008).

Phan, Tri Giang, Simone I. Strasser, David Koorey, G. W. McCaughan, J. Rimmer, H. Dunckley, L. Goddard, and S. Adelstein. "Passive Transfer of Nut Allergy after Liver Transplantation." *Archives of Internal Medicine* 163, no. 2 (January 27, 2003): 237–39.

Rabeyron, Thomas, and Carolyn Watt. "Paranormal Experiences, Mental Health and Mental Boundaries, and Psi." *Personality and Individual Differences* 40, no. 4 (March 2010): 487–92.

Ramachandran, Vilayanur S., Luke Miller, Margaret S. Livingstone, and David Brang. "Colored Halos around Faces and Emotion-Evoked Colors: A New Form of Synesthesia." *Neurocase* 18, no. 4 (November 2011): 352–58.

Ramachandran, Vilayanur S., and Diane Rogers-Ramachandran. "Hey, Is That Me Over There?" *Scientific American*, May 1, 2010.

Rimland, Bernard. "Savant Capabilities of Autistic Children and Their Cognitive Implications." In *Cognitive Defects in the Development of Mental Illness,* edited by G. Serban. New York: Brunner/Mazel, 1978.

Ring, Kenneth. *Heading Toward Omega.* New York: William Morrow and Company, 1984.

———. *The Omega Project.* New York: Quill/William Morrow, 1992.

Ro, T., D. Shelton, O. Lee et al. "Extrageniculate Mediation of Unconscious Vision in Transcranial Magnetic Stimulation-induced Blindsight." *Proceedings of the National Academy of Sciences* 101 (2004): 9933–35.

Roach, Mary. *Spook.* New York: W. W. Norton and Company, 2005.

Rodrigues, Tori. "Compulsions Can Follow Trauma." *Scientific American* website, posted September 1, 2012.

Rogo, D. Scott, ed. *Mind Beyond the Body: The Mystery of ESP Projection.* New York: Penguin Books, 1978.

Ross, Colin A., and Shaun Joshi. "Paranormal Experiences in the General Population." *Journal of Nervous and Mental Disease* 180, no. 6 (1992): 357–61.

Royte, Elizabeth. "The Caged Bird Speaks." *New York Times,* November 9, 2008.

Rufus, Anneli. "Book Review: Return to Life." *Spirituality & Health,* November–December 2013.

Ruthsatz, Joanne, and Jordan B. Urbach. "Child Prodigy: A Novel Cognitive Profile Places Elevated General Intelligence, Exceptional Working Memory and Attention to Detail at the Root of Prodigiousness." *Intelligence* 40, no. 5 (September–October 2012): 419–42.

Sabom, Michael. *Recollections of Death: A Medical Investigation.* New York: Harper & Row, 1982.

Sacks, Oliver. "A Bolt from the Blue." *The New Yorker,* July 23, 2007.

———. *Migraine.* Berkeley, Calif.: University of California Press, 1992.

Sadibolova, Renata, and Matthew Longo. "Seeing the Body Produces Limb-Specific Modulation of Skin Temperature." *Biology Letters* 10, no. 4 (April 23, 2014).

Safina, Carl. *Beyond Words: What Animals Think and Feel.* New York: Henry Holt and Company, 2015.

Salinas, Joel. *Mirror Touch: Notes from a Doctor Who Can Feel Your Pain.* New York: HarperOne, 2017.

Savage-Rumbaugh, Sue. *Kanzi: The Ape at the Brink of the Human Mind.* New York: Wiley, 1996.

Schneider, Tamera R., Joseph N. Lyons, and Maria Williams. "Emotional Intelligence and Autonomic Self-Perception: Emotional Abilities are

Related to Visceral Acuity." *Personality and Individual Differences* 39, no. 5 (October 2005): 853–61.

Schultz, Mona Lisa. *Awakening Intuition.* New York: Harmony Books, 1998.

Schwartz, Jaclyn, and Staci Bilbo. "Sex, Glia, and Development: Interactions in Health and Disease." *Hormonal Behavior* 62, no. 3 (August 2012): 243–53.

Seaberg, Maureen. "Meet the Nurse Whose Superpower Is Feeling Your Pain—Literally." *Glamour,* March 1, 2018.

Shallis, Michael. *The Electric Connection: Its Effects on Mind and Body.* New York: New Amsterdam Books, 1988.

———. *On Time: An Investigation into Scientific Knowledge and Human Experience.* New York: Schocken Books, 1982.

Sheikh, Anees A., ed. *Imagery: Current Theory, Research and Application.* New York: John Wiley & Sons, 1983.

Sheikh, Knvul. "Do You Hear What I Hear? Auditory Hallucinations Yield Clues to Perception." *Scientific American,* August 10, 2017.

Sheldrake, Rupert. *Dogs That Know When Their Owners Are Coming Home: And Other Unexplained Powers of Animals.* New York: Three Rivers Press, 2000.

Shermer, Michael. "Anomalous Events that Can Shake One's Skepticism to the Core." Originally published as "Infrequencies," *Scientific American* 311 no. 4 (October 2014): 97.

———. "Demon-Haunted Brain." *Scientific American,* February 10, 2003.

———. *Why People Believe Weird Things.* New York: W. H. Freeman and Co., 1997.

Siebert, Charles. "An Elephant Crackup?" *New York Times Magazine,* October 8, 2006.

Simmonds-Moore, Christine A. "An Interpretive Phenomenological Analysis Exploring Synesthesia as an Exceptional Experience: Insights for Consciousness and Cognition." *Qualitative Research in Psychology* 13, no. 4 (July 2016): 303–27.

Simmonds-Moore, Christine A., and Stephen L. Moore. "Exploring How Gender Role and Boundary Thinness Relate to Paranormal Experiences, Beliefs, and Performance on a Forced-Choice Clairvoyance Task." *Journal of the Society for Psychical Research* 73, no. 3 (July 2009).

Smith, Dana. "Anxiety about Certain Things Can Be Hereditary." *The Atlantic,* December 17, 2013.

———. "Can Synesthesia in Autism Lead to Savantism?" *Scientific American,* December 4, 2013.

Smith, Karen A., and Karen R. Gouze. *The Sensory-Sensitive Child*. New York: HarperResource, 2005.

Smuts, Barbara. "Child of Mine." In *The Smile of a Dolphin: Remarkable Accounts of Animal Emotions,* edited by Marc Bekoff. New York: Discovery Books, 2000.

Spraggett, Alan. "Nandor Fodor: Analyst of the Unexplained." *The Psychoanalytic Review* 56A (1969): 128-37.

Stein D. J., K. C. Koenen, M. J. Friedman, E. Hill, K. A. McLaughlin, M. Petukhova, and A. M. Ruscio et al. "Dissociation in Posttraumatic Stress Disorder: Evidence from the World Mental Health Surveys." *Biological Psychiatry* 73, no. 4 (February 15, 2013): 302–12.

Sternberg, Esther M. *The Balance Within: The Science Connecting Health and Emotions*. New York: W. H. Freeman & Co., 2000.

Steuwe C., R. A. Lanius, and P. A. Frewen. "Evidence for a Dissociative Subtype of PTSD by Latent Profile and Confirmatory Factor Analyses in a Civilian Sample." *Depression and Anxiety* 8 (August 2012): 689–700.

Stevenson, Ian. "Birthmarks and Birth Defects Corresponding to Wounds on Deceased Persons." Paper presented to the Eleventh Annual Meeting of the Society for Scientific Exploration at Princeton University, June 11–13, 1992.

———. "Phobias in Children Who Claim to Remember Previous Lives." *Journal of Scientific Investigation* 4, no. 2 (1990): 243–54.

———. *Twenty Cases Suggestive of Reincarnation*. 2nd edition. Charlottesville, Va.: University Press of Virginia, 1980.

Stillman, William. *The Soul of Autism*. Pompton Plains, N.J.: New Page Books, 2008.

Stokes, Deborah A., and Martha S. Lappin. "Neurofeedback and Biofeedback with 37 Migraineurs: A Clinical Outcome Study." *Behavioral and Brain Functions* 6, no. 9 (February 2010): 1–10.

Storr, Will. *Will Storr vs. The Supernatural*. New York: Harper, 2006.

Sutherland, Cherie. "Psychic Phenomena Following Near-Death Experiences: An Australian Study." *Journal of Near-Death Studies* 8, no. 2 (Winter 1989): 93–102.

Tangley, Laura. "Natural Passions." *National Wildlife,* July 2001.

Taylor, Gordon Rattray. *The Natural History of the Mind*. New York: E. P. Dutton, 1979.

Terasawa, Yuri, Yoshiya Moriguchi, Saiko Tochizawa, and Umeda Satoshi.

"Interoceptive Sensitivity Predicts Sensitivity to the Emotions of Others." *Cognition and Emotion* 28, no. 8 (February 2014): 1435–48.

Terhune, Devin B. "The Incidence and Determinants of Visual Phenomenology During Out-of-Body Experiences." *Cortex* 45, no. 2 (February 2009): 236–42.

Terhune, Devin B., David P. Luke, and Roi Cohen Kadosh. "The Induction of Synaesthesia in Non-Synaesthetes." In *Sensory Blending: On Synaesthesia and Other Phenomena,* edited by Ophelia Deroy, 215–47. Oxford, UK: Oxford University Press, 2017.

Terr, Lenore C. "Childhood Traumas: An Outline and Overview." *American Journal of Psychiatry* 148, no. 1 (1991): 10–20.

Thalbourne, Michael A. "Transliminality: A Review." *International Journal of Parapsychology* 11, no. 2 (2000): 1–34.

Thalbourne, Michael A., James Houran, A. G. Alias, and Peter Brugger. "Transliminality, Brain Function, and Synesthesia." *Journal of Nervous and Mental Disease* 189, no. 3 (March 2001): 190–92.

Thalbourne, Michael A., and John Maltby. "Transliminality, Thin Boundaries, Unusual Experiences, and Temporal Lobe Lability." *Personality and Individual Differences* 44 (2008): 1617–23.

Thomson, Helen. "We Feel Your Pain: Extreme Empaths." *New Scientist,* March 10, 2010.

Torrence, Fiona. "Experience: I Feel Other People's Pain." Interviewed by Gary Cansell. *The Guardian,* March 18, 2011.

Treffert, Darold A. "Savant Syndrome: An Extraordinary Condition." *Philosophical Transactions of the Royal Society* 364, no. 1522 (April 12, 2009): 1351–57.

Tsakiris, Manos. "The Multisensory Basis of the Self: From Body to Identity to Others." *Quarterly Journal of Experimental Psychology* 70, no. 4 (May 2016): 597–609.

Tucker, Jim. "The Case of James Leininger: An American Case of the Reincarnation Type." *Explore* 12, no. 3 (May/June 2016): 200–207.

———. *Return to Life: Extraordinary Cases of Children Who Remember Past Lives.* New York: St. Martin's Press, 2015.

Tyberg A., and W. H. Frishman. "Animal Assisted Therapy." In *Complementary and Integrative Medicine in Pain Management.* Edited by Michael I. Weintraub and Marc S. Micozzi. New York: Springer, 2008.

Van de Castle, Robert L. *Our Dreaming Mind.* New York: Ballantine Books, 1994.

Vargas, Diana L., C. Nascimbene, C. Krishnan, et al. "Neuroglial Activation and Neuroinflammation in the Brain of Patients with Autism." *Annals of Neurology* 57, no. 1 (January 2005): 67–81.

Vedantam, Shankar. "Variation in One Gene Linked to Depression." *Washington Post,* July 18, 2003.

Walker, Caroline, Paula Krakowiak, Alice S. Baker, Robin L. Hansen, Sally Ozonoff, and Irva Hertz-Picciotto. "The Role of Preeclampsia in Autism Spectrum Disorders and Cognitive Function." Paper presented at the 2012 International Meeting for Autism Research, May 18, 2012.

Ward, Jamie. "Emotionally Mediated Synesthesia." *Cognitive Neuropsychology* 21, no. 7 (October 2004): 761–72.

Watson, Lyall. *Elephantoms: Tracking the Elephant.* New York, Norton, 2003.

———. *Jacobson's Organ and the Remarkable Nature of Smell.* New York: W. W. Norton & Company, 2000.

———. *Lifetide: The Biology of the Unconscious.* New York: Simon and Schuster, 1979.

Weingarten, Gene. "Something About Harry: Gene Weingarten on Why Old Dogs Are the Best Dogs." *Washington Post,* October 5, 2008.

Wiens, Stefan. "Interoception in Emotional Experience." *Current Opinion in Neurology* 18, no. 4 (August 2005): 442–47.

Weintraub, Karen. "A Newborn's Placenta May Reveal Autism Risk." *USA Today,* April 25, 2013.

Weintraub, Michael I., and Marc S. Micozzi, eds. *Complementary and Integrative Medicine in Pain Management.* New York: Springer, 2008.

Weiss, Sarah, Martin Sack, Peter Henningsen, and Olga Pollatos. "On the Interaction of Self-Regulation, Interoception, and Pain Perception." *Psychopathology* 47, no. 6 (November 2014): 377–82.

Whitlock, F. A., and J. V. Hynes. "Religious Stigmatization: An Historical and Psychophysiological Enquiry." *Psychological Medicine* 8, no. 2 (May 1978): 185–202.

Williams, Donna. *Autism and Sensing: The Unlost Instinct.* London and Philadelphia: Jessica Kingsley Publishers, 1998.

———. *Nobody Nowhere.* New York: Times Books, 1992.

Wilson, Sheryl C., and Theodore X. Barber. "The Fantasy-Prone Personality: Implications for Understanding Imagery, Hypnosis, and Parapsychological Phenomena." In *Imagery: Current Theory, Research and Application,* edited by Anees A. Sheikh, 340–87. New York: John Wiley & Sons, 1983.

Wise, Stephen M. *Drawing the Line.* Cambridge, Mass.: Perseus Books, 2002.

Wolf, E. J., C. A. Lunney, M. W. Miller, P. A. Resick, M. J. Friedman, and P. P. Schnurr. "The Dissociative Subtype of PTSD: A Replication and Extension." *Depression and Anxiety* 29, no. 8 (August 2012): 679–88.

Wolf, E. J., M. W. Miller, A. F. Reardon, K. A. Ryabchenko, D. Castillo, and R. Freund. "A Latent Class Analysis of Dissociation and Posttraumatic Stress Disorder: Evidence for a Dissociative Type." *Archives of General Psychiatry* 69, no. 7 (July 2012): 698–705.

Wood, David. "Bomber Down." *Washington Post Magazine,* August 8, 1999.

Wurzman, Rachel, and James Giordano. "Differential Susceptibility to Plasticity: A 'Missing Link' Between Gene-Culture Co-evolution and Neuropsychiatric Spectrum Disorders?" *BMC Medicine* 10, no. 37 (2012).

Yong, Ed. "Maternal Antibodies Linked to Autism." *The Scientist,* July 9, 2103.

Young, Emma. "Researchers Have Identified a Group of Patients Who Are Especially Prone to Out-of-Body Experiences." posted on the British Psychological Society website, "Research Digest," on July 6, 2018.

Young, Louisa. *The Book of the Heart.* New York: Doubleday, 2003.

Index

About the Author

Anna Gross

Michael Jawer is a Washington, D.C.–based writer, speaker, and researcher. His focus is the nexus of personality development, body/mind, emotion, and spirituality.

Jawer is the author (with Marc Micozzi, M.D., Ph.D.) of two previous books: *The Spiritual Anatomy of Emotion* (Park Street Press, 2009) and *Your Emotional Type* (Healing Arts Press, 2011).

His papers have appeared in *Frontiers in Psychology—Consciousness Research, Journal of Interpersonal Neurobiology Studies, Science & Consciousness Review, Explore, Seminars in Integrative Medicine,* and the *Journal of the Society for Psychical Research,* while his feature articles and interviews have run in *Psychology Today, Spirituality & Health, Aeon, Nautilus, Minding Nature, Advances in Mind-Body Medicine, Edge Science, Noetic Now, Epoch Times, Scientific American,* and on PsychCentral.

Jawer has spoken to organizations including the American Psychological Association, the Society for Humanistic Psychology (APA Division 32), the Association for Comprehensive Energy Psychology, and the Jung Society of Washington, D.C.—and guest lectured at Georgetown University, the University of Maryland, Drexel University, George Mason University, and the University of Virginia. Jawer also blogs for *Psychology Today* ("Feeling Too Much").

To learn more about his latest book, *Sensitive Soul,* associated articles, public appearances, and more, go to **www.michaeljawer.com**.